JACQUES
BREL

La Vie Bohème - A Biography Of Jacques Brel
by Alan Clayson

A CHROME DREAMS PUBLICATION
First Edition 2010

Published by Chrome Dreams
PO BOX 230, New Malden, Surrey,
KT3 6YY, UK
books@chromedreams.co.uk
WWW.CHROMEDREAMS.CO.UK

ISBN 978 1 84240 535 2

Managing Editdor   Rob Johnstone
Cover Design   Sylwia Grzeszczuk
Layout Design   Marek Niedziewicz

Printed in the UK by CPI William Clowes Ltd, Beccles, NR34 7TL, Suffolk

JACQUES
BREL
LA VIE BOHÈME

ALAN CLAYSON

Contents

Acknowledgements

Particular debts of gratitude are owed to Inese Clayson, Ian Drummond, Oliver Gray, the late Garry Jones, Frederic Pierre and Marthy Van Lopik-Grundy for their invaluable assistance with translation of French, Flemish and Dutch source material.

I am also beholden to Hans Alehag, Graham Bartholomew, Robina Baine, Roger Barnes, Robert Bartel, Carolyn Begley, Dave Berry, Jane Bom-Bane, Bruce Brand, Penny Braybrooke, Jonathan Bridger, Chris Britton, Arthur Brown, Lara Carballo, Mark Chapman, the late Russell Churney, Harry Clayson, Jack Clayson, Pete Cox, Don Craine, Paul Critchfield, Kathryn Cutts, Margaret Cutts, Jean-Luc Dancy, Tim Day, Kevin Delaney, Des de Moor, Jackie Doe, Peter Doggett, Ray Dorset, John Forrester, Helen Drummond, 'Wreckless' Eric Goulden, John Harries, David Harrod, Tim Hill, Hilary James, Robb Johnson, Barb Jungr, Andy Lavery, Brian Leafe, Spencer and Anne Leigh, the late Jon Lewin, Kenny Lynch, Steve Maggs, Fraser Massey, Glen Matlock, Phil May, Simon Mayor, Dave McAleer, Ralph McTell, Jim McCarty, Tony McGregor, Sandy Newman, Rob Norris, Reg Presley, Nick Pynn, Joan Redding, Amy Rigby, Imogen Setterfield, Dave Shannon, R. Shepping, Mark. St. John, Attila the Stockbroker, the late Lord David Sutch, Dick Taylor, Lee Taylor, the late Jake Thackray, James Tomalin, John Tobler, John Townsend, Twinkle, Cedric Vandenschrik, Martin Vincent, Mike Watkinson, John Whittaker and Pamela Wiggin. Let's have a big hand too for the BBC Music Library, Irregular Records, the National Sound Archives, Westminster Music Library, the British Library, Colindale Newspaper Library, Wordplay of Caversham and New York Public Library.

Very special thanks is in order for Rob Johnstone, Sylwia Grzeszczuk, Marek Niedziewicz, Cathy Johnstone, Angela Turner and the rest of the team at Chrome Dreams for their encouragement as I worked at this new edition, and for seeing it through to publication.

It may be obvious to the reader that I have received help from sources that may prefer not to be mentioned. Nevertheless, I wish to express my appreciation of what they did. Much new and rediscovered evidence was brought to light as I waded through oceans of press and other archives, and screwed myself up to interview complete strangers. Crucially, though it concerns a historical figure potentially as dry and academic as any other, this biography is meant to be as entertaining as the music that inspired it.

Notes On Translation

Just as a Londoner's understanding of the word 'tramp' is different from that of a New Yorker, so is a Parisian's comprehension of a French-speaking Belgian's idiomatic expressions. Consequently, as Brel tended at times to speak and write in aphorisms, and dwelt for long periods in both Belgium and France, certain of his lyrical fragments defy adequate interpretation (like Cockney rhyming slang or a sentence like 'the star's latest single is a smash' might confuse a French translator). Even a modern day Englishman might scratch his head over an archaic phrase like 'cheese him on the snitch' (i.e. biff him on the boko, punch him up the hooter, hit him on the nose).

In 'Le Plat Pays', for instance, the old cathedrals are decorated with 'des diables en pierre décrochent les nuages si gris qu'un canal s'est pendu' - which is rendered literally as 'devils in stone that take down clouds so grey that a canal hangs itself', but these splendid metaphors seem more succinct and make more sense as 'gargoyles bringing the clouds so low the canals are lost. Then Brel sings in 'Quand On N'A Que L'Amour' of joining forces with those whose only battle is 'de chercher le jour' (for to seek out the day') - while a couplet from 1967's 'La La La' - 'Je boirai donc seul ma pension de cigal/Il faut bien être lorsque l'on a été' - appears to mean 'I have drunk so alone my pension of insect/It is necessary well to be when one has been'. Not above half, I don't think.

I have, therefore, been inclined not to quote his lyrics directly, but to paraphrase their substance. Laffont's *Oeuvre Intégrale* (see bibliography) and a comprehensive French-English dictionary are recommended for supplementary investigation of Brel's *chansons*.

Otherwise, listen to the records. Robert Alden of the *New York Times* wrote of a New York concert in 1965 that 'it was possible for a member of the audience who did not understand a word of French to understand emotionally and to be swept along by what Mr. Brel has to say.'

To Gordon and Rosemary

'As in the case of painters, who have undertaken to give us a beautiful and graceful figure, which may have some slight blemishes, we do not wish them to pass over such blemishes altogether. The one would spoil the beauty, and the other destroy the likeness of the picture'

- Plutarch

Prologue

'I Am Not A Poet And I Am Not A Musician'

Jacques Brel remains both a figurehead and *éminence grise* of twentieth century songwriting, despite penning not a single libretto that wasn't French (or, on one solitary occasion, Flemish) and an indifference towards success in foreign dominions beyond banking royalty cheques for myriad translations of his *chansons*, and being paid as per contract for obligated recitals in Britain, the United States and Russia. In 1967, he withdrew from the concert stage altogether to embark on non-musical enterprises that were ambitious but, collectively, of no great merit, whilst continuing what would become a snail-paced recording career.

During the twelve years between Brel's retirement as a performing *chansonier* and his early death, pop music was upgraded from ephemera to Holy Writ, and its under-used brain jolted into quivering action - an inevitability traceable to Bob Dylan's stream-of-consciousness literariness; fans scrutinizing of every inch of the *Sgt. Pepper's Lonely Hearts Club Band* sleeve for veiled but oracular messages; the aural event-structures of rock, jazz and post-serialism that was Frank Zappa's Mothers of Invention; the widening chasm between 'progressive' rock - which only the finest minds could 'appreciate' - and the so-called junk culture that is mainstream pop, and the correlated elevation of the album format to something more than a pig-in-a-poke, slopping with musical swill and a hit single.

Brel, however, was as tangential to both 'prog rock' and the Top Twenty as Mel Tormé, Peggy Lee, Perry Como, Frank Sinatra and their 'quality' kind, all beyond needing chart strikes. No more than they could he be marketed as a provider of entertainment for the ordinary young adult in Huddersfield, Laramie or Brisbane, even without the language barrier.[1]

Yet Brel was to burn his brand on the output of such discerning and diverse English-speaking wordsmiths as Mort Shuman, Rod McKuen, Ray Davies, Leonard Cohen, Victoria Wood, David Bowie, Glen Matlock of The Sex Pistols - yes, really! - Billy Bragg, Jarvis Cocker and, the foremost interpreter of his work, Scott Walker. It sometimes required effort, but the gist of his verses - like those of Dylan - could be appreciated without music.

Unlike Dylan's younger self, however, Jacques Brel did not preach about, say, fairer shares for all or war being wrong. He was above truisms and protest. Instead, like the best creative artists, Brel was simultaneously personal and universal; subversive but encroaching upon public consciousness through the popular media; romantic but pertinent to real life interactions and outcomes within likely human situations. In the only interview he ever gave to a British music paper (*Melody Maker*), he explained that 'I'm obsessed by those things that are ugly or sordid, that people don't want to talk about. I can't get excited about anything that isn't a battle. I like to be afraid. I like to learn - and I like to take blows in the face too.'

If he had to be brutish or foul-mouthed, he was gifted with a forgivable arrogance and the sureness of touch to say enough without too much lingering intimacy or detail but with the subtleties that Marxist playwright Berthold Brecht would call *Verfremdungtechnik* - detached comment that provokes thought rather than social validation - or, as Scott Walker noted, 'Brel rarely offers solutions yet states the confusion beautifully.'

As such, he represented an updating of the mediaeval minstrel's vernacular lyric poetry - especially that of François Villon, a vagabond bard of the fifteenth century whose escapades almost overshadowed in retrospect the bitter humour of his *ballades* - some of which were adapted by Brecht and Kurt Weill for *The Threepenny Opera*. However, rather than get too frightfully erudite, perhaps we could turn to a simpler illustration in the 'Allan-A-Dale' character played by Elton Hayes in the 1954 Walt Disney movie, *The Story Of Robin Hood And His Merrie Men*. This roving troubadour's bursts of sung reportage served as both a recap of the plot and encapsulation of the Common Man's dim view of the Sheriff of Nottingham's ruthless campaign to capture Hood and gather Prince John's crippling taxes. It didn't do much for me, but a hamlet of villeins verily fell about with thigh-slapping mirth at Allan's sardonic 'Now Robin Hood doth hunt the deer that in the woodlands prance/But oft times shoots the Sheriff's men - by sorrowful mischance!'

Jongleurs like Allan-A-Dale, Villon and their Belgian compatriot, Michel de Ghelderode - in common with the black bluesmen of an unimaginable future - were also inescapably more identifiable with the essence of their songs than the so-called 'serious' composers paid to cater for the recreational whims of duke, bishop or like paymaster - olde tyme equivalents of radio station programmers.

Though an obituary in the *New York Times* nutshelled his life as 'that of a romantic in perpetual search of his personality', Brel, when an established star in 1963, could afford the following divulgence to *Le Parisien Libéré*: 'In this job, you tell of who you are - tell yourself of who you are. Me, I work for myself. What is essential is that I appreciate myself - because if you sing to please someone other than yourself, you cannot (unless you are perilously unconscious of it) help but feel that you are prostituting yourself. Personally, I refuse to be servile.'

Nevertheless, if the peasants didn't like what they heard - or saw - the lynching of the vocalist was not unknown. Even in this computer aeon, black Nat 'King' Cole was beaten up - for being too 'uppity' - by racial extremists midway through a show before an unsegregated audience in North America's Deep South. The country-and-western legend Hank Williams was to encounter similar extreme strategy - and, one evening, Brel came within an ace of physical injury by an audience rendered hostile by the content of his act.

To sidestep such dangerous occupational hazards, it was incumbent upon singers to defuse potential unrest by presenting challenging material in an admissably diverting way. As well as an acceptable vocal style, considerable dramatic qualities were needed to involve onlookers in both the song and its performer. This Brel learned quickly in the early 1950s when working the unsalubrious cabaret clubs that littered Paris and his native Brussels - where he and most of the other *chansonniers* were as vulnerable - psychologically at least - as the troubadours of old.

If accompanying himself on guitar rather than lute, Aristide Bruant is recognised generally as the missing link between the likes of Villon and the modern *chansonier*. If the name is unfamiliar, Bruant's image - black wideawake hat, long red scarf and cavalier boots - is that celebrated in the post-impressionist posters of his better known contemporary, Toulouse-Lautrec. Bruant was likewise a denizen of Montmartre cafes where he enacted *chansons* that dealt not with the ooo-la-la Paris of hansom cabs, berets and the Eiffel Tower, but its artistic fringe; its often unnerving *arte pour l'arte* aestheticism; its underworld of pimps, whores and criminals, and the posturings and indiscretions of its politicians and aristocracy.

Among Bruant's most direct descendants is Charles Aznavour. Though as much a professional Gaul in the eyes of the world as Maurice Chevalier, Aznavour was of a different feather to 'those who sing of the beauty of Paris, of the girls of Paris, of the Champs-Élysées. My Paris is not like that. My Paris is rude and earthy.' Brel, the least French of all the famous *chansoniers*, saw the city in a similar light during years of commuting between there and Brussels. Considered by France, if not himself, as an artist who defected from and, arguably, ridiculed his own country, Brel became so much part of France's cultural furniture that he would be claimed as one of her own, just as Van Morrison's Belfast beat group, Them, would be categorized as English 'when we had a couple of hit records'.

As Belgian as Morrison was Irish, the inscription below the name and dates on the memorial plaque above his South Sea island tomb was to read *Auteur, compositeur, chanteur, né a Bruxelles*. His origins were obvious to anyone who listened to him in speech and in songs such as 'Les Flamandes', 'La Bière' and 'L'Ostendaise'. For all the many vistas like these that he opened into the meaner lives of his kindred, Brel was not unproud of what he called his 'belgitude'. This was, perhaps, his most singular contribution to Gallic - as against strictly French - *chanson*.

His post-war period also witnessed the ascent of Charles Trenet, Leo Ferré, Félix Leclerc (from Canada), Gilbert Becaud, Boris Vian, late-comer Aznavour and, crucially for Brel, Georges Brassens: all members of a national resistance movement to US pop and jazz intrusion (even if it was Trenet who introduced swing rhythms to the *chanson*). The man-in-the-street in Quebec, Marseilles, Ghent and Algiers knew their songs and public images well, but to his compeer in the parallel Anglo-Saxon dimension, how many of these artists are just as obscure now as they were in the 1950s? Much the same applies to younger *chansoniers* like Adamo, Jacques Dutronc, Barbara, Marie-Paule Belle, Georges Moustaki and even Soeur Sourire, the Singing Nun, who, if more affected by pop's internationalism, was steeped in the same cohesive traditions of what might be the most mature and cultivated form of popular song.

This was endorsed by Pierre Seghers, the old and respected Parisian publishing firm's inclusion of the outstanding *chansoniers* in its series *Poètes D'Aujourd'hui* - though both Brel and Aznavour, each unable to divorce their own lyrics from musical settings, were uncomfortable with this exploitation of them as printed poems. 'Poetry is for the old times,' thought Aznavour, 'and the great poets I love are from the old times. Poetry today has to walk the streets. It has to be in the air.'

Brel, the more self-depreciating and pragmatic of the two, appeared to regard his work as no more or less of a craft than carpentry or bricklaying: 'I am not a poet and I am not a musician. I haven't that many things I can say. I challenge you to clearly express the slightest idea in three verses. Presently, I am writing a song which will probably be called "A Child". Give me ten pages, and I'll explain to you how I see childhood, but the song only lasts three minutes - so ten pages have to be reduced to one verse. One crucial line - "Children kill off your lovers and mistresses" - is likely to be unnoticed. I can say no more than that without unbalancing my song - or be more concise. Free verse offers more freedom. Poetry is less restricting than the disciplines which control songwriting. Of all the arts, I know of none other that is as stilted.'

The *chanson*, however, infiltrated language and music faculties in British and US universities as a subject for serious study - with Brassens the composer most prone to analysis. A lot of post-graduate research, however, has produced academic tomes in English that are as unreadable in their fashion as *Poètes D'Aujourd'hui* to the Average Joe with his GCE 'O' Level (failed) in French.

When first I failed French, I could listen to the *chansoniers* with as little awareness of each one's distinctions as a shopper has between wedges of supermarket musak. To ask my opinion about Brassens, Trenet or Dutronc was like asking me about railway lines or donkeys' false teeth - because I couldn't say anything objective. They were just there.

I discovered Brel via Scott Walker, and Aznavour more precisely through his one-song spot on some ITV variety programme in 1972. While everyone else at college seemed to have caught the overall post-Woodstock drift of ham-fisted heavy metal, vainglorious pomp-rock and twee singer-songwriters, my record collection included all three volumes of *Aznavour Sings Aznavour* and the first four Scott Walker albums. Later, teenage Europe would be treated to a Clayson and the Argonauts version of 'The Ham' (*'Le Cabotin'*), described by a *New Musical Express* reviewer, blast his impudence, as 'a slice of Aznavourian breast-beating that was all too appropriate in the circumstances.' When we toured Holland, I acquired second-hand copies of *Jacques Brel À L'Olympia* and *Brel '67*, which, initially, were purely for display.

It was only after around three years in my possession that they gained further scratches and surface hiss, principally because Inese, my girlfriend - with her honours degree in French - started spinning them on our shuddering monophonic Dansette. After I became as intrigued, I found out, with a kind of despairing triumph, that records by him were only then available in Britain on expensive import. There seemed to be no sheet music either apart from an 'If You Go Away' buried in a Dusty Springfield songbook. Therefore, Inese and I put Brel on our mental list of wanted items during our habitual scouring of local bazaars, charity stalls and bric-à-brac emporiums.

Over a decade later, Jacques Brel trickled into the kingdom on compact disc. When in New York in the mid-1990s, I had also stumbled upon a portfolio of some of the numbers from the *Jacques Brel Is Alive And Well And Living In Paris* musical. I'd hoped to find the elusive chord sequence to 'My Death' for a purpose that was then non-specific, having been faintly shocked at how different the composer's harsh 'La Mort' blueprint was from the *legato* orchestral dovetailing on 1967's *Scott* LP. Unhappily, *Alive And Well* contained only its words.

Actually, the relatively simple 'My Death' chords had been staring at me from my piano keyboard all along - for, while Brecht and Weill were able to combine potent librettos with interesting music via a hybrid of opera and *Alive And Well*-like quasi-cabaret, melodies by Brel and fellow *chansoniers* are sometimes little more than a repeated series of notes used to carry lyrics that might be weakened by stronger underlying elaboration. Two notes only, for example, are the bedrock of Brel's 'Ces Gens-Là'.

By contrast to most modern Anglo-Saxon pop, words, therefore, dominate the *chanson* as they did when Victorian and Edwardian drawing rooms and theatres were set a-tremble with sonorous refrains about street urchins, fallen women, early graves, meticulously mannered courtship and embattled honour. If hard to perform without affectation nowadays, 'The Newsboy's Debt', 'Had She Listened To Her Mother', 'The Little Shroud', 'Come Into The Garden Maud', 'Grandma's Last Amen', 'Don't Bring Shame On The Old Folks' and even the more rollicking likes of 'Burlington Bertie', 'With Her Head Tucked Underneath Her Arm' and 'Where Did You Get That Hat' are often as handsome in their choice of words as any *chanson* defined by Aznavour as 'a song you can't dance to', however much Brel, in alliance with Aznavour again, would insist that 'music loses a lot when it is aligned with a text. We must not forget that it is the music - that everyone hears but nobody listens to - that will get a song onto the radio and get it performed in music halls between a tightrope walker and a juggler'.

Like it was in Britain, they were named 'music halls' because each act was expected to make use of the pit or onstage orchestra if only for a rumble of timpani as doves fluttered from a magician's mysterious sleeves. Usually the bill would contain a wholly musical turn, an individual *chansonier* more often than not. Closer to formal concerts than lusty Drury Lane singalong, there was less emphasis on backchat with the audience. Though the lyrics could be funny, the singer was seldom a comedian too - or anything else for that matter. Without fuss, he'd stride centre stage to deliver the goods with the stoic deliberation of one whose every utterance seemed to have been wrenched from his very soul, getting so 'gone' that he could manage only a *sotto voce* 'merci' after each cadence died away.

To most foreigners who were aware that French pop had any depth or domestic character at all, Brassens and Brel in the 1950s - and Brel and Aznavour later on - were seen as opposing forces. As with Fellini and Antonioni to pseudo-intellectual movie-goers, it wasn't done to like both Brel and Brassens. Yet there were basic similarities in each *chansonier*'s recurrent themes (love, tenderness, liberty, parting, death, abandonment, human stupidity and a rueful patriotism); a confrontation of life's problems and stresses (seldom touched upon by, say, Trenet); his frosty wit and sense of irony, and a casually shocking frankness that rode roughshod over a circuitous and irresolute political intervention.

'What is amusing,' confessed Brel, 'is that if you talk to a group of young Communists, they will say to you, "Brel? He's a Communist" - because I took part in a festival of *L'Humanité* and a world congress of youth in Helsinki. However, they forget that I do not take part in these sort of events because they're political or religious, but because I believe that I will find something in there which resembles generosity - generosity, not charity. I hate charity. I spend my time being charitable simply because I am too weak to stand up for justice.'

The older Brassens was never so conclusively non-committal either in interview or song. More verbally complex than Brel, he cloaked (rather than blunted) his lyrical intentions in self-protecting imagery, allusion, parodic hyperbole and projection into alien realms such as a past century. Under his influence, many of the more Germanic Brel's early *chansons* were of like kidney until a shift from narrative to the implications of what his characters and situations *were* rather than how they operated, and a growing preponderance of aching commiseration with the lost and the weak alongside the scowling contempt elsewhere. The texture of his songs darkened too from pastoral softness to neo-Machiavellian grey. This was conspicuous in his questionable, if caustically amused attitude towards the sexes: 'Oh! the women are frightened! It isn't their fault. I am convinced all the same that seeing the Tower of Pisa for the first time, a man says to himself, "That's beautiful!"; a woman says to herself, "Wait! It's going to fall down."'

Evidence suggests that, after a slow start, Brel was a devil with women. Though an admirable person in many ways, other dubious attributes surfaced as my profile of him assumed a sharper definition. It is sometimes dismaying to investigate the private life of a given celebrity, especially a musical one. If he turns out to be a Right Bastard, the records may never sound the same, too many illusions can be shattered. Contradicting fanciful accounts - including his own - of his climb to fame, Brel was not, for example, the cliched Misunderstood Artiste who Left His Family in order to Suffer For His Art by Starving for two years in a Rat-Infested Garret on the Left Bank. Furthermore, the myth of Brel as a hardened drinker and hellraiser smokescreens a profoundly spiritual (or, if you prefer, superstitious) man with a deeply-rooted respect for the forces of good and evil - though it was a violent reaction to the upbringing that instilled this in him that underscored his subsequent career.

Alan Clayson, January 2010

NOTES

1. In 1995, Brel didn't figure at all in French pop magazine Juke Box*'s 'Collectors Top 50' - which was topped by Johnny Hallyday.*

Chapter One
'The Navel Of The World'

There are thousands of Brels - and tributary surnames like'Breel', 'Br-ijl' and 'Bruegel' - listed in telephone directories throughout the Low Countries. Though traceable to the Crusades, Jacques Brel's ancestry was no more distinguished than that of any other with the same name. However, as with most families, there was a real or invented genealogical link with someone vaguely famous. Jacques would claim one with a Georget de Brelles, musician of the Flemish school during the fifteenth century 'golden age of polyphony', who was cathedral choir master in Cambrai, a city then unsure whether it was French or German.

Four hundred years later, an identity crisis persisted in the area, despite Belgium becoming an independent (and, in theory, perpetually neutral) kingdom in 1831; its people having revolted against union with Holland imposed after the fall of Napoleon. Largely as a result of being the centre of avaricious squabbles between France and Germany over the centuries, Belgium had evolved into a crowded and divided nation that embraced two distinct cultures and languages.

As in Canada with its French and British partitions, there are effectively two Belgiums - one centred on Brussels with its French street names, and another round Ghent and Bruges in Flanders, home of the mediaeval dukes who, if Burgundian by affinity, found it practical to learn the Flemish tongue of those, high and low, who were the flesh-and-blood of trade and commerce from Dunkirk to the Rhine.

The main language in Belgium today is French - in most respects, the same as that spoken in Paris - though Flemish continues to be a compulsory subject for its school children as Welsh is for their opposite numbers in, well, Wales. If derived from the same Old Celtic and Low German mixture as Dutch, differences in pronunciation and dialect become more marked the further one travels across Belgium from Holland. Jacques Brel in his cradle caught and held a northern accent more akin to that heard in Amsterdam than Flanders. Yet he thought, spoke and dreamt in French - for though he'd be able to follow Flemish (and Dutch) conversations, he could not participate very effectively in them because, as a boy, he'd had scant contact - outside his Boy Scout troop - with anyone whose first language was Flemish.

If of Flemish stock, both Brel and his father Romain's fierce sense of national identity and loyalty - to be expressed by Jacques in 'Le Plat Pays' (most conspicuously in 'the flat country which is mine' hook) - was tempered by an unflagging (and often over-generalised) criticism of the strain of Flemish fanaticism that was always doomed to be ineffectual. 'They amaze me,' Brel *fils* would exclaim, 'These people that no-one understands and who are trying ineffectually to make everybody speak their language.'

Like most of his generation, Brel did not learn the old national anthem, 'La Brabançone', such was the extent of its suppression after its French lyrics were considered insulting to the Flemings' Dutch blood-brothers. However, this and other appeasements weren't enough to stop cells of Flemish nationalism from employing radical tactics to isolationist ends, whether painting over French street signs or, in 1900, firing attention-seeking bullets at the visiting Prince of Wales. Nearly thirty years later, the government was defeated over a bill relating to linguistic problems - and, during the German occupation in the Second World War, the Flemish were wooed by the invaders' Propaganda Ministry as fellow Teutons who ought to join in the overthrow of the deluded Allies.

No Brel was stirred by any such overture. Indeed, while regarding himself as Flemish, Romain as a mature student had been hospitalized, allegedly, as a result of a punch-up that had developed from a discussion over the issue with some militants.

A combination of nineteenth century custom and Roman Catholic hit-or-miss birth control methods had resulted in Romain being the last of ten children sired by Louis Brel, baker of Zandevoorde. This village lay near Ypres, the future Great War battleground that bordered both France and the Flemish-speaking territory of Belgium.

Romain was a bright, self-motivated and academically adventurous young man. In his late twenties, he had the confidence to chuck in a secure office job to start a master's degree course in the comparatively new subject of chemical engineering at the University of Louvain. It might have been attributable to the fight with the Flemish activists, but he abandoned his studies, grew a moustache and, in 1911, gained a post in the Belgian Congo as an agent for Cominex, a firm that exported groceries, hardware and selections from Belgium's eight hundred brands of beer while importing the colony's coffee, palm oil, ivory and rubber.

During a lonely three years based in Popokabaka, Our Man Brel applied himself diligently to the task in hand, frequently taking an intense and unwelcome interest in the furthest-flung branches of his allocated district. On long, mosquito-ridden expeditions - mostly on foot - as well as the expected interviews of clients and inspections of workshops and factories, he prodded indolent colleagues and sly sub-contractors about why this shipment was late, where that percentage had come from or why so-and-so had been granted this franchise. Delighted that they'd got a representative who was more than a time-server, Cominex pushed Romain Brel further up the ladder, extending his brief to cover bordering Angola by the outbreak of the Great War.

When 'gallant little Belgium' (as it was named in condescending British journals) was overwhelmed by the might of the Kaiser, and even the fields of Zandvoorde became filled with military graves, King Albert I's appeal for British and French help ensured that part of the country remained in Allied hands. The youngest in a large family, Romain Brel was exempt from conscription. Neither did he step forward for active service. Instead, he enjoyed a holiday in London - and became a lifelong Anglophile - before returning to central Africa to consolidate his position with Comitex.

After the Armistice was signed, Brel wondered whether thirty-six wasn't a good age to look for a wife. He wasn't a bad-looking fellow, was he? He stood straight as a lance, and was over six feet tall in the bowler hat worn when he walked out with a lady. These occasions were rare because, even in Leopoldville (later, Kinshasa), the Congo's very capital, eligible females weren't especially plentiful. Therefore, with the beginnings of an Imperial beard, he appeared in Brussels in 1919, just as Belgian troops commenced the occupation of the North Rhine. Not stressing his negligible hand in the Kaiser's downfall, Romain entered polite society through acquaintance with a Madame Van Adorp, rich widow of a stained-glass window maker. It was at one of her *soirées* that he met

Elisabeth 'Lisette' Lambertine, a pretty, slim brunette, thirteen years his junior.

Reader, she married him - and, back in the feverish heat of the Congo, the twins Nelly and Pierre, conceived on the wedding night, were born on 13 August 1922, only to die weeks later of the typhus that, with other tropical diseases, always lurked behind the beauty of the blue lagoons, rich jungle and pearly mountains. This finished Romain Brel with Africa, and he took his wife home.

She'd been raised in the more uptown area of Schaerbeek, a north-eastern suburb of Brussels, where she and Romain - now cycling daily to a city office - found 138, Avenue du Diamant, the white stone house where, on 19 October 1923, the couple were blessed with a second son. For the sake of morbid tradition, he was baptised Pierre, and Lisette chose the name Nelly for the daughter she hoped - in vain - would be next. She mitigated her disappointment by sometimes calling the boy that arrived instead 'Nelly' - though everyone else in his immediate family would come to know him as 'Jacky'.

Jacques Romain Georges Brel had been prised into the world in the early hours of Monday, 8 April 1929, a dry day which a biting northeast wind hit like a hammer. Such raw weather was commensurate with that evening's performance of *Siegfried* at the city's Théâtre de la Monnaie. That same year, Simenon's first detective story was in the shops, and Hergé drew the maiden adventure of Tin Tin. Along with Adolphe Sax, designer of the saxophone, Simenon and Herge were to be foremost among precious few Belgians renowned beyond its frontiers.

The wider world was then preoccupied with 1929's Wall Street crash after US overseas investment dried up. So began the Great Depression: the global collapse of all sizes and manner of business enterprises with attendant multitudes suddenly unemployed. Yet Belgium finished the decade in a better situation than most, thanks to rapid development of industry since the War. City boundaries had expanded, swallowing smaller communities on the way as road, river, and rail connections fanned out in all directions. Myriad manufactured products - pen-nibs to steamship boilers - were shunted daily from cavernous warehouses in over-populated connurbations, haphazard and huddled. In the years before phrases like 'environmental health' had been coined, giant chimneys were trained on the clouds like anti-aircraft guns, belching chemical waste from Belgium's blast furnaces and factories, and caking their surroundings with soot as indelible as Lady Macbeth's damned spot.

In the more heavily industrial zones, the summer sun was as obscured by smoke as it had been in cordite-riddled Ypres during the war. Perhaps this is why outsiders tend to visualise Belgium's flat landscape under permanently murky skies. The delusion would be perpetuated in 'Le Plat Pays' which, alloting a verse each to the four winds, has that from the east calling up an 'infinity of mists to come', and glooms about 'cathedrals the only mountains' and those 'gargoyles bringing the clouds so low that the canals are lost.'

Any encircling depression, meteorological or otherwise, did not yet trouble a curly-headed infant with grey-green eyes, whose family had left Schaerbeek when, as the economic malaise gripped tighter, they were obliged in 1931 to move to Boulevard d'Ypres, the fortieth floor of a new apartment block where the air was lacerated by the churn of city centre traffic and tugboat whistles emitting the same lone note from the Canal de Charleroi. During this sojourn of no fond memory, Jacky - prone to chest and sinus infections - was encouraged to play within the warmth of the gas cooker.

With little to lose, Romain gave notice to Comitex, and landed on his feet as co-director of a brother-in-law (and majority shareholder), Amand Vanneste's flourishing cardboard carton merchandising concern. 'Vanneste and Brel' continued to grow - as did Romain's standing as a fair-minded if fastidious employer of a conscientious firm supplying sturdy goods. In 1967, Jacques would speak of 'my industrial father' and complain that he didn't wish to become an 'industrialist of song'.

Nevertheless, though Romain could be included among the bourgeoisie derided by his son in both *chanson* and press conference, he was a moderate liberal politically, and only a nominal Roman Catholic. Certainly, Romain was far less conservative than Amand who swooped unquestioningly to the defence of Church, monarchy and the established order, and had a statue of the Virgin Mary erected at the factory gate.

Jacques would turn out to be more like his father than he'd ever liked to imagine. As well as a shared view about Flemish militants, his feelings about parental responsibility and male superiority evolved from information received tacitly from Romain who never discussed work with Lisette just as he didn't expect her to drag him into unnecessary matters to do with housework and child-rearing. The place of a Belgian woman - who hadn't yet been granted the vote - was in the home. Papa never changed nappies.

'Fatherhood doesn't exist,' Jacques Brel would pontificate, 'Motherhood does, and it is the affection of the mother which is indispensible for a child. However, it is almost impossible for a father to establish a proper dialogue with his children apart from baby-talk, but that doesn't go very far. I don't see any sense in children greeting each evening a man with nothing to say to them - who's going to sit down, put on his slippers, break wind at the end of a meal, and then watch TV after yelling for them to go to bed.'

A parallel may be drawn between the urbanised Brels and the well-to-do rural English family of William Brown, Richmal Crompton's outrageous eleven-year-old whose first exploit, *Just William*, was published in 1917. Mr. Brown rarely showed any overt emotion towards his ideally seen-but-not-heard younger son beyond an icy irritation - particularly if interrupted during his customary relaxation over a post-dinner crossword. Not an easy fellow with whom to make small-talk, he was, overall, a rather remote figure in William's life - like a Victorian *paterfamilias* who governed his children's behaviour even when absent via 'just wait till your father gets home' litanies whenever they were naughty.

If not as hostile towards him as William's brother, Pierre - approaching puberty when his sibling was at kindergarten - hardly spoke to Jacques, who had even fewer areas of contact with his male Vanneste cousins - who were all older too.

With the best of intentions, the adult Brels and Vannestes, knowing few who lived much differently from themselves, would instill into their respective broods what *ought* to be admired about achievement by effort - as exemplfied by Jacques, at Papa's behest, taking on a weekend baker's round to learn the value of money. More ingrained was the 'decent' sir-and-ma'am propriety that was the norm behind front doors with silver letterboxes. The sugar was in its bowl, the milk in its jug, the cups unchipped on their saucers on an embroidered tablecloth during Mama's coffee mornings with their gossip, betrayed confidences and murmured suspicions: there's something between her and that young bricklayer. I can perceive no good in it, indeed I can.

Like Mrs. Brown, Lisette cared more about social standing and the good opinion of her peers than her children's happiness. As such, she was a dutiful rather than doting mother. 'She didn't much like you loving her,' remarked Jacky, 'It didn't mean much to her. Anyway, she hid it well.'

In the throes of sweeping the carpet, his mother would surprise her youngest lying on his stomach under the dining room table with his head in a comic. A more obvious symptom of a certain 'apartness' was a reluctance to let himself be seen in family portraits as demonstrated by the frequency that the back of his head appears in them compared to the many times his toothy grin was to be prominent in photographs with his Wolf Cub pack. Such contrasting behaviour may have been regarded by the adults of the family as mere unmindful perversity - like a parrot that curses when the vicar is visiting and reverts to 'pretty Polly' the minute after his scandalized exit.

Today's psychologist might interpret Jacky Brel's attitude as a 'rejecting' response to progressively more emotionally inattentive parents by one so innately affectionate that a letter to them would read: 'Dear Papa, sweet Mama, If my pen could only go as quick as my heart and even my tongue, what a long letter you'd receive from your little Jacky.'

A bigger Jacky would come to believe that 'we all lack tenderness because we do not dare to give it or receive it - also, perhaps, because the tenderness that ought to come from our parents is eroded when the family is no longer what it was. Tenderness disappears little by little and isn't replaced by anything.'

His was, therefore, a realm of taciturn men but vivacious women who threw themselves into sundry parish activities with a zeal that their working class sisters may have thought excessive. Tombolas, fêtes , and other ostensibly charitable functions were very much part of the scheme of things for Jacques' mother and aunts - role models for 1959's 'Dame Patronesse' maybe - as they were for fictional Mrs. Brown and her neighbours. The smell of home-made jam was a lasting memory of Jacky's boyhood - as was that of cabbage soup at his maternal grandmother's flat.

Lisette would refute her son's later assertion that he had lived more with his grandparents than parents - but he was delivered for them to mind many times whenever the presence of a visibly bored child was likely to mar grown-up occasions. Otherwise, his face was scrubbed and his hair combed until his entire scalp was sore. He was then dressed like a miniature version of besuited, starchy Papa, and compelled to conduct himself with nicely-spoken and fatuous affability whenever some banal platitude was directed at him. Another formal event where Jacques was permitted to open his mouth was divine worship where he sang and recited the holy sounds that were novel and unintelligible at six, over-familiar and rote-learnt by twelve.

When grown to man's estate, Brel would never renege on an unremarkable - even dull - Catholic upbringing. Neither would he ever regard the rich as necessarily wicked. Indeed, his later comments on the properous lassitude described in many of his lyrics would betray an inbred awareness that happiness is hardly the product of money: 'I'm not a sociologist, but I know that the more conspicuous your spending, the greater your status, the greater your worry. A rich child, without doubt, ages quicker than a poor one.'

This opinion had been compounded during a decade when, through a dogged quest for custom, Vanneste and Brel expanded to the point where a pattern could be established whereby the proprietors' families went onwards and upwards to homes that were always improvements on the ones before. Romain got the ball rolling by moving Lisette and the boys from the hated Boulevard d'Ypres to 26, Boulevard Belgica in Belgicalaan suburb - albeit within view of a hideous war memorial - then to more upmarket 7, Rue Jacques-Manne.

Needless to say, Pierre and Jacques attended a private academy rather than a state school. Yet an unimaginative and often frightening regime was prevalent in both. Mid-morning passers-by would catch multiplication tables chanted mechanically and *en masse* to the rap of a bamboo cane on a teacher's inkwelled desk.

Jacky, gaberdine-raincoated and short-trousered, commenced his official education at École Saint-Viateur where he was remembered as a courteous and tractable pupil. Both arithmetic and Flemish would always be trying subjects, but he was sound enough in reading and writing, and a retentive memory facilitated a mature and sometimes encyclopaedic understanding of people and places, interactions and outcomes. Though he needed little coaxing to sing in public, he was generally poor at music theory which was then taught as a kind of mathematics that proved the conjecture that a tone-deaf person could compose a symphony.

Of extra-mural activities, he was keenest on the Cubs where he became known as rather a show-off. In the Scouts, he fell in line as the 41st Brussels troop's resident funnyman for his impersonations of Hitler and Charlie Chaplin; the informal clowning in camp fire sketches, and an affected chuckle - machine-gun plus concluding yelp - that earned him the nickname 'Laughing Seal'.

An important date on the Scouting calendar was the summer camp. Other major encounters with the Great Outdoors took place during Brel family holidays that included sailing, swimming (only at the height of summer) and outings along the forty miles of Belgium's North Sea coastline from rented accommodations in resorts such as Ostend, Zeebrugge, Blankenberger and Knokke-le-Zoute (the location of an annual song festival).

En route to the seaside, Jacky would gaze fixedly from train window or car windscreen for the first exciting glimpse of distant waves. These, he knew, could turn cruel when they breached the sea walls and swept across the low-lying hinterland, spreading havoc like marauding Vikings. Brel's affinity to the cold, grey waters and those who fought them would surface in such as 'Amsterdam' - and 'Le Plat Pays' with its mention of fisherman who sail away in November and return in May.

Back home in landlocked Brussels, he'd plunge down into the deepest ocean fathoms, brave the snowy wildernesses of Alaska and ride in Red Indian scalping parties via the ripping yarns of Jules Verne, Jack London, Sir Henry Rider Haggard and Fenimore Cooper. In 1944, he'd complete two of his own: 'The Vagrant' with a bitty if lyrical plot that filled forty-seven frequently illegible pages of an exercise book (and contained a guileless beauty named Madeleine and a businessman father who is a crook), and the shorter but laboriously typed and illustrated novelette, *Kho-Barim*, about the revenge of Egyptian gods on an English archaeologist who plundered a pharaoh's tomb.

He would show these nascent samples of his dark humour to no-one because, regardless of, say, *Kho-Barim*'s actual geographical setting, it was a soothing flight into what its creator, like other Gallic youngsters, would refer to as the Far West - a private universe that should have ceased to exist like the tooth fairy had already from the morning after she failed to swap the molar under his pillow for a silver coin.

Beautiful myths and never-never lands nurtured and then casually destroyed can turn a sensitive child into a distrustful cynic. This can occur the second that the lost paradise of childhood evaporates into the overcast skies above 'factory courtyards, traffic lights and policemen,' sighed Jacques Brel, 'I never had a Far West after all. In the same way, adults promise you Father Christmas, and assure you that love is eternal - until the day when they suddenly tell you, "Sorry, that was all a joke." Nowadays, children are so much in love with the Far West that they get dressed up as cowboys until the Far West no longer exists. For that reason, I get a sinking feeling from time to time. I know that there are no more heroes or villains, that there are no more Indians. There are instead people who are sometimes Indians and sometimes Buffalo Bills.'

While there may have been no more story-book villains, a German soldier was a close approximation of one to the average Gaul. This had been confirmed by Hitler's rape of Belgium in April 1940 when, after eighteen days of resistance, Leopold III had ordered the national army to surrender and advised his ministers to flee to London. His conduct may have been deplored by others, but shirtsleeved fathers brandishing patriotic pokers in breakfast rooms did not blame their king, and if no Brel was a hero of the war, neither was he a collaborator. Indeed, Romain listened illicitly to the BBC at home, and he, Lisette and the boys followed the advances of the Red Army, then seen as more likely deliverers than the departed Allies.

At Vanneste and Brel, however, pragmatism ruled because establishments that did not accept German rule or behaved provocatively were likely to be shut down and their executive bodies terrorized by Gestapo hitmen. Antwerp's Ancienne Belgique variety theatre, for example, was closed when, for reportedly singing what was deemed to be an anti-Nazi song, a certain Bobbejaan Schoepen had been escorted from the stage and sent to a labour camp at the behest of the Gestapo.

In the factories, there were comparable perils of denouncement to the Reich authorities - particularly if some ambiguous utterance was overheard by the wrong person now that tensions between French and Flemish were in sharper focus than ever. Moreover, Pierre Brel, a foreman by then, was of an age whereby he could be pressganged as a labourer to be worked to death in a worse spot in occupied Europe.

Whenever this possibility seemed most distinct, he was sheltered in the house of Georges Dessart, Jacky's godfather, until the heat was off again. Too close for comfort already had been the descent into Gestapo dungeons of two clergymen known to the Brels - and the Jewish father of Robert Kaufmann, Jacky's best friend in the scouts, wore the degrading yellow star ordained by the Nazi high command.

In their own capital city, many buildings and streets were now *verboten* to Belgians whose every town had become a realm of queues for items of food and clothing so scarce that you could only buy them with weeks of saved-up ration coupons or on the black market. When their mother couldn't acquire groceries by either means, Jacques and, when available, Pierre cycled into the countryside with the determination that if there were eggs, butter, potatoes and similar prized commodities to be had there, they were going to have them.

To Jacques' chagrin, one of the few constants unaffected by the new regime had been his schooling. The cosy, guiltless era of École Saint-Viateur was over when, in September 1941, he transferred to L'Institut Saint-Louis within earshot of the Gare du Nord, Brussels' principal railway station. Its masters a mixture of cassocked clerics and Eton-collared laity, this seat of learning was more permissive than most. Yet, though eight o' clock mass was optional, Brel Minor - unlike his classmates - was there every morning for two terms in the fourth year. Rooted in credulity rather than a sudden attack of true spirituality, he may have been supplicating the Almighty for a report that would read more optimistically than the 'could do better' that had emerged from each one as regularly as rocks in the stream.

At the outset, he'd buckled down almost eagerly to his lessons. An interest in history had been rewarded with good marks, and, despite appalling spelling, he'd often been first in French; his essays incorporating realistic dialogue riven with the low slang that intrigued him. He'd won a prize too for a *précis* of Cervantes' *Don Quixote*, the only humourous fiction he'd maintain he'd ever read.

During his second spring at L'Institut, he'd decided to start a class newspaper, but lost interest partly because his father felt that it would interfere with 'proper' school work. This argument was undermined by Abbé Duchamps, a forward-thinking language teacher, who organised a drama club in which an initially reserved Jacques surfaced as a leading light (and something of a ham).

Such attainments weren't sufficient, however, to prevent him having to repeat his first year - and falling further behind during a demoralized transformation from a well-meaning if uninvolved student to a known troublemaker whose pranks included setting off an alarm clock in class. Picturing himself as a most terrific desperado, he was also a sharer of dirty jokes and magazines of female lingerie, and - like Pierre before him - an initiate of a caste who'd graduated from the innocence of tooth-rotting boiled sweets to the lung-corroding evil of cigarettes. Tall for his age, Jacky had no qualms about putting up his fists, looking fierce and hoping for the best rather than swallow insults or shrug off the bullying of his meeker pals by older children.

During the lunch hour and immediately after lessons, he and his blazered cronies would gawp at hoity-toity girls from a sister school, parading down the Boulevard du Jardin Botanique. Though L'Institut Saint-Louis boys weren't automatically threatened with detention for fraternizing with anyone with a different set of hormones who wasn't a relation, Brel - for all his observed brashness - hadn't yet the gall to make even the most polite and bashful approach. In 'The Vagrant', he'd pondered whether Madeleine had any conception of how vulnerable teenage boys can be. Moreover, his self-esteem was in any case at rock-bottom because, by his fifteenth birthday, Jacques was slacking among lads three years his junior.

Had he been familiar with Wordsworth, Brel might have muttered a dry 'to be young was very heaven' as he took stock of what was becoming a miserable existence. Retreating from the pressures to 'be good', to 'be worthy' of all his parents had given him, he began a neatly-written secret diary to which he added collages and drawings. Like *Kho-Barim*, it alluded to little that was going on around him. This was an apparent attempt at expressing feelings otherwise suppressed, and idealising a drab childhood via a process that was revealing - and prophetic in the same sense that 'Bruxelles', a *chanson* he'd pen twenty years later, dealt not with the metropolis of his youth - 'because I didn't like it very much, and because it had nothing to say to me' - but that flickering, monochrome Brussels of the turn of the century with its horse-drawn carriages and silent cinema. Even so, he would comment disparagingly that 'Brussels in my song could well be Bordeaux or any other town.

Belgium in general was as much of a muchness to Jacques Brel. The war hadn't altered its essentially conservative conventions - particularly in rural districts where life was regulated by seasonal whims (as when 'the merry south wind causes the meadows to tremble beneath July' in 'Le Plat Pays'), harvest yield and the eternal verities in which human kind was inexorably involved. Even in the most unprepossessing industrial settlement, old traditions lived on in carnivals, beer festivals and brass band tournaments that finished - as was proper - with the massed ensembles blaring out the national anthem (or *a* national anthem). When composing 'La Bière' in 1968, Jacques would be amused by an adolescent memory of *basso profundo* tubas blown by blokes with bellies full of ale.

Like the Welsh and their Eisteddfods, folk choirs and dance troupes connected with local Cercles Folkloriques societies donned national costume to present material from time immemorial at weddings, fêtes and school concerts - though the form was often corrupted by accompanists making do with modern instruments like chromatic accordion, dance band drum kit and yellow-keyed parish hall piano.

If he wearied of the hearty clubbism of these worthy hands-on archivists, Jacques Brel absorbed enough of Belgium's musical culture for it to have a bearing on his own creative output long after his voice broke to a baritone that would one day be dredged from vocal cords husky with chain-smoking the untipped mega-tar weed that would kill him. Eventually throwing away up to five empty packs of Gauloise daily, he claimed that the habit was the fault of his father: 'He had every right to smoke, but it was a shame that the odour of his fine tobacco made us feel like trying it too.'

An infinitely less harmful life-long addiction was to the cinema. It was always fun during his weekly escape (usually on the half-day holiday each Thursday afternoon) to Le Cinema Pax: the convulsions of laughter at the same joke; telling yourself that it's only acting in the sad bits; the lump in the throat giving way to giggles at mawkishness, and the muted buzz as the half-lights dimmed before the main feature.

In his 1962 *chanson*, 'Madeleine', a movie was designated in vain to supply Brel's stood-up courtly lover with seclusion of sorts for his whispered sweet nothings, but sub-titled *film noir* Hollywood was at its callous and neurotic apogee during the 1940s: all platinum blondes in sleazy dives; rain-sodden nights lit by neon advertisements, and lonesome, defeatist anti-heroes like James Cagney and Humphrey Bogart. Moreover, when Belgium was liberated by the Allies in September 1944, the United States seemed more than ever to be the wellspring of everything glamorous from Coca-Cola to the Ink Spots whose crooning would enrapture the Théâtre de la Monnaie during their European tour in 1947.

Many a Gallic entertainer gained a second-class and, questionably, counterfeit status by aping whatever was going on over the Atlantic - and across the Channel - but among those fighting back were the likes of Cora Vaucaire, Lucienne Delyle, Lys Gauty, Charles Trenet, Jean Sablon, Pierre Dudan, Georges Brassens, the dancing vocalist Mistinguett, goofy singing comedian Fernandel - to France what Bob Hope was to the States - and, most illustrious to a wider world, Maurice Chevalier. As a prisoner-of-war for over two years, Chevalier had been advantaged by an acquisition not only of an engaging 'ow-you-say grasp of the English language, but also the trademark straw boater and Noel Coward smoking jacket for a one-man show of jauntily urbane characterisations that included mime, comic monologue and songs, some of them self-penned. Before an Eiffel Tower backdrop, he was rendered inseparable from 'Zank 'Eaven For *Leedle* Gurls, 'Ah *Lurve* Paris' and the rest of them after he Made It as a caricature Frenchman on stage and screen in the USA and Britain - where few Gallic artistes had made much headway.

In much more qualified fashion, Jean Sablon - as a bilingual French 'answer' to Bing Crosby - and Fernandel were to be Hollywood-bound too, but being enormous within French-speaking territories could be enormous enough. Though as well-placed to do so as Sablon, Trenet, for instance, didn't try to permeate an international market. Moreover, if more unknown globally, Georgius, the 'Chevalier of the suburbs', was assured well-paid work for as long as he could stand before a microphone for an energy and epic vulgarity that matched that of Britain's Max Miller.

More germane to this discussion is the case study of Bobbejaan Schoepen. After his wartime sufferings, he emerged as a balladeer, songwriter and all-round entertainer, who was able to adapt just enough of prevailing North American trends - most conspicuously the cowboy suits and rehearsed 'sincerity' of country-and-western - to not alienate a Flemish-speaking home following that bought his discs by the ton from the dawn of his recording career in 1948 - with 78 rpm 'The Yodeling Whistler' - making him one of the richest men in Belgium.

He achieved worthwhile, if limited, recognition by his mid-twenties, but, more typically, Chevalier, Georgius and Fernandel's respective times had come when they were older, thus fuelling the mitherings of Belgian parents and teachers that, unless you'd been born into showbusiness, it was unwise to see it as a viable career. It was a facile life anyway, a vocational blind alley. Chevalier and his sort apart, no-one lasted very long.

Besides, Brussels was beyond the geographical limit of the pool from which the entertainment industry, centred in Paris, was usually prepared to fish for its talent - and, in households like the Brels, the very idea of a boy venturing onto the professional stage as a singer in the popular style was almost as deplorable as a girl joining a burlesque troupe. Regardless of who was present, a middle-class father would often switch off a wireless set if it was broadcasting what was taken to be 'jazz', and fly into a rage if his adolescent - not 'teenage' - son came downstairs in an American tie. With geometrically-patterned lino the only hint of frivolity in many such homes, the youth would glower through net curtains at the early evening street lamps, and wonder if this was all there was: get up-get to work-get home-get to bed.

Condemned to be both well-bred and intelligent, Jacques and two similarly-placed school chums, Jacques Seguin and Jean Meerts, channelled part of their pampered frustration into issues of a four-page duplicated magazine, *Le Grand Feu*, published in May and June 1947. Seguin's self-depreciating editorial stated its anti-materialistic aims and a desire to unite the young people in the district against the bourgeoisie.

Under a pseudonym, 'Raoul de Signac', Brel's principal contribution was a short story, *Frédéric* - the name Jacques would insist he'd have given his son if he'd had one. It began with a man on his death bed urging his grandson to run away while the rest of the family discuss the burial, thus anticipating vaguely 'Le Moribund' and 'Le Tango Funèbre'. More shrouded indications of what was to come were contained (under another *nom de plume*) in two poems, 'Rain' and 'Spleen'. When declaimed, they tend to sound like bombastic 'why, oh, why' ramblings - dying souls, weeping clouds and all that. Maybe the rest of *Le Grand Feu*'s executive body thought so too because nothing by Jacques appeared in the second number - and, in spite of working up a readership of around two hundred, the gazette petered out during the summer recess, belying promises of a third edition in September.

Never mind, it had been great fun, but, if pretentious and slightly infuriating, *Le Grand Feu* had had the impact of a feather on concrete on 'The System', 'Society' *et al*. Finally, the three principals had to face the fact that being 'subversive' was a folly to be cast aside on departure to the sadder Real World.

Jacques had quit L'Institut Saint-Louis before he was expelled. His final term report was summarized by the bald statement that 'he has lazed about as he is going to leave' from a master who - like the majority of his colleagues - had been as anxious for Brel to go as the lad himself was. In later years, he'd express regrets for his slothful and disorderly behaviour, but, in 1947, Jacques had gone along with whatever would placate Romain and Lisette after his academic failure. So he joined Vanneste and Brel with hardly a murmur, furtively pleased at the idea of receiving a man's wages.

His hours were an inflexible 8.30 to 1 p.m., 1.30 to six. In a suit rather than overalls, he was put to task fixing prices and liaising with clients from a desk in the corrugated cardboard department - though he was soon to be sent to the new branch in Flanders for several weeks in hopes of improving his Flemish.

This trip was among few highlights of a weekly grind as humdrum as school. With fist supporting forehead, Brel's mind grew numb with the monotony of convertible debentures and compound interest in francs and centimes. An exasperated attempt to elicit his mother's sympathy only brought to the fore how little she ever considered not only what his ambitions or aspirations might be, but whether he even had any.

He had already absorbed the habits of idler co-workers; stopping the service lift between floors for a quiet smoke or, after a glance over his shoulder for the nosier members of staff, tinker on scrap paper with fragments of verse or prose for a then unknown purpose. These small covert rebellions symbollized how removed his concept of self-advancement was from that of one who'd borne the brunt of the Depression.

Romain - now over sixty - was, to all intents and purposes, no more than titular head of the firm now, having been poleaxed by a stroke. The reins of administration were in the hands of Amand Vanneste Junior, nearly thirty and very much a chip off the old block. On the board too were Amand's brother-in-law and Pierre Brel who, likewise understanding the dictates of modern commerce, had authorized the laying-off of a considerable percentage of the work force after the installation of automation.

Jacky did his bit by representing the family in the company's soccer team. Otherwise, he beheld its social activities with the disinterest of the completely jaded. Self-contained as young Monsieur Jacques was in the office, few who saw him there could have visualized a radically different Monsieur Jacques who made a spectacle of himself at a cramped Christmas Eve party thrown by a certain Hector Bruyndonckx and his wife Jeanne.

The couple were the only thirty-somethings present as the former *Grand Feu* revolutionary became the life-and-soul of the gathering - as if trying to regain a reputation lost by an apparent capitulation to capitalism. Fixing listeners with a penetrating stare, he turned on Brooding Intensity, false paranoia and self-assumed celebrity in rambling and contradictory accounts of his life, his tortured genius, his Blows against the Establishment. Revelling in his wickedness, he bragged that (gasp!) he didn't go to Church any more (though, in fact, he still went to Mass every Sunday to humour not so much his parents as the Vannestes).

Man, he was obnoxious. Nevertheless, Hector Bruyndonckx, a university drop-out, was a tolerant host who recognized a 'good kid' who was probably ranting about losing his faith for effect. He was from a good home, wasn't he? In his heart-of-hearts, he must still believe, mustn't he - even if the power of prayer hadn't brought better school reports? 'When you say to a Catholic that X or Y is no longer a Catholic,' Brel would observe later, 'they are always surprised. As far as they're' concerned, only Sartre escaped the net. However, they are sure that Camus was still a Christian.'

Yet Jacques relished the warm, open-handed atmosphere at Jeanne and Hector's. It was so different from that at home where a subject like, say, atheism was so monstrous that it was mentioned only in a pained murmur. Bruyndonckx's get-together was also Brel's closest encounter with anything that he could perceive as a *demi-monde*. It wasn't just the nicotine clouds and the table lamps dimmed with headscarves. Hector's house, you see, was a liberty hall of rapid-fire intellectual debate. That *chez* Bruyndonckx welcomed even defrocked priests and non-believers was regarded as border-line abominable in the late 1940s.

As a measure of both the nature of Brel's sheltered upbringing and the *ennui* of post-war Brussels, Bruyndonckx and his circle seemed to a highly-strung eighteen-year-old to be the hottest action going - with the charismatic Hector as seer, prophet and guru. He was one of these boisterous muscular Christians and right-wing progressives, who tended to stare appraisingly at whoever was addressing him, and pass judgement on what was said in carefully polished and resounding one-liners. 'Belgium is the navel of the world' was one memorable Bruyndonckx-ism. The only subject he was reticent about was his daytime employment at his father's garage.

In 1941, he and his missus had founded La Franche Cordée - FC - a mixed-sex Church youth club. Its motto was 'More Is Within You'; its emblem, Christ's crown of thorns. It was also very discerning in its membership selection. Among those barred were prototype *yé-yé* - youths from the poorer quarters, recognisable by seedy-flash garb that only the boldest homosexuals and American GIs on passes would be seen dead in: zoot-suits, 'spearpoint' shirts, black-and-white footware and hand-painted ties with Red Indians or baseball players on them. They were not unlike Britain's pre-rock 'n' roll Teddy Boys either with their brilliantined ducktails, brass rings adorning fingers like knuckle dusters, belts studded with washers stolen from work - and a musical preference for the less slushy shades of US pop music, lumped together derisively as 'swing' by Bruyndonckx.

Like the Teds too, they modelled their personalities on *film noir* ne'er-do-wells when prowling the streets of Brussels in swaggering phalanxes with hunched shoulders, hands rammed in pockets, and chewing gum in a half-sneer, their women trailing forlornly behind them. A lone pedestrian would cross over to avoid them as, bored silly, they looked for things to destroy, people to beat up.

Both were potentially available in parochial FC headquarters where sports jackets, 'sensible' shoes, cavalry twills and short-back-and-sides marked you as a serviceable husband material for tweedy, earnest maidens who looked as if they couldn't wait for a game of chess or ping-pong, followed by a chat about life-after-death over an orange squash. As the motto implied, Bruyndonckx's steep and rugged pathway had a predictably wholesome, self-improving reek about it. Sport, purposeful hobbies, charity work and the open-air was just the ticket to take your mind off nature's baser urges and any other distractions from loftier ideals.

When not out canoeing, hiking or booting a soaking-wet piece of leather about, the young people - not 'youths' - of La Franche Cordée watched a slide-show or engaged in a 'Brains Trust' on topical issues like Sabbath Day opening, universal suffrage (Hector was against it) and the monarchy (Jacques was more a republican) - all the subjects never thrashed out at Rue Jacques-Manne. Yet Romain and Lisette were not displeased about wayward Jacky's increasing participation in the FC - so much so that he was permitted to use a factory van and even Romain's Studebaker car for its outings, fund-raising fêtes , religious retreats or delivery of home-made condiments, second-hand garments and like hand-outs to orphanages and old folks homes.

Though unrecompensed for petrol, Jacques did whatever willingness and energy would do to further the FC cause as if to make up for his shortcomings at school and work. Here was a mission, something in which he could be a credit to his parents - like he would be when elected FC president in 1949. Now at last he could be taken seriously, innovate, contribute to the good of mankind - and be seen doing so.

Mama smiled fondly when he reported back after the Saturday afternoon when, robed as St. Nicholas (rather than pagan Father Christmas), he'd stopped the traffic with his processional cross so that the FC entourage could cross the road on the way to give an entertainment to hospital patients. Among his party pieces was a dramatized reading of Antoine de Saint-Exupéry's *Le Petit Prince* in a literary cabaret. Though the Brels weren't an especially musical family, there was an upright piano in the house on which Jacques by ear had figured out 'Für Elise' and, on request, could bang it out with digits on auto-pilot as others would 'Chopsticks'. He had also acquired a guitar and, his fingertips hardening with daily practice, taught himself a handful of chords to provide accompaniment to his sung adaptation of Villon's 'La Ballade Des Pendus' - an appeal for divine justice - and other items in keeping with the FC's devotional repertoire.

This may be seen now as one of few signs of the ultimate destiny of the seemingly pious youth group leader who'd been dubbed 'Abbé' Brel as much for his resemblance to some nerdy young curate - the wire spectacles, the beanpole frame, the sticking-out teeth and the shadows of both greying temples and a wispy moustache. All he lacked were the dog-collar, the damp handshake and the halitosis.

Yet the disruptive Institut Saint-Louis schoolboy of yore still peeped out on FC trips with Jacques solely in charge. During his turn at the wheel, he'd pull over to buy everyone a drink in wayside bars, surprising some passengers with his colloquial turns of phrase and rich fund of rude jokes. After a few beers, they'd zoom off on wings of song, winding down the car windows to thump a beat on the roof, and shout insults at passers-by. As disgraceful was 'Abbé' and an accomplice lighting-up boldly during a midnight mass in Brussels, stage-whispering a giggled 'la Sainte Cigarette!' during a silence in the proceedings.

This antic was a blip on the test card of a phase in Brel's life which, like certain Russian novels, had him looking onward at a dismal, futile eternity. The FC may have provided an outlet for otherwise thwarted artistic expression, but an equally strong motivation was that it gave him licence to fraternize - but not much else - with girls. In the years before the birth pill and the Swinging Sixties, pre-marital gropings were a bigger step to take. A young man might boast of his conquests, but everyone knew that they were either exaggerations or downright lies. Her whole being might be screaming for sex, but a 'nice' girl of both La Franche Cordée in particular and the late 1940s in general 'saved herself' for her future husband.

Probably because of his high office and his known abuse of it, 'Abbé' Brel got on well with sillier FC females to whom he spoke in a jokingly confidential fashion about sex as if he had inside information about it. Others, however, did not feel libido flood their nervous systems whenever his runaway tongue unfurled a cuss-word. Among them was no-nonsense Thérèse Michielsen - 'Miche' - a *petite*, blue-eyed blonde with a *retroussée* nose. Nearly three years older than Jacques, Miche was also, perhaps, half a class below him, being the daughter of a commercial traveller. Her background was even more ordinary: convent school, Girl Guides and a business studies course embracing typing, stenography, accountancy, commercial law, German and English. All trackways of her life thus far lead the same way - to an administrative post with Saks the clothing manufacturers, and enrolment in the FC.

Miche was not an active participant in the organization's more theatrical endeavours. She was, however, within an audience that heard Jacques Brel's first performances of his own compositions. Some like waltz-time 'Le Fou Du Roi' had a mediaeval flavour melodically - and lyrically in their neo-sacred portrayal of heterosexual love. In 'Priére Païenne', a subdued suitor proffers his poetry as a gift to the Virgin while in mournful 'Heureux', a recurring 'blessed' stresses the purity of the mutual adoration between separated sweethearts. Yet, past straightforward narrative, Brel was already concerned with the implications of what the situations in his *chansons were* in essence rather than how they unfolded.

Some items betrayed more blatant clues of that which lay unthinkably ahead. Pretty-but-nothing 'Ballade' didn't, but 'Le Troubadour' sang love songs without believing in them, and 'Les Deux Fauteuils' ('The Two Armchairs') pre-empted 1963's 'Les Vieux'. Though an untitled *chanson* of which only the hymnal chorus is extant was deist rather than overtly Christian, most of Brel's early efforts had been tailored to suit the with-it bible-bashing of the FC. This would remain discernable in 'Les Dames Patronesses' and 'Les Despèreres' with their New Testament phraseology, and in the tenor of further later songs that were even more like secular hymns in their preoccupation with redemption and the wrongs of Brel's immediate environment.

In acute need of a change from it during 1948's rainy summer, Jacques anticipated National Service by volunteering a year before his call-up papers were expected. All told, it was to be as painless a stint as he could have had; certainly light-years from the vile transit camp scenario of 'Au Suivant'. Following basic training in Limbourg, Rifleman A 48-2567 was sent to the 15th Division Transport and Communication sector in Zellik on the outskirts of Brussels, and less than five miles from Vanneste and Brel.

Because he arranged for an influential lieutenant to have use of the Studebaker - that Romain could no longer drive - Jacques was treated with an unfair favouritism that included undeserved promotion to corporal; a 'cushy' indoor position requisitioning and distributing underwear and regulation dung-coloured shirts, and a longer convalescence than was necessary when he caught bronchitis. The officer also turned a blind eye during an initiative test when Brel, required to find his way back to barracks without any money from a point thirty miles away, simply hailed a taxi to the doorstep of the family home where Mama paid the fare.

Furthermore, he was still able to attend Franche Cordée meetings and continue what had become an open pursuit of Miche who, overlooking the disparity in their ages, now perceived a strength of personality in him unnoticed when she'd first caught him surruptitiously studying her whilst feigning indifference. He'd screwed himself up to ask her out, and within weeks of that first date, they crossed the impalpable barrier between inferred companionship and declared love.

Naturally, Jacques the bohemian did not believe in wedlock - 'I believe that men are nomads, without peace in their soul, always attracted to the other side of the hill'. More knuckleheadedly, he'd latched onto the machismo values and dual code of morality whereby Belgian men could mess around with other women, but wouldn't put up with any infidelities from their wives. Nevertheless, Jacques the compliant scion of a respectable family proposed to Thérèse Michielsen on New Year's Eve 1949 - and, two nail-biting days later, she accepted. 'Women always take more than they can give,' Jacques would confide one day to a journalist's tape recorder, 'They disorientate us in the long run because they oblige us to give them everything that we possess.'

Six months after announcing the betrothal, Jacques was demobbed. After absurd contemplations about becoming either a cobbler or a poulter, the security of the old firm seemed a sounder option for a chap with marriage in mind. The job description now included debt-collecting and assignments as far afield as Paris, a visit endured rather than relished as it didn't take him far outside a claustrophobic industrial estate as faceless as those around Vanneste and Brel. As depressing was the discovery that Belgians were the butt of jokes about disorientated provincial bumpkins as much by the French there as they were by the Dutch.

Yet, with a steady job, a sagacious *fiancée* and his parents' financial safety-net, the story might have ended happily ever after with The Wedding on 1 June 1950 in the Maison Communale registry office, and a religious ceremony eight days later. Romain was too poorly to attend either, but he was amenable to the pair using the car for the long journey (with another couple) to the honeymoon location on the Cote D'Azur - and a drive back to Brussels that was as dispiriting as Jacques had presumed it would be. Still, it was inevitable, he supposed, as he and his bride settled into 29, Avenue Brigade-Pironlaan, a rented ground floor flat - sitting room, bedroom, kitchen, bathroom - a tram journey away from both Vanneste and Brel and the electricity company where Miche was now a secretary. 'In my view, Brussels has always been a tramway,' grimaced Jacques, 'I used to have to ride the tram for an hour and a half every day.'

Outside the working week, Jacques and Miche were eager to splash vivid hues on whatever spare time was theirs. They might, therefore, be At Home for a throng of invited guests; pushing furniture against the walls to create room. While Miche served the finger food, Jacques needed only token cajoling to strum the *chansons* he still wrote. Other Saturdays would find them jollying everyone along at holiday camps for deprived youngsters, and, as sure as the sunrise, there'd be a chicken dinner, preceded by grace, every Sunday at Rue Jacques-Manne with the expectant grandparents - for Chantal, the first of Miche and Jacques' three daughters, was to enter the world on 6 December 1951.

Somehow, it was all too pat, too dovetailed, too *decent*. Months passed and the intensifying tedium of keeping up a respectable front inspired Jacques to pen 'Belle Jeanette', one of his first non-doctrinal creations, and a poke at those who pretend to be contented because their social equals appear to be. The junior Amand Vanneste would recall Brel remarking that he wanted many more children, but the stifling environment drove him to hang around in bars with various mates in the era just before television became an indispensable household fixture. 'The word "Papa" meant nothing to him,' his youngest daughter France would note without rancour, 'Brel as a father never existed because he refused to play the part.'

As well as his carousing, Jacques would be 'talked of' with other women, but any cheery flirtations did not adulterate his emotional allegiance to Miche as would be demonstrated in small public fondnesses and in the respect shown to the mother of his children. In turn, unable to rein it, Miche would always indulge his later routine unfaithfulness for those private sweetnesses that forbade her from ever not loving him. 'Love is an expression of passion. Compassion is something else,' he'd explain, 'Passion disappears one day, while compassion stays forever.'

Among members of her family who hadn't approved of Thérèse going out with Jacques Brel was her brother René - at whose nuptials in 1952, his brother-in-law was introduced to Angèle Gullet, presenter of a popular radio programme, *La Vitrine Aux Chansons*. Age and the moderating guidance of Miche had braked the look-at-me affectations displayed at Hector's party, and Brel's more cunning intertwining of modesty and self-projection led Madame Gullet to rub a professional chin when he gave a brief recital during the reception.

What she heard didn't much excite her, but this Jacques wasn't an obvious no-hoper. It would do no harm, she guessed, to try him out with a couple of numbers on the show. Leaving nothing to chance, however, perky 'Il Peut Pleuvoir' - almost a parody of Trenet - and 'La Diable (Ça Va)' - outlining Satan's satisfaction with twentieth century humankind's bellicose activities - were pre-recorded with Angèle issuing orders to Jacques from a glass-fronted booth of tape-spools and switches in a room about the size of the average hotel bedroom.

Reaction to the broadcast was surprisingly gratifying, and an in-person slot followed. Mildly shocked by his sudden fame - and, perhaps, with an apprehensive weather-eye on his parents - Jacques chose to hide behind the *nom de théâtre* 'Berel' as he had with the *Grand Feu* pseudonyms. It might have been just as well because, badgered by Angèle, one of the appointed judges, Berel entered a radio talent contest to be networked all over the Netherlands and France. On the day, however, there was a hitch: Gullet was flat on her back with 'flu. Without his champion, Jacques, fraught with misgivings, discharged his brief turn with a cautious politeness and misjudged extemporizations. After he thus died a death, one of the panel - a Frenchman - wondered on air what on earth Angèle Gullet could see in this hopeless singing composer with an 'unintelligible' Brussels accent you could slice with a spade.

On the premise that anyone who could stoke up so much negative response must have something going for him, Angèle persuaded her husband Clement, a power at the Brussels wing of the Philips label, to grant Jacques an audition on 17 February 1953. When re-running the tape afterwards, Clement heard in the very guitar-and-voice starkness of the three *chansons* a quirky beauty, a freshness - like a rough-hewn Brassens - that might prove marketable.

A debut single - pressed on brittle 78 r.p.m shellac - of 'La Foire' and 'Il Y A' shifted two hundred copies - faintly promising at a time when sales of sheet music far outnumbered those of discs. With the arrival of a royalty statement, Jacques was elevated from amateur to semi-professional status with the correlated broadening of his performing spectrum from the protective bubble of soft-drinks-only youth clubs to cabaret bars like the Grand' Place, the Coup De Lune and, in particular, La Rose Noir in the very heart of Brussels. These were run by hard-nosed managements who paid little because their establishments - so they made clear - attracted slumming showbiz moguls among a late night underworld of gamblers, racketeers and prostitutes: all those that Brel had been taught to despise and fear.

The personality of a given act was, nonetheless, usually secondary - a background noise - to boozy chatter. Brel's knees knocked with terror, but after a while, he grew braver, quite thrilled whenever he was able to extort a spatter of applause. From ignored inertia, he started to get noticed. Intrigued, Jacques Nellens, son of the director of the Casino in Knokke, suggested that Berel or whatever his name was should take part in the next festival - but, out of twenty-eight contestants, Jacques, glistening with embarrassment, came twenty-seventh; one jurer calling him 'ridiculous'.

As his mother often reminded him, rather than just waiting for six o' clock to roll around, he could choose to make more of an effort at Vanneste and Brel - and thus be on the board of directors within ten years and maybe vice-chairman by the time he was forty. Instead, Jacques Brel kept such a noxious vocational decision at arm's length for as long as there remained even the remotest possibility of a more glamorous alternative.

Chapter Two
'Ask Pierre To Bring A Jar Of Nescafé'

The discovery that, execrable though you might be, an audience of responsible adults is actually listening to you singing and playing an instrument can create false impressions of personal abilities in a vulnerable mind. So began the transfiguration of Jacques Brel - possessor of provocative originality rather than orthodox talent - to stardom because, as Brel himself would tell you, 'If I had any talent, I wouldn't waste my time making songs. Our vanity pushes us to actions at the depth of our thoughts.'

His first deep thought on the matter was that he lived in the wrong place. While it contained a plethora of radio stations and recording concerns, back-of-beyond Brussels might have been years rather than miles away from Paris.

Next came the motivation to uproot himself when, via the Gullets, a copy of his single landed on the desk of Jacques Canetti, a showbiz jack-of-all-trades in the French capital. With his Philips talent scout's hat on, he had 'discovered' Georges Brassens - and the label was as voracious as any other for newer faces to exploit and discard for a fickle public. Of late, Canetti had taken on French Canadian expatriate Félix Leclerc, and become 'interested' in Boris Vian, jazz trumpeter, journalist and composer of satirical pieces such as 'Le Deserteur', which took the form of a letter from a newly-drafted soldier to the President of the Republic, and containing the daring line: If blood has to be spilt, Mr, President/Set an example by spilling yours.' Yet neither he nor Leclerc was yet shaping up either as even *a* new Brassens, let alone *the* new Brassens.

So what's with this 'Berel'? As the disc span its little life away, Canetti decided that while neither 'Il Y A' nor 'La Foire' was a masterpiece of *chanson*, they were promising enough for the fellow to be summoned to Paris for a try-out. Canetti had heard about the poor showing at Knokke, but this was mitigated by Angèle Gullet's faith in the songs if not the artist. Shall we say 20 June?

Though a recording deal was far from in the bag, just the sniff of one was sufficient excuse for Brel in 1953, twenty-three years old and nauseated by the thought of his present drudgery stretching ahead of him, day upon day, unto the grave. He'd long seen the crunch coming, but not making the impending decision any easier was the imminent arrival of another child. If anything, Miche - a handy peg on which to hang his frustrations when he slammed in from the office - was more objective about the occupation that kept the family's heads above water financially but crushed her husband's spirit. Fearing that one day, Jacques might snap, Miche was, therefore, supportive of any marginally feasible means of escape.

She'd go back to work, she said - and, as soon as she was able after the birth of a second daughter, France, on 12 July, she was to operate from home as a typist, copying endless quires of student theses amid the close smell of soiled nappies and correcting fluid. 'Maybe I was very brave' was her understatement, 'I was the anchor he needed.'

The galvanizing telephone call from Canetti was the culmination of an age of interminable evenings of the same arguments coming up over and over again, building from a trace of vapour on the horizon to Wagnerian thunderstorm. With his wife's concurrence, Jacques went the whole hog by resigning from Vanneste and Brel - where he'd become quite used to being ribbed about having ideas above his station - and announcing his immediate departure to make his name in Paris as a *chansonier*.

He was, however, surprised (and, perhaps, a little dismayed) that neither of his parents prevailed upon him to be sensible. Indeed, after raising quizzical eyebrows, Papa - who, at near enough the same age, had walked away from a 'good' job to go to university - advanced him a year's salary (to be repaid with ten per cent interest) and promised him that, as it had been when he'd returned from the army, Jacky's old job would be waiting for him after he'd flushed this singing nonsense out of his system.

With more confidence and hope than he could possibly justify, Jacques flung his arms round Miche and Chantal before heaving guitar and suitcase onto the long, high train to Paris where he knew no-one apart from Vanneste and Brel affiliates - no-one at all really. True, he had Canetti's business card, but the two hadn't yet communicated face to face, and Brel didn't want to jinx anything by popping round there before the session. It might put Canetti off.

On the Big Day, Brel did precisely this. Before a note was heard , Canetti became less enthusiastic than he'd seemed on the wire, and the seemingly final verdict took Brel's breath away. Yes, he had acquitted himself well, made nice music, but Canetti, anxious to keep his plum job with Philips, explained that the problem was Jacques' manifest deficit of...how can I put this?...sex appeal. Look at Charles Trenet's athletic frame, curly blonde hair and graceful stage movements or svelte newcomer Phillipe Clay, with his imposing height, handsomely angular features and the stage presence of an updated Chevalier. Then there was Gilbert Becaud, who, so Canetti had just heard, was being bombarded with screams and even female underwear the moment the curtains swept back a few dramatic bars into his 'Monsieur Pointu' signature tune.

What could 'Berel' with his staid and whiskered demeanour offer *les midenettes* - France's 'bobby-soxers'? As well as the long jaw and buck teeth - more Fernandel than Clay - he was gangling and skinny. He'd be all arms and legs, a human stick-insect, in front of an audience when he abandoned the guitar - for abandon it he'd have to if he was granted a contract because it was the done thing then to front an orchestra, unencumbered by an instrument.

From the disobliging way Canetti put it, you'd think he was talking about Quasimodo, but he kept his options open so that Brel couldn't say that he had actually been turned down. Yet, with perfunctory kindness, Canetti advised him to set his sights on working to order as a backroom songwriter with a publishing company that would endeavour to place his stuff with suitable acts in an age when the demarcation line between composer and singer was the norm, and a jobbing tunesmith was an indispensable part of the music trade.

Jacques had not yet become so uncompromising an artist to splutter 'I'd rather not, sir' to Canetti's face. Nevertheless, the very next morning, with pride smarting, he made it a point of honour that, even if had to dial his index finger to a stub, he'd get signed to another company and sell so many millions that his horse face would peer at Canetti from every record store window in Europe. He wasn't going to answer to 'Berel' anymore either.

At any rate, he couldn't go back to Brussels without something to show for it. Besides, feeling infinitely patient then, he liked the image of himself living *la vie bohème*, even finding a vague enchantment in imagining that it might go on forever. Indeed, mentions of his early struggles were to bring out his tall stories of sleeping on park benches; subsisting on soup made of leftovers from street markets; burning furniture against the chill of winter, and dressing like a tramp at the mercy of the parish.

These tales weren't so much improved with age as total fiction. Throughout his first sun-filled residency in Paris, Brel stayed in hotels around Montmartre which, within the shadow of the Basilica De Sacre Coeur, had an intimate ambience of bistros where you could sit for hours; street-sweepers with twig brooms, and, lacing the air, the purr of accordions and an aroma of coffee and Gauloise.

The haunt of Modigliani and Sartre, Montmartre was also the traditional home of existentialism with its 'nothing matters' engrossment with self-immolation and death. Yet Brel's noted complaint about bedbugs to room-service was hardly romantic squalor. Neither were his restaurant meals and even the novel idea of cooking for himself after dashing off a request to Miche for 'a frying pan, plates, pepper and salt cellars (full ones please), a corkscrew and a tin-opener.' Expecting to see his big brother soon - in Paris on a Vanneste and Brel assignment - he added 'Please ask Pierre if he has a burner (alcohol not petrol). Ask him to bring a jar of Nescafé.'

The inconvenience of the so-called Hotel Idéal not having a telephone could scarcely be seen as any great hardship either. All the same, poor Jacques was compelled to make and await calls in a nearby café. Dejecting in their curtness were those 'too busy' to ring back or answer his letters. Others were 'in a meeting', 'out to lunch'. Jacques who? Try again tomorrow.

Getting nowhere with record companies and radio, he scanned the cabaret clubs, thinking that here at least he could pick and chose. 'Chez Giles,' he reported to Miche, was 'too snobby' and L'Écluse 'too small, only seventy seats.' By way of market research, he attended concerts by Becaud ('too relaxed and full of himself'), baby-voiced Suzy Solidor ('very pretty dress') and Yves Montand ('no-one can present his songs like him. The way he uses his hands motivated me to write some poems to recite without guitar').

One evening, Brel was granted an audience with Brassens at the prestigious Bobino where Georges was preparing for a show. If too young to be losing his hair, there were a lot of miles in his eyes. Furthermore, guaranteed work for good money for as long as he could stand, the Great Man had the means to be paternal. Yes, he'd like to hear M. Brel sing a *chanson*. Drawing on his beloved pipe and nodding with apparent pleasure while the last chord yet reverberated, Brassens decided to help out. There and then, he wrote a general letter of recommendation for the young Belgian to make this unresponsive stage director or that bemused club owner sit up.

Perhaps Georges was sufficiently soft-hearted to do the same for every supplicant - for his endorsement combined with further pavement-tramping and rounds of telephone calls did not improve Brel's prospects - or his mood. Capitalizing on, rather than shrinking from his vexation, he channelled it into the *chansons* that were now streaming from him: 'In these, I can work out my anger, though I do not deal with particular people. A song will not be about one woman, but a certain type of woman; never one man but about ten men at the same time.'

Often, there were so many ideas chasing through his mind that it was all he could do to write them down. Shards of inspiration cut him during a ten minute walk to a newspaper stand. Others imposed themselves in bed, jerking him from a velvet-blue oblivion. Dawn would seem a year away as he figured out a chord sequence to fragments of melody or rhymes to form a couplet. From just a mere title, the ghost of an opening verse, maybe a sketchy chorus too, would smoulder into form, and an unshaven, red-eyed impartiality and a private quality-control would engross him until daylight found him dozing over his instrument, surrounded by cigarette butts, smeared coffee cups and pages full of scribbled lyrics and notation peculiar to himself.

As he'd never learned to sight-read or write musical script at more than a funereal pace, Brel was untroubled by the do's and don'ts that traditionally affect creative flow. There were only the stylistic cliches and habits ingrained since he'd positioned yet uncalloused fingertips to shape an E chord on six taut strings when he was fifteen. Handsomely endowed with a capability to try-try again, he grappled with his muse, drawing from virtually ever musical and literary idiom he had ever encountered and trying to disguise sources of inspiration in hopes that nothing would remain infuriatingly familiar.

On days when little would come, all he could do was dream or despair, lying full-length on the bed, hands under head, smoking, smoking. He'd wander over to the window to gaze glumly at the cobbled courtyard below. Then, in a ritual of thwarted eroticism, he might position himself with his guitar in front of the wardrobe mirror, and perform to thousands of ecstatic fans that only he could see.

Feeling no end of a fool afterwards, he'd earn a night's repose by finding a few clean sheets of paper and writing home. He was a multi-faceted correspondent. His mother might have suspected otherwise, judging by the frequency with which she mailed him money and food parcels, but his chatty letters to her were freighted with life's small change and general assurances like 'Everything's fine. These are splendid times.' To Miche, however, he'd spill out his fears and longings as if the therapy of putting it down in black-and-white made him more likely to stumble upon answers than through fretting and getting more depressed.

Miche and Lisette were each recipients of blithe quotations such as 'At the top, the air is too thin to be able to survive' from Charles Morgan, a Proust-like English novelist highly regarded in France - and Jacky's own Bruyndonckx-type *bons mots* like 'Conscientious people must have friendship.' In a letter to Hector himself, he related a telling tale of a cabin boy who emerged as both a man and a skilled navigator during a single voyage. Afterwards, he sailed off alone to uncharted oceans rather than repeat the same voyage.

Bruyndonckx's preachy reply - hinged on the directive 'Listen to what God says to you. He is never far away' - never quite got to the point that others were having no qualms about making: that Jacques had tried, but the fish weren't biting, and he ought to pack it in.

Well, why not? He felt almost foredoomed to cast the weight off his shoulders. This driving and clearly futile urge to be a *chansonier* was a handicap as surely as if he was schizophrenic or addicted to heroin - and, despite himself, he was missing Brussels as much as Mama had in the Congo. He was now firing off missives to Miche daily, and had discovered himself glowing with patriotic pride when Belgium qualified for a tennis championship against the USA. He was also knocking back an increasing and exclusive capacity of Belgian beer. One evening, its short-lived magic wore off, and Jacques Brel saw that, after two months, the adventure was over.

On the day of departure, he stored up memories of the Paris that would soon be behind him. It would be a morose journey with painfully slow departures before he climbed down stiffly onto the platform in Brussels where everything would be the same as he'd left it. There'd come the ignominy of 'I told you so' recriminations, but to those less inclined to crow, he'd be able to exaggerate his exploits and his familiarity with Brassens. He'd be attractive in his phlegmatic candour about sacrificing all for his wife and children. Folk would start to believe that he had, indeed, once Hit the Big Time, and Chantal and France - his 'little apples' - would brag to playmates about their famous Papa.

To his grandchildren, they could bequeath his scratchy old seventy-eight, and, within days of dumping his luggage in the front room of Avenue Brigade-Pironlaan, 'Adieux', 'L'Ange Dechu', 'Suis L'Ombre Des Chansons', 'Les Enfants Du Roi' and twenty or so further *chansons* he'd taped - with a franc sign over every fretful quaver - in a miniscule Brussels studio where acetates were pressed and cut while-you-wait.

Inherent in the prodigal's return was the hypothesis that, with secret relief, he'd resume the path of secure anonymity at Vanneste and Brel. Jacky, however, proved incorrigible. If his singing career hadn't left the runway in the outer world, he was determined to be a local hero by flaunting his modest achievements on home turf for all they were worth. By consolidating media connections, he'd cling on somehow or other. Yet back on the trivial round of local engagements - with occasional side-trips into the provinces and the borderlands of Holland and France - he shook his fist in the direction of Paris as the old impasse loomed again, and beyond it the unwanted opportunity to pick up where he'd left off, keep his nose clean, graft his way up the firm's hierarchy, and slip quite comfortably into honourable old age -with aberrations of a flaming youth to be unmentioned in his obituary.

What else was there apart from just enough incentive to carry on as an entertainer? Canetti still hadn't passed a final judgement - though with every passing week, it seemed less probable that it would be favourable. Even an encore was sufficient to feed hope nowadays. For many an artiste, records (if any were released) were only adjuncts to earnings on the variety circuit where it was possible to keep up at least an illusion of professional employment for years on the same bill as vile comedians, fat-thighed dancing girls, jugglers, accordionists, trick cyclists and pierrots with names like 'Dut' and 'Spak'.

This road was generally obscure and quiet, a dusty, wearisome road that didn't look as if it led anywhere important - but there was always a chance that it might. A venue in Antwerp where you'd gone down well changes its policy and you don't belong any more, but then you get a week second-billed to Rico's Creole Band nearer the heart of things in Lille. Becaud had tinkled piano in bars until a minor hand injury 'gave me the opportunity to sing'. Next thing you know, he was headlining at the Olympia, France's premier music hall. For God's sake, Edith Piaf - now a French cross between Vera Lynn and Judy Garland - had busked in the streets for centimes before turning to streetwalking. According to long-circulated but disappointingly erroneous hearsay, one of her clients had engineered her first big break.

Another who'd been in the right place at the right time had been Serge Gainsbourg, only a year older than Brel. He'd been a mere jobbing song-writer and pianist in and around Paris before he was cajoled into sing-ing in public, his stage fright interpreted by onlookers as part of an act that procured stray paragraphs in the national press and the first covers of his songs, some entering the stage repertoire of newly big-time Phil-lipe Clay.

It wasn't how good you were, it was who you knew, wasn't it? Sacha Distel, a more well-connected showbiz brat than Gainsbourg, had be-come a respected jazz guitarist before his seventeenth birthday in 1950, often sitting in with distinguished Americans visiting Parisian clubland. He played hard in other respects - with Brigitte Bardot and bohemian icon Juliet Greco among his amours. With lost business innocence too, he'd invested wisely in music publishing, switched smoothly from jazz to singing mainstream pop, and was full steam ahead for his first million.

Brel was sodden with bitter ruminations. It seemed daft to be anything but pessimistic - and, in some ways, the worst was yet to come. Yet the tide started to turn with majestic slowness after another call from Can-etti. It wasn't quite what Jacques wanted to hear, but it would suffice for now. Perhaps it was Brassens' luvvie-like praise that had done the trick, but Canetti – a booking agent too - had an off-peak night that Brel could fill in September at the Théâtre Des Trois Baudets, just off Boulevard De Clichy in Montmartre.

Rather than the roughhouses Jacques was used to, this converted cine-ma attracted students, middle class beatniks - all berets, ten-day beards and holey sweaters - and tourists looking for something less polished than the Moulin Rouge. It may have been because the clientele wanted more than incidental accompaniment to revelry that it was common for Trois Baudets entertainers to be roundly booed if they didn't provide it. Conversely, a grotesque cameraderie could accumulate after an initially gawping crowd tuned into the most unlikely hopeful that an audacious booking policy had procured. During his traipsing the clubs in summer, Jacques had learned too that the Trois Baudets could also be a shop window for anyone who wanted to move up to somewhere more fashionable on the Left Bank like, say, the Quod Libet, Club L'Échelle de Jacob in St. Germain des Prés, its Club Geneviève rival, the smaller L'Écluse or over the river to Milord L'Arsoille, capacious and steeped in history. It could even be a springboard to the 2,300-seater Olympia, France's premier music hall and, as the likes of Phillipe Clay - a club regular only two years earlier - was soon to show, an avenue to a Chevalier-sized index of possibilities.

A new urgency impelled Brel to over-rehearse his act to the last syllable of the patter between songs. On the night, he stood motionless before the unsettling hush with his four-eyed geekiness and a faintly ludicrous 'rustic' stage costume. You didn't quite like to laugh - especially as this clodhopper conveyed the impression that he was unaware of his own inadvertent pricelessness. He stepped forward to make an opening announcement in an intonation that sounded both alien and 'common' to those Parisians who view the Belgians with the same insular arrogance as many Londoners view the Irish, i.e. as ignorant, good-for-nothing Micks.

A snigger set the whole house off. From then on, it was murder. Someone bawled 'peasant!' during a shaky 'La Diable (Ça Va)'. Further taunts, howls of derision and sporadic barracking drew verbal retaliations from Brel, his predetermined continuity in ruins. Finally, the curtain came down, and he quit the building within five minutes.

'Defeats but no surrender,' he told Miche. Other foreigners had shown what was possible, hadn't they? Iberian tenor Luis Mariano and Tino Rossi from Corsica had 'arrived' from small beginnings in Parisian watering holes. Even Belgium-born Rocco Granata - a mere babe-in-arms by comparison - was on the way up. Therefore, partly because there'd been a handful entranced by his efforts on that night-of-nights in September, Brel applied for a work permit and looked for a flat for - to give a sentence in one of his letters a free translation - 'I must stay on because Paris is where it's all happening.' He was going to brazen it out by maximising the fact that he'd actually played the fabled Trois Baudets, regardless that it was, let's say, an incomplete success. From now on, every engagement would be a triumph in retrospect.

Another ace up his sleeve - admittedly, a rather dog-eared one - was Brassens' written laudation. More than silver-tongued guile, this lurched the weather vane of approval in Brel's direction for Suzy Lebrun, owner of Club L'Échelle de Jacob. To his amazement, room was made for him to do a turn that very evening. As non-stop preparation had blighted his Trois Baudets debut, so the exhilaration of the impromptu and an unbottled exuberance brought him safely into harbour at Suzy's place.

Small, bossy and neurotic, she scuttled round him like a mother hen, bringing about a transformation from clumsy hick to one more attuned to what Parisian agents and record label supremos expected of a singing money-maker. He had to wear, she said, stylish but not too way-out suits - or smart casuals akin to the turtle-neck pullover and slacks that Phillipe Clay had when leaving the runway at the Trois Baudets. The glasses and moustache would have to go. He hadn't the face for them. He had to focus himself on every customer, not just the nearest tables; had he ever come across the term 'back-projection'? As for stage dialogue, it might be better if he dispensed with it altogether under the circumstances.

Mme. Lebrun accorded more concrete assistance by lending the young man cash for a new one after some dastard stole his guitar. Furthermore, he'd be among favoured artists invited up to her apartment after hours for a supper of omelette or, the night spot's speciality, avocado stuffed with tuna.

The ego massage of such attentions resulted in *bravura* recitals from a smartened-up and slicker Brel for up to two hundred drinkers. Ideally, he'd end by sweeping into the wings, leaving 'em wanting more - but, even minus the rose-tinted spectacles, rival entrepreneurs began casting covetous eyes on Suzy's find, and soon he was administering his musical elixir in Club Geneviève in split-shifts with Charles Aznavour, a twenty-nine-year-old Armenian. The most gratifying sign that Brel was breaking through at last was a second chance at the Trois Baudets. This time, the taunts and slow handclaps from those who remembered metamorphosed into amused cheers and then considered ovations.

Within weeks, Jacques was cramming in twenty-minute spots in up to six different clubs per evening between Montparnasse and Montmartre. Some lines to Pierre, a motor-cycle enthusiast, joked 'Rallies? I go on them every night!' A lasting and beneficial effect of this exhausting but exhilarating schedule was that it wrought in him a more workmanlike stagecraft. With most loose ends now firmly tied, Brel started to deliver casually cataclysmic performances with a sweaty intensity rarely sampled on Parisian club stages, and was soon triggering a spontaneous cessation of conversation the instant he walked on.

Up and about by late morning, he was being recognized in the immediate vicinity. Subtle boasting that let Miche guess more than was said was the burden of his news that 'a woman stopped me in the street to tell me how useless my third song had been - one of Brassens' too. Charming!'

Mingling the songs of others with his own was a genuflexion to a lingering critical dictate about the necessity of including a generous portion of old favourites and entries in the newly-established record and sheet music sales charts. An uninterrupted set of your own stuff wasn't on because what the powers that be were looking for was overall competence and versatility rather than individuality - and Brel, though adept enough to give daytime guitar lessons when money was shorter than usual, was no Sacha Distel.

Yet Brel's deserved if small-scale knot of devotees had deduced that, yes, he wasn't a genius musician, and form still overruled content, but he was developing a stage presence that, if not pretty, was compelling. He had also taken his clubland impact to its limit. When they heard about this over in Brussels, it'd been one in the eye for detractors, tangible or otherwise, who were alighting with nit-picking hope on the faintest indication of his fall.

Jacques was aware, nonetheless, that unless he pulled another stroke soon, he might be superceded by a newer sensation and consigned to the oblivion from which he was still emerging. Of course, there was the temptation to throw the race before he was beaten. He'd seen the Promised Land, hadn't he? He could die easy. Instead, he investigated the vexing question of how to progress onto the next level.

Some man who turned out to be less high-ranking than he'd represented himself had promised to get Brel on Radio Luxembourg. Jacques continued to behave as if this was still feasible long after the trail went cold. Success was always just round the corner too for everyone else with whom he was on terms of fluctuating equality. When paths crossed in café or backstage corridor, out would pour the boasts of imminent tours of outlandish countries or a certainty of opening for Fernandel at the Olympia. Yet through an informal sense of solidarity, any competitiveness would often dissolve rivalry into ribald cameraderie.

During one uproarious rendezvous, Jacques Brel entered, with deceptive casualness, into the life of Catherine Sauvage, a diva with a fondness for the *chansons* of Leo Ferré- who sat at the right hand of Brassens in the Valhalla of French popular culture. It would be quite a feather in Brel's cap if she sang his compositions too, but she gave it to him straight that the melodies were too simplistic. Ostensibly, they were professional comrades, but only Brel's married state and the feeling that this personable blonde was out of his league reined him during long and dangerous moments when they might have become more.

'I know in Brussels they all think that I've been sowing my wild oats,' wrote Brel to a friend, but life was too complicated to embrace full-scale love affairs. He added that he seemed to be suffering from a constant slight influenza. If psychosomatic, it may have been brought on by paranoia about the tardy mailing of the work permit - and financial worries. The dwindling of the amount borrowed from Romain was not staved off by Jacques' income which, on aggregate, was about a thirtieth of that of a dustman. At one club in the Latin quarter, he was worth less than the resident pianist who backed him.

Late in the year, a false dawn broke when Canetti ceased procrastinating and, in the teeth of executive doubts, issued eight Brel *chansons*, swamped in orchestra, on one of these new-fangled ten-inch 33 rpm longplayers - LPs - somewhere between the twelve-inch albums yet to come and the seven-inch EP - extended play - that, replete with picture sleeve and title track, was a more common (and economical) release than the 45 rpm single that had superceded the seventy-eight.

Jacques' delight when 'Il Peut Pleuvoir' and, a contradiction of enjoyable melancholy, 'Sur La Place' picked up a few scattered spins on radio was dampened when his eponymous LP was rubbished by reviewers.

Typical was a *France Soir* hack who counselled him to board the next train back to Brussels.

Not even the prospect of spending Christmas alone could draw Jacques away from Paris, but his creative well was now as dried-up as his bank balance. His wits dulled by the cold of the bedsit he'd found above a dance studio, more often than not, he'd brood for hours, clutching a guitar that might as well have been a coal shovel. 'I'm so tired,' he moaned to Miche as the New Year wore on, 'My spring is broken. Over the past seven months, I haven't composed a single song. Suffering in order to "arrive" is bad enough,' he continued grandiloquently, 'but to have to suffer to uphold and defend your ideas is dreadful, believe me. Men, especially poets (I consider myself to be a poet), need their muses. Mine are 350 kilometres away. They are called Miche, Chantal and France. My only muse is myself, and the water flowing from it is undrinkable.'

Yeah, well...getting the message, Miche - fed-up with being a single mother anyway - set wheels in motion for her and the 'little apples' to join Jacques in Paris by summer when, despite the housing crisis being worse in France than Belgium, they would put down a deposit on a house. On Jacques' instructions, she sold both the furniture and his shares in Vanneste and Brel, and wheedled some more cash from her father-in-law on the grounds that he'd just stumped up for Pierre to go on a lengthy motor-biking vacation.

There wouldn't be space for four in Jacques's box designed for one, so Miche and the girls stopped in a revenue-draining hotel until the entire family moved into 71, Rue Du Moulin À Vent in suburban Montriel Sous Bois, In this functional two-up two-down with no bathroom, washing had to be done either in the kitchen or in the street, using a pump which froze in winter, but the mortgage was cheap enough for the Brels to buy their first car - a Renault - on hire-purchase, and a tape recorder. Later, a forthcoming appearance on television by Jacques would prompt the purchase of a TV.

In 1954, however, they'd barely unpacked when Jacques was agonised with toothache so severe that he was prevented from singing for three weeks prior to his last minute addition to a July evening at the Olympia. Unbilled, he wasn't permitted a dressing room, and had to take the stage, fuddled with pain-killers, while the customers were still filing in, foreheads bestowed with pinpricks of perspiration from early evening sunshine. Nevertheless, Brel gave a fair account of himself after an aetherial fashion, and the venue's manager, Bruno Coquatrix, despite considering him a 'poseur', rebooked him.

It made sense too for Canetti to squeeze Brel into a very imminent round-France package tour. Kicking-off in Troyes on 29 July, it also included Phillipe Clay - in the first flush of a four-year run of hit records - neo-operatic Dario Moreno and bill-topping Catherine Sauvage, and would do battle with the varying public address systems and acoustics of provincial theatres, cinemas, casinos, sports pavilions, village institutes and, a new innovation, boarded-over swimming pools.

Driving, driving, driving to strange towns and stranger venues, Brel's first trek of this nature was not all it was cracked up to be. Uncertain about whether he'd even be sleeping comfortably that night, he'd endure overcoats for blankets, shampooing in toilet washbasins and waking up shivering to Moreno snoring open-mouthed a yard away. All part of a day's work too were overcharging alternators, flat batteries, jammed starter motors and long waits for mechanics who may or may not fix them.

Not purposely snubbing him, the others spoke of parties he hadn't been to, venues he'd never played, people he didn't know. In striving not to put his foot in it with some inanity, Jacques' reserve was construed as haughtiness, and rumbustious dressing room repartee would turn suddenly nasty as the rest poked ruthless fun at him, exhuming the 'Abbé' nickname, and using language that would shock a drunken marine as the former president of La Franche Cordée fought to control his features.

Swiftly, he learned rejoinders and made additions to the stock of dirty words that had encrusted his adolescent boorishness. Thus he defused the teasing, but couldn't stop himself being sucked into the behind-the-scenes vortex of sullen exchanges, moody discontent and the squabbles that exploded like shrapnel between any given combination of the human cargo hurtling from town to town, and continued on arrival backstage. The sophisticated Catherine usually reared up at Brel. Her assessment of him as a *chansonier* was unaltered. She thought his freshly-concocted 'Il Nous Faut Regarder', for example, was 'too Flemish', meaning too Franche Cordée goody-goody. He took to heart too her vitriolic (and unjustifiable) comments about a presentation that gave those rotten songs no help whatsover.

An assumption that closer acquaintance has caused La Sauvage to dislike him was not true - far from it - because she was at least watching Brel perform while paying little heed to Clay and Moreno with their scripted grinning and wonderful-to-be-here vapourings. She sought his particular comradeship to the degree that it was accepted that he travelled in her car (despite his own apprehensions after a hair-raising mountain ride down to Nice with Catherine taking bends too quickly).

Initially, he was almost like an eighteenth century *cavalière servante* who, with no romantic intentions, was on hand to listen to tearful reminiscences of her two years with an Italian who had just finished with her. On the rebound, she was cherishing a caprice to entice Jacques into her bed. When she succeeded, he spoilt what might have been no-strings frivolity by getting jealous and sulky when all she'd needed was someone who didn't care. Jacques, see, couldn't cope with her daunting independence. Apart from whores, women only went all the way if they were besotted, didn't they? How could Catherine possibly desire men like men desire women?

When the trek wound down on 31 August, Brel was both confused and, for all his philosophical objections, wracked with Roman Catholic guilt. Recipient of only the odd postcard from him, Miche guessed as much from tacit signals perceived during an excruciating afternoon when Catherine dropped by, and Jacques reverted from the untamed man-about-Paris to a tongue-tied boy from Brussels, terrified of eternal punishment for sin. Both women, however, retained a façade of self-composure and would remain on civil terms even after Jacques spluttered out his infidelity during the frank exchange that followed the caller's departure.

Brel pledged to spend the rest of his days making it up to his wife. So unnerving were his verbose histrionics and mental self-flagellations that, so he wouldn't do himself a mischief, she accepted hurriedly his sweetener of a holiday in Morocco that they could ill-afford. Calming down, he articulated his plea on paper: 'I humbly beg your forgiveness for the moral wrong I have done you and, moreover, for the doubt that I have created in you. As you know me so well, you will realize that I must be really ashamed in order to have the courage to write to you in this way. As you see (and as I have known for some time), without you I lose my strength - which I need to be a better man and a better entertainer.' He closed with 'I think a long night is coming to an end, but nights aren't important. What matters is that daybreak will find us morally and physically hand-in-hand,' signing himself 'Madame Brel's new fiancé'.

His penitence seemed genuine, and long-suffering Miche came to terms with the escapade, blaming it on his prudish parents and their symbollic castrations for the sake of propriety. Consequently, she shouldered many of his day-to-day trials and tribulations - ringing the agents, typing the publicity hand-outs, posting the supplicatory epistles. If nothing else, it occupied her while she grew accustomed to his increasingly longer absences.

The Renault would pull up outside a hotel - or wherever else its driver was staying - in a faraway town. Meanwhile, in Montriel Sous Bois, Miche wondered what he was doing until the rattle of keys in the front door would herald one more deliverance from the treadmill of the road. 'When I've been travelling,' he confided fatly to Guy Bruyndonckx, Hector's visiting brother, 'I just want to sit in comfort in an armchair at home. I like to be king of the castle. After about three days, I've had enough. I have to go.'

In short, he wanted to have his cake and eat it. When home, his daily routine was rising after the girls had been escorted to school by Miche. After breakfast, he'd tune his six-string for the day's songwriting labours. When Chantal and France came back, it often stirred in him the onset of tickling, pillow-fighting high spirits and repetition of in-jokes, side-splitting to no-one beyond the walls of Number 71.

In any family, there is territory forbidden and inexplicable to outsiders. How else can be explained the enigma of the Brels, epitomized by the daughters' adoration of a neglectful father who'd be almost permanently away by the time Chantal reached secondary school. The more salacious amongst us would like the impossible: videos of scenes that busied the rooms, or sampling with our own sensory organs Miche's feelings about her husband's taste for illicit sex that - after the Sauvage episode became history - would verge on the satyric.

He'd carry himself with a ruttish swagger onto the stage. Up there, he'd have licence to lock eyes fleetingly with any girl who looked as if she might, well, you know... Soon to become second nature to him, unchallenging procurement of erotic gratification would be sealed between performances with a beatific smile, a torrent of desire and an 'All right then: I'll see you later.'

A lady of perennial good nature, Miche was to become more abstractedly tolerant of - or indifferent to - stray mutterings about other attachments whilst gripping hard on her dignity as the official spouse. It wasn't as if mistresses and one-night stands were uncommon or even a purely Gallic phenomenon - though it was a Gallic homily that ran 'The chains of marriage are so heavy that it takes two to carry them, and often three'.

Neither Miche nor Jacques were chaste but lovestruck Franche Cordée hand-holders anymore, and she wasn't so naive to presume that, living for the moment on tour - and with a tired wife not looking - he wouldn't tilt for the downfall of some chorus girl's knickers or succumb to come-ons from stage door Jezebels aspiring to an orgasm at a musicianly thrust.

It was Villon in 'Ballade Des Femmes De Paris' who stated that 'only Parisian mouths are worth kissing,' and it would be a girl from the city who'd float the Brels' free-and-easy marriage into another choppy sea. In her early twenties, Suzanne 'Zizou' Gabriello's surname had opened doors when she elected to follow the footsteps of her Papa, a singing actor, forever on national television. This furnished her with both the best and worst start because, though Les Filles À Papa, her trio that included others with fathers who were illustrious entertainers, gained engagements on the strength of it, theirs was one of the corniest acts in Paris, finishing as it did with the three donning masks of their better-known parents' faces.

A solo vocalist by 1954, Zizou's name was in bigger lettering than Jacques Brel's on his second national tour. He was charmed but not quite easy when she chose to occupy the passenger seat in his car, particularly as - like Catherine - she wasn't keen on his *chansons*. She'd been struck mostly by his humour. After the backstage lionising that followed a particularly well-received show in St. Valery-en-Caux, a coastal town near Dieppe, the charged-up troupe repaired to a local palais where saturnine Zizou took the initiative by asking Brel to dance. Light-hearted smooching took a serious turn, and the pair spent the remaining nights of the expedition together.

As *omerta* is to the Mafia, a vow of silence concerning sex on the road has always persisted among roving minstrels. Brel - battle-hardened by the Sauvage fling - and Zizou - still living with her parents - brought what had been a pleasant diversion to an amicable halt, and went separate ways. However, on meeting not really by chance in Canetti's office shortly afterwards, they left arm-in-arm, both reconquered.

Brel bid farewell to both wife and mistress that October to fulfil a contract in Algeria where, despite a very recent earthquake and growing hostility to French imperialism, the bands played on - on this occasion, backing Dario Moreno, North American entertainer Sydney Bechet, a bland vocal group named the Milsons, Jacques and a volcanic female compère. The visit was characterized by tempestuous off-stage quarrels and *primadonna* tantrums loud enough to be heard in the galleries. A hidden long term blessing, nonetheless, was Brel's instant rapport with thirty-year-old Georges 'Jojo' Pasquier, one of the Milsons. Neither he nor Jacques knew then to what extent their lives would interweave.

Scarcely a week after sleeping off the African excursion, Brel was away to Holland to warm-up for Pierre Dudan at Amsterdam's De La Mer theatre for promoter Jo Van Doveren as part of a deal with Canetti. If out of the way, it proved a pivotal event of sorts when, with no preconceptions about him by someone else's audience, he stole the show. In an apt bright-red spotlight, he'd sidled into the sinister preamble to trusty 'La Diable (Ça Va)'. Building from muttered trepidation to strident intensity, it carried more acclamation-earning weight nowadays because the situation in Algeria was getting worse. Next up was loose-limbed 'Les Pieds Dans Le Ruisseau', pastoral and subdued, before concluding - in defiance of Catherine Sauvage - with 'Il Nous Faut Regarder', an amalgamation of some of the salient points of its predecessors.

'I don't work for applause,' he'd affirm, 'I like it, but only like a bootmaker who is complimented for making a good pair of shoes. For me, the singer is an artisan.' By now, he did not 'consider myself to be a poet' any more as he studied the 'hit parade' as a stockbroker would a Dow Jones index. 'Pop' music was, after all, a commodity to be bought, sold and replaced when worn out just like, say, a cardboard carton. When asked years later to contribute to a poetry anthology, he shrugged, 'I'm no poet. I'm a variety singer. I *make* songs, that's all, never more than eight a year.'

If he wasn't to be the overnight sensation he may have once convinced himself he'd be, Philips marketing division had distributed over 2,000 copies of his LP, but the maintenance of at least a minimally decent standard of living for the family depended mainly on a hectic succession of one-nighters. A three hundred mile round trip to Angers in the Loire to play in a Christian youth hostel (which his repertoire still suited) wasn't unusual.

There were recurring dates in Ostend, Namur and elsewhere in Belgium, but Brel was reluctant to venture into Brussels where he'd be no-one's lion - especially at the Franche Cordée concert that Hector Bruyndonckx was only too willing to organize for any mutually convenient weekend. Miche fogged Hector with an intricacy of prior bookings and rather patronizing alternatives: Jacques would send a tape or, failing that, she'd come and read out some of his lyrics. For the fee that Bruyndonckx was offering, that was all that a rising star of Jacques Brel's calibre could manage.

That's what Jacques himself slid into the conversation when holding court at the Trois Baudets where he reunited with Jojo, then an ex-Milson working for a petroleum company, installing pipelines. They went back for coffee at Pasquier's rented room near the gardens of Luxembourg. In the sock-smelling frowsiness, Jacques was diverted by the accidental junk-sculptures of parts of Jojo's second-hand Czech car on plinths of back-issues of *Le Monde* and *France Observateur*.

Eccentric and well-informed, Pasquier was good company, and he and Brel, if not exactly David and Jonathan, became best pals, the differences between them only consolidating their brusque empathy. Burly where Brel was slight, Jojo was a Breton by upbringing, and steady by nature. Living at a slower tempo to Jacques, he was content to be a passive listener as his friend, angry or sardonically amused by everything, held forth during their wanderings, giving his lightning-bright imagination its arm-waving head.

On the next stool during three-in-the-morning bar-hoppings, Jojo would soon be fulfilling several functions for Brel: father confessor and healer of psychological wounds; straight man in a double-act that would palliate the daily grind of road-dressing room-stage-hotel, and a 'Dutch uncle' who'd never be so beglamoured by Jacques' future fame that he couldn't offer criticism or give honest, constructive answers when ideas were bounced off him.

Brel's cash flow would enable Jojo to ditch his day job to become Jacques' general factotum for the rest of his pal's stage career. He would deal with more and more of Miche's paperwork, and cope with the tactical problems of getting artist and retinue from A to B. Once at B, Pasquier would buttonhole promoters, shoo unwanted guests from dressing rooms, sign chits and bills, assist in rehearsing whatever accompanists had been hired, and, like an army batman without the uniform, attend to Brel's dietary, accommodation and recreational requirements.

Jacques would also be fortunate in his choice of business manager. Born into showbusiness finance, Charley Marouani, a Tunisian, was around the same age as Brel - his first success - but had infinitely more contacts as well as an instinct for the manoeuvres needed to give that extra push up the ladder - all the way when the time came - and the know-how to sidestep the sly quagmires and downright thuggery of the music industry.

Yet, after he took formal charge of Jacques' professional life, their relationship would be based always as much on friendship as profit. It was an attraction of opposites, but a different opposite to Jojo. Retiring and be-suited, Charley had the tenacity and cautious confidence to strike a bellicose stance in negotiation, and a brain that could at a moment's notice spew forth dizzying facts and figures. On these occasions, eyelids would grow heavy, but if Charley was tedious, at least his yap was in his client's best interests, and Jacques would think enough of him to once declare that 'if Jojo is my brother, Charley is my cousin'.

On the road in the early days, Brel would gaze most often at Pasquier tunnelling into a meal across a wayside café's formica table with the jukebox playing some other *chansonier*'s record. While still unaccustomed to singing so frequently, Brel's vocal cords would sometimes weaken to a gravelly croak, bubbling with catarrh, and curable only with medication and enforced silence. However, he often went down just as well with a strained ranting conveying such exquisite brush-strokes of enunciation and inflection that a fractional widening of *vibrato* during a sustained note could be as loaded as the most anguished wail on lyrics that would touch and dissect lives as blighted as their creator's after 'Quand On N'A Que L'Amour' - main selling point of a five-track EP, and Brel's first hit - fell from its peak of Number Three in the domestic chart.

Chapter Three
Hit The Road, Jacques

Perseverance was rewarded, but until 'Quand On N'A Que L'Amour' inched to its tantalizing apogee, Jacques Brel had been more effective on stage than on disc in ratio to the continuing improvement of his microphone technique and finger-style guitar playing - though how effectively he put on the agony varied because, in the highest tradition of jazz, he had good and bad nights.

A lot of the allure of Brel's chart breakthrough - its 'gimmick', if you like - lay in the ear-catching extraneousness of his Belgian brogue, now no longer such a turn-off. A similar asset would be crucial to The Beatles' more exportable rise from Merseyside obscurity to national (and then global) eminence in the 1960s. Moreover, from the non-retractable realm of the studio, 'Quand On N'A Que L'Amour' owed much to producer Canetti's knack for picking a raw hit and squeezing it into the lushly orchestrated mould of the day: 'decent' pop that programme planners for national radio thought the public *ought* to want. Inherent in this mandate was veneration for pop's elder statesmen - hence the antics of ensembles like Les Filles À Papa.

This meant that there was little middle ground between nursery rhymes and Maurice Chevalier. Teenagers had to put up with the same music that their elders and younger siblings liked; the first stirrings of rock 'n' roll warranting cursory spins before being brushed under the carpet as another US fad as transient as the Cha-Cha-Cha or hula-hoops.

The title of 'Paris, Tu N'A Pas Change', a mid-1950s smash by Jean Sablon, summed up the stranglehold that its cautious overseers would have on France's electric media well into the next decade. Unless you toed a clean, winsome line, you wouldn't have a hit record. If you did, the industry would look after you, keep you in work when your time in the main spotlight was up, and the circle would remain unbroken. There was no reason why business couldn't carry on as usual with pop performers who were exactly that: purveyors of harmless, ephemeral doggerel to be hummed, whistled and sung imperfectly by the milkman while another ditty was prepared by reworking the same precept with either the same act or a new one developed from a similar formula.

As long as Brel didn't do anything that the music establishment didn't like, even one best-seller would place him in a favourable if short-term negotiating position for more rumunerative and respectable work in variety, cabaret and even TV shows and advertising instead of the thankless zig-zag of far-flung and often mismatched one-nighters through bookers who sold his services like tins of beans - with no money back if they tasted funny. Now that Jacques was getting to know the ropes of a business rotten with time-serving incompetence, mental sluggishness, short-sightedness, cloth-eared ignorance, fake sincerity, backstabbing and the contradiction of excessive thrift and heedless expenditure, he was less willing for it to be taken for granted that he existed only to vend transient entertainment with a side-serving of cheap insight. More pragmatically, his Top Ten penetration gave greater leverage to submit compositions to other artists and, if he desired, churn out assembly-line pop for the masses by joining a songwriting 'factory' within the music publishing offices, management concerns, record companies and studios that clotted in Paris.

Yet 'Quand On N'A Que L'Amour' was of more substance than the boy-meets-girl piffle with which it sat uncomfortably in the Top Ten. The melody was as catchy as any of these, but its libretto looked past moon-June travesties - though youthful idealism (notably, that love is all) persisted as this anthemic *chanson* dwelt on humanity's conquest of its disordered nature through the detours of Art, a theme than runs through the works of both Albert Camus and Jean Cocteau.

Under film director Cocteau's avant-garde wing was Juliette Greco, the Thinking Man's French actress. Like Brel, her destiny was also bound up with Philips who had seen pop star potential in this willowy and spectral high priestess of popular existentialism. Stark facial cosmetics - skull-white (lipstick too) relieved only by the darkest mascara and eye-shadow - straight black hair, tent-like sweater and trousers blended with an intellectual aura that would make her the heroine of middle-class Arts undergraduates in dimly-lit bedsits with Man Ray on the walls. That someone so counter to the usual run-of-the-mill singing sensation had proved a commercial success had stirred in Brel and other modern *chansoniers* vague hope that the weather-vane of pop convention was about to lurch in another direction.

Greco would scrutinize portfolios of any interesting up-and-coming tunesmith for likely material - and a sign that Jacques might be going places was her cover of 'Le Diable (Ça Va)'. Though it swiped at 'lads full of ideals' who become terrorists, it was, felt Juliette, 'a song difficult to defend - extremely subversive, extremely violent,' but, when she came by the Trois Baudets, what a performance there was by this Belgian that everyone was talking about! 'He had eyes like charcoal,' she'd recall with uncool awe, 'He began to sing and I was bedazzled, filled with wonder.'

Beyond the pale of Paris, less eminent mouths fell open too during Jacques' provincial engagements where, in the wake of 'Quand On N'A Que L'Amour', he'd moved up to more salubrious venues with tiered seating, heavy drape curtains and dressing room mirrors bordered by light bulbs. No more was he changing in the lavatory or being paid in loose coins as dates unfolded for nearly a year into the future. Most onerous financially were those contracts settled when he'd been an also-ran, but otherwise he took the sweep of events in his stride. Admitted to one particular venue's inner sanctum, a local journalist had the rare treat of watching Brel seizing the first opportunity to shave in three days. Sometimes, there wasn't time to remove stage make-up, and he'd doze with the road buzzing in his ears as sidekick Jojo drove through the night in order to reach the next evening on time.

While it circumscribed serious composition, flashes of inspiration in cars, restaurants and train journeys could be revised and developed in hotel room quietude. 'When an idea comes to me, or an expression comes into my head,' Jacques revealed, 'I note it down in an exercise book. Then I leave it until I can work out the whole song. It takes me a few hours once I get started.'

Despite - or because of - the pressure of work, he embarked on his most prolific period as a songwriter; a creative rush commensurate with increases in both booking fees and record sales. His second album, for example, found ten thousand buyers; a third, four times more.

These and the one that followed were laden with aged fixtures in his repertoire; every nuance and crochet cut-and-dried over hundreds of hours on the boards. Mostly, they'd been not so much scathing indictments of society as quasi-sermons like 'Sur La Place' ('a hymn of love and kindness,' said the author), affirmations of his belief in enduring love, and 'poetic' observations about the recurring joys of nature as in 'Les Pieds Dans Le Ruisseau', 'L'Aventure' - which could be adapted for singing at a primary school assembly - and, most markedly, 'Au Printemps', which blended a breezy contemporary arrangement with ersatz mediaevalisms about the 'new green of nature' causing adolescent sap to rise.

Because it exposes a point of view, all lyrics - even soppy 'Ballade' - may be construed as political. War was, indeed, wrong because people get killed in it, averred Brel in 'La Haine', but, as there were no combustible references to, say, the trouble in Algeria, the nuclear arms race or east-west, black-white confrontations, it was nearly as acceptable an opus for mid-morning radio as tame 'Au Printemps' - as was 'La Bastille' which echoes 'Le Diable (Ça Va)' in its detestation of strong-arm tactics. Also propelled by a square-bashing beat and martial brass *ostinatos* was 'Le Colonel', which concludes with a mortally wounded officer in the front line of some unnamed 'minor war', who in a reverie about his sweetheart, finds it in him to smile at death.

The inclusion of radio-friendly items like 'Sur La Place', 'L'Aventure' and, most markedly, 'Au Printemps' on his LPs helped appease industry watchdogs about tougher *chansons* that the endlessly inventive Brel may have completed a week before the session: ones that laughed callously at broken-hearted lovers, that inserted rude words, that looked up a girl's skirt (in perky 'Les Blés'), that stepped outside pop's then stagnant limits. 'The difference in tone between my former songs and my new ones,' he explained, 'came about because, at the start, there I was, twenty years old, in all my stupidity, *naiveté* and innocence. Today, you've got me relating to the outside world.'

That Brel was finding his feet as a writer was evidenced by a confident disregard of audience reaction as he gave fierce and direct vent to feelings about what he understood of myriad social, cultural, environmental, religious and other factors that had made him what he was. Like pus from a lanced boil, all manner of frustrations, prejudices and disgust accumulated from earliest youth were bursting forth via a wryly watchful, literate lyricism that, mingling humour and gloom - sometimes in the same line - would press progressively harder on the nerve of how far he could go. 'It is an eternal need in me to combat all which is filthy and ugly,' he cried, 'I attack all that which is unspeakable as if I was touching a wound needing to be treated. I get violent though I am naturally timid - but I have no choice.'

Yet, however justified his tirades, Brel would sympathize with his victims such as the soldier in 'La Haine', dying 'as children die', artlessly and pointlessly. Those ignorant of his background might have assumed that the man who'd done his indolent bit in the 15th Division lived the role he delineated so piquantly in both 'La Haine' and Latin-tinged 'Grande Jacques (C'est Trop Façile)' - with the giveaway phrase, 'you who never were the same as a soldier' - and was knowing beyond his years when he referred in ironic interview to 'the boys who tell you of a peace, just and lasting.'

As the scurrying accompaniment in 'La Haine' embraces befitting snare drum rolls and extemporized dissonance from a trumpet, so 'holy' organ would whine below the surface of the Yuletide recitation, 'Dites Si C'Était'. Likewise, 'L'Air De La Bêtise' - the follies, narcissisms and baser undercurrents of the adult 'socials' he'd endured in Brussels - is an appropriate burlesque of classical *lieder*, complete with a tapping baton calling the tuning-up orchestra to order, and Brel's abnormally plummy *bel canto* eloquence. In parenthesis, at over four minutes, it's also around twice the length of most other *chansons* on disc in the late 1950s. As deceptively light-hearted is 'Le Boureé Du Celibataire' - which, while it wouldn't have been out of place in Edward German's Edwardian light opera *Merrie England*, had a passing lyrical and melodic resemblance to Irving Berlin's 'The Girl That I Will Marry' (from the 1946 musical *Annie Get Your Gun*).

Though not reconciling easily on the same 1957 album, Brel's stylistic range extended to the polite small-hours jazz shuffle of 'Pardons' - and 'J'En Appelle' which pre-empted the heartbreak balladeering of British pop singer Billy Fury. To a similar end, a lone guitar would launch 'Seul', a key Brel composition in that its stoicism in the teeth of separation from a desired object would recur in 'Madeleine', 'Chanson Sans Paroles', 'Mathilde' and 'Les Bonbons'.

In 'Je Ne Sais Pas', a companion piece to 'Seul', harp, flute and sombre strings convey an apposite late evening mood for its description of night 'playing me like a guitar' (anticipating Dylan's 'Ain't it just like the night to play tricks when you're trying to be so quiet' in 1966's 'Visions Of Johanna') as the forsaken swain hastens through the streets of his god-forsaken town to watch, concealed by pitch-blackness, as his girl and her new beau depart on a train.

Conversely, the rival leaves alone while the other protagonists remain in the final frames of the 1954 film, *East Of Eden* starring James Dean as a character with whom Jacques Brel's younger self might have identified: a teenager whose good intentions were misunderstood by a strict father. A prototype rock 'n' roll rebel, the fated Dean's next movie, *Rebel Without A Cause*, illustrated that you didn't have to come from the wrong side of the tracks to qualify as a sullenly introspective outcast.

As well as not dying in his early twenties in a messy road accident, Brel was, perhaps, too long in the tooth to present himself - had he wished - as a Gallic 'answer' to Dean. Moreover, as the most perfunctory study of his frequently hilarious lyrics can verify, his image would never be that of a surly pariah, even during what his public would apprehend as the darkest hours of his life. Tending to grin with eyes rather than lips, he was, he assured us, 'a happy person - even if I don't look as if I am, even if I am in despair. "Bitter" is a word that I refuse to acknowledge'.

It wasn't, however, all smiles in his private life, *circa* 1958. His romance with Zizou - now less renowned than he - was blighted by deafening explosions of temper and even temporary break-ups sparked by incidents such as Jacques showing up late for Zizou's spot in a Montmartre cabaret, tossing back a double whiskey and making an immediate exit.

Into the bargain, her father was most distressed by his Suzanne's liaison with a married man. He'd bought her an apartment in Rue Versin on condition that she gave Brel up, but on learning of its use by the sinful pair for discreet assignations, the deceived M. Gabriello telephoned the newly pregnant Mme. Brel to turn her generalised suspicion into fact. To his chagrin, the strategy backfired when the wronged party seized upon the news as an excuse to return to a Brussels seen through a golden haze, so homesick had she become in the isolated sideroad among neighbours whose Parisian intonations Chantal and France - and Jacques - were picking up. Miche had always assumed that the stay wouldn't be for ever, and was becoming anxious not so much about her husband's extra-marital shennanigans as his deepening entrenchment in *la vie Parisienne*.

She had not, therefore, erupted with anger when confronting him with this latest nonsense. Gently, she implored Jacques to help her grasp what was going on, groping once more for any avenue for forgiveness - but, after weathering the old circular arguments and cliff-hanging silences for a decent interval, he headed for the front door to ease his emotional fatigue in the arms of Zizou.

There was relief on both sides when Miche and the girls departed in February 1958 for Brussels and a flat in 71, Avenue du Duc Jean, near the basilica where Jacques had once lived with his parents. Nevertheless, after the initially liberating effect of inconvenient Miche not being around anymore, the excitement of flaunting his shame by squiring his girlfriend openly round the clubs palled for Jacques well before the gossip dried up. He chose not to move in with Zizou - argumentative, impetuous and prone to bouts of sulking - but to reside alone in a *pied-à-terre* within a Regency town house, a mere stone's throw from the Trois Baudets.

Though Brel had spoken of divorce to Zizou, it had never cropped up in even the most candid discussions with the eclipsed Miche. The affair muddled on because neither he nor Zizou had enough motivation to finish it. A 'friend' spilling the beans about the birth of the Brels' third daughter, Isabelle, that August, could draw from Zizou only the cold comment, 'I hope she never finds out what a rogue her Papa is.' For the new baby, Jacques penned a lullaby ('Isabelle'), but the muse for another new *chanson*, 'Ne Me Quitte Pas', had been Zizou.

He wasn't immune to twinges of conscience as the enormity of his domestic unheavals sank in. Among those confidantes who'd wondered aloud what he was playing at was Françoise, wife of François Rauber, Isabelle's godfather and the maestro with whom Jacques felt most relaxed both in session and on the boards.

All good men and true, Andre Popp, Michel Legrand, Andre Grassi and others had accompanied Brel with the nonchalant proficiency expected within the self-contained caste of middle-aged middle-of-the-road bandleaders who had first refusal of virtually all record dates in Parisian studios throughout the 1950s. It was as if French pop couldn't be done in any other way or with any other players than those bound by the rigidity of radio-imposed conservatism and union officials who would spring to the defence of any pedant who yelled 'time's up!' in the middle of a take.

Twenty-five-year-old Rauber was more understanding about awkward talent like Jacques Brel, and, unlike most conservatory-trained musicians, was not self-depreciating about his knowledge and love of pop, having tickled the ivories for years in an all-styles-served-here combo common to a cache of vocalists on a given bill. This had included Brel one 1956 night in Grenoble. Intrigued by his way with words and his accuracy of pitch in the most stubbornly chromatic tunes, François looked forward to working with him again.

Flung together on a string of engagements a few weeks later, François and Jacques passed many a moonlit mile listening to classical music on the former's car radio; Rauber's enthusiasm for Wagner and Fauré rubbing off on Brel. Tightening the bond between the connoisseur and the Belgian *parvenu* was the cultivated Mme. Rauber's informal tutorials concerning what authors were worth reading - such as Teilhard de Chardin (no, I'd never heard of him either) as well as the usual Zolas and Sartres.

The realisation that he and his new pal might be a winning combination professionally led Jacques to rely more and more on François Rauber's expertise. Allowed increasing control of his destiny as a recording artist, Brel was taking a greater interest in arrangement rather than merely presenting lyrics (often radically altered later) and a basic tune, and leaving the rest to his producer. Head-to-head with Rauber, he would *dah-dah-dah* the scoring required, and mull over suggestions about counterpoint and further concepts never previously considered.

It was foreseeable that the two would collaborate as songwriters - Brel's lyrics with outlines dissolving over musical imput. One of the first fruits of the partnership was 'Voici', an attempt to compose a fugue, according to Brel. What he had been driving at was translated by producer Canetti as a ponderously majestic effect achieved by lugging mobile equipment into a church to tape Rauber at its organ. This was the bedrock of this lesser *chanson* in Brel's canon that might not have supported such magniloquence had it been reduced to the acid test of just voice and piano - and neither would schmaltzy 'Dors Ma Mie Bonsoir'. More substantial early examples of the Brel-Rauber hook-up are 'La Lumière Jaillira' - from the same location as 'Voici' - and 'L'Homme Dans La Cité'; a foreboding bolero pulsing beneath a libretto about a Messiah-like revolutionary whose 'anger was pure, young and beautiful like the thunderstorm'.

Another principal of the *dramatis personnae* of Brel's artistic career was Gerard Jouannest with whom he would write over forty *chansons* (including 'Ne Me Quitte Pas', 'Jackie' and 'Madeleine'). Jouannest had been functioning as pianist to the Three Minstrels (of much the same bent as the Milsons) in 1957 when Brel - with whose work he was unfamiliar - asked him to deputise for an indisposed Rauber at a charity concert. As adept at improvisation as reading dots, Jouannest so rose to the occasion that he was charged with forming a permanent backing unit for Brel - who was finding a perpetual turnover of personnel prohibitive.

This outfit - and those that followed - were subject to a policy that permitted musicians a longer leash and a deeper engrossment with rhythm than on record. Though utilizing conventional rather than home-made instruments, the line-up was akin to skiffle, the craze that was gripping young Britain and, to a lesser degree, France (with Hugues Aufray *et son* Skiffle Group its foremost executants). Yet while adhering to the conventions of double bass and standard drum kit, Gerard Jouannest, had he been given a freer hand, might not have hired an accordionist - whose sound, he thought privately, was cheap-and-nasty, but agreed that it would serve to stress Brel's *belgitude*. Nonetheless, it would be an Italian who'd fill the post after Brel, on holiday in the Cote D'Azur, spotted one Jean Corti accompanying a *chanteuse* in a quayside bar.

Though he was lumbered with a wife and brats who wanted him home in the evenings, laconic Jouannest, a staunch Communist, let himself be put upon more and more after he moderated an initial dislike of garrulous Brel for whom wealth was second nature. Yet, give him credit, Jacques was a generous front man, never failing to introduce the boys in the band (Gerard sometimes as 'Nikita' Jouannest after Khrushchev, the Soviet president), and direct the adulation of the horde towards them.

With his new group, Brel headlined at the Bobino, the venue where he'd once cleared a hesitant throat and sang his song for Brassens in a dressing room. Now he was singing six of them beneath the proscenium to a paying audience - and the next day, *France-Soir*, the journal that'd told him to clear off back to Belgium, would be full of 'the rise of a new singing star.'

At last, the proverbial 'overnight sensation' five years after his first record release, a vista had been opened to a wider world, but Brel's Gallic purity would remain defiantly unadulterated; his *belgitude* shining most brightly (and provocatively) in 1959's 'Les Flamandes'. To rising key changes and a purposely clodhopping bounce, he transports the listener to what might be a vicarage fête somewhere in Flanders where unsmiling women, fancy-dressed perhaps like Breughel peasants, perform a country dance mechanically, emblematic of what he perceived as the joyless and unmindful conformity of an ignorant, servile populace to social and religious expectations, and Vicar Of Bray-esque compliance ('Nazis during the war and Catholic in between, you swing constantly between rifle and missal').

It was a hit in France where Brel was still regarded in many quarters as a Fleming - not a Belgian - who sang in French. Nevertheless, 'Les Flambardes', understandably, did not endear him to the targets of its derision. Throughout the Netherlands, media critics piled into 'Les Flamandes' and, by implication, all other Brel records with the malicious glee of those who'd been betrayed and deceived by their own kin. The furore was yet resounding when the viper in the bosom came to Knokke Casino for the first time since he'd been panned by 1953's festival judges. Jacques couldn't help but visualize the venue and its staff as it'd been then - and, sure enough, there was Nellens the younger, peering through a minute tear in the backcloth at a murmurous crowd that he'd guessed was determined to hate the main event.

To Jojo and the rest of the team, Brel seemed no more nervous about Knokke than anywhere else - and, other than isolated catcalls, each number went by without interruption; contentious 'Les Flamandes' ending with long seconds of silence before a grudging outburst of clapping. This was better than everyone may have imagined, but reaction to both Brel's recordings and in-person appearances would be more subdued in his native land than anywhere else for years to come - and, following much discussion, 'Les Flamandes' suffered an airplay ban on Flemish-language radio.

In France, however, triumph followed triumph. Colliding with the falling 'Les Flamandes' in the charts was *accelerando* 'La Valse de Mille Temps' (with an opening quote from 'The Blue Danube'). In the ascendant too would be 'La Dame Patronesse' - as mickey-taking after its fashion as 'Les Flamandes' - and march tempo 'La Mort' established Brel as a perpetrator *par excellence* of the death disc, one of pop's hardiest forms. Yet 'La Mort' was neither *kitsch* nor melodramatic. Past caring about the afterlife, Brel advocates outwardly that we try to live in a cheerier 'constant present' than the existentialists; that we eat, drink and be merry in the sphere of our sorrow, stick around for our friends, and hope to be taken when in sexual congress. This would be all very well if not for being brought up sharp by lines like 'death waits for me in the lilacs that a gravedigger will toss over me to make the future' and unsettling reiteration of the phrase 'the time that passes'.

Death is defied as vainly but with iller humour in 'La Colombe'. Like a prequel to Scottish-Australian songwriter Eric Bogle's morbid 'And The Band Played "Waltzing Matilda"' homecoming, it focusses on a railway platform resonating with fanfares, left!-right! bellowings, the hissing of steam engines and the general hubbub of soldiers going off to the war. One of two central and interrelated images is of a resentful and bewildered new recruit and his girlfriend reflecting as the evil hour 'where our childhood ends' approaches, and that the cause he may well die for might be less noble than they'd been led to think. The second is in the chorus (borrowed from the French folk song, 'Nous N'Irons Plus Au Bois'): a dove - universal symbol of peace - pursued to its death by an unwilling young hunter.

Like the question 'Why?' in 'La Colombe' and 'the time that passes' in 'La Mort' - and, for that matter, the title in Perry Como's '(I Love You) Don't You Forget It', incessantly on the radio all over Europe then - 'ne me quitte pas' is repeated over and over again in Brel's most famous song. A milestone and a millstone, it would become to Jacques what, say, 'Be Bop A Lula' was already to Gene Vincent, and 'A Whiter Shade Of Pale' would be to Procol Harum, i.e. the customers would never let him quit the stage unless he gave 'em his 'Ne Me Quitte Pas'.

Its general drift had been previewed in 'On N'Oublie Rien', a concert favourite not yet put on record. 'Ne Me Quitte Pas', however, has its entreating suitor even madder with obsessive, fevered love via desperate, irrational promises to one beloved to the point of veneration, but who, like most divine beings, does not deign to reply verbally. Nevertheless, the supplicant keeps trying to elicit some response other than indifference. His abandoned undertakings - buoyed by the song's soaring bridge passage - include reactivating extinct volcanoes, drawing rain from a clear sky, and inventing a nonsense language - as if what he wants to say is too deep for orthodox articulation (or orthodox instrumentation, epitomised by the use of an *ondes Martenot*, a monophonic keyboard capable of a variety of unearthly tone colours). Finally, the wretchedness of his devotion gets so painful that, returning melodically to the narrow dynamic range of the verse, he brakes his ravings to solemnly accept his degradation, the complete loss of self-respect, in the silent presence of an emotional tyrant.

If as bigoted a male chavinist as ever walked the planet, he makes the 'Ne Me Quitte Pas' person unmanly in his pleading despair - for, like many so-called extroverts, Jacques covered a hesitancy with respect to women as well as more general insecurities by brutalizing himself. On one occasion, for instance, he urinated into a piano provided as per contract but not quite in tune. Though the most homophobic of men, he would express in song a preference for male company in such as 'Jef' and, especially, 1964's neo-misogynistic 'Mathilde'.

Worth quoting at length here is Brel's sexist attitude towards his distant family obligations: 'Domestic routine ruins everything. From my point of view, I insist absolutely on seeing my daughters from time to time and taking them with me, say, on tour so that they can see a man who is fulfiling his proper function as a man because as soon as you take away that function, he's nothing but a ridiculous sight. Have you ever seen a great surgeon playing billiards? That interests no-one - certainly not his children. It is much finer for them to look up to a surgeon at the operating table than a surgeon playing billiards. Children everywhere are being raised by surgeons who play billiards.

'The mother is above this sort of criticism because she is always playing billiards metaphorically. The average father is only at home at a time of day when he's worth nothing and has nothing to give. It's worse with the sort of parents who argue from the start of one year to the next - who just stay together out of habit or laziness. They throw plates at each other - and are surprised later that their children become traumatized. Have you noticed the number of them who can't stand noise? A plate breaks and they jump. I've known grown men start to sob when just a knife or fork falls on the floor.'

Brel's fights with Zizou - who wouldn't stomach domestic conduct tolerated by Miche - were becoming almost continuous. Yet she held on to a belief that he was worth keeping, and that his intentions were honourable - or would be but for the apparently complaisant wife in Brussels.

It was thanks to Zizou's petitioning of Jean Michel Boris, Bruno Co-quatrix's assistant, that, in 1959 - with Zizou herself as MC - Brel first topped the bill at the Olympia, albeit sharing the accolade with Philippe Clay - whose name was in larger type on the poster, but whose star seemed then to be on the wane. Predictably, Brel won the day to rabid and sustained cheering that would get louder every consequent time he played there.

Television appearances consolidated the Brel phenomenon, and so did the promotional films that found their way onto the short-lived 'Scorpi-tone', a video juke-box prevalent in the early 1960s. In these mediums, Brel, rather than straightforward synchronization with a musical per-formance, projected himself into dramatic situations, albeit while de-pendant on few props. As the sozzled alcoholic in 'L.'Ivrogne', for exam-ple, he decants the dismal platitudes of the sozzled alcoholic, just seat-ed at a table, tumbler in hand - while 'Les Toros' required only matador fancy-dress from the wardrobe department against a featureless white background.

Noticing viewers' spontaneous attentiveness whenever the on-screen Brel flashed into both living room and wayside café, a foreign corre-spondent with the *New York Times* would proclaim, 'He has held Paris in the palm of his hand. No other singer of his generation can claim quite the same allegiance.' In his field, Jacques was now on a par with Gener-al de Gaulle who, that same year, had become first President of the Fifth French Republic. Neither Jojo nor Brel were admirers of de Gaulle's mil-itarism, but were struck that his *kepi* was as distinctive a personal idio-syncracy as Hitler's moustache - or Chevalier's boater.

That governing bodies could envy the pop celebrity's easy manipula-tion of the minds of millions lent creedence to the homily, 'I care not who makes a nation's laws as long as I can write its songs' - and, to the man-in-the-street, Brel was pinpointing iniquities to greater purpose than any number of dissembling politicians could via his musical snapshots of life, then and later, that, by laying into the Church, the family ('Ces Gens-Là'), the army, school ('Rosa'), you name it, emphasized a solidarity with disaffected consumers - of all ages.

Diving straight into the heart of a situation, Brel (like Dylan after him) bypassed the implied generalities of pluralised titles like 'Les Flaman-des', 'Les Paumés De Petit Matin', and 'Les Bigotes', and pared them down to a wordscape as detailed as a Giles cartoon. As mere entertainment, these *chansons* were more digestable too than fidgeting through, maybe, three acts of some Théâtre of the Absurd play, though Brel compositions were often constructed in similar roundabout form.

Co-written by Jean Corti (and propelled by his accordion), 'Les Bourgeois' acquaints us with 'Jojo', 'Pierre' and fat 'Adrienne', all thoroughly half-educated, who spend a carefree youth drinking, having pseudo-intellectual discussions and making fun of each other and the staid, elderly barristers they encounter in a chosen watering hole. The refrain embraces their favourite taunt: 'the bourgeoisie are like pigs, the older they get, the more bestial they become'. However, heralded by a switch from smug horns to twinkling celeste, we move forward in time to the same hotel bar where the boys have matured into tired men-of-law themselves, swollen by obesity and *what's-the-matter-with-kids-today?* venom, and recipients of their old porcine insult from a new brood of moneyed young tearaways.

While 'Les Bourgeois' exemplifies Brel's incisive habit of dehumanizing institutions and social groups, the likes of 'La Colombe', 'Les Biches', 'Les Singes', 'La Statue', 'Les Toros' and 'Le Cheval' personify animals and inanimate objects as if they'd stepped out of one of Aesop's fables. Elsewhere, he homes in instead on a solitary person - 'La Parlote', 'L'Ivrogne', 'Jef' - who frequently does little more than hang around (as would the fellow in 'Madeleine').

Always, Brel glorified individuality, and revelled in the unmasking of hypocrisy: seemingly charitable deeds that bolster the doer's social standing rather than exorcise demons of compassion ('La Dame Patronnesse'), and old maids keeping at arm's length men who wouldn't give them a second glance anyway ('Les Bigotes'). Of the same kidney are the dancers of 'the oldest tango in the world' in 'Rosa', bracketed by a 'kiddie' chorus at odds with those who, past youthful aspirations (e.g. 'I will never be Vasco de Gama'), can only indulge in trite and counterfeit pleasures.

Shades of Zola's *L'Assommoir* pervade 'Les Paumes Du Petit Matin' as a vision of carousers holding each other up on the way home along the echoing streets of early morning is rendered as sound via the clack of rim-shots on a muted tom-tom and the drowsy good-time brass section of what seems like a tipsy band wrapping up for the night.

Brel himself was rarely intoxicated, though he was a heavy enough drinker to have had a whiskey-and-cola ('fuel', he called it) handy in the wings, onstage perspiration diminishing its effect. Afterwards, when unwinding in, perhaps, a nearby bar, the tension would gradually flow out of him as the liquor flowed in, and he'd burble away convivially - all word-play and, never going beyond talk, ideas like compiling an entertainers' directory of open-all-hours restaurants. He was inclined to bond there with those others who either weren't in the mood for sensible conversation or, like him too, suffered from insomnia.

He'd take cat-naps with a book over his eyes during a punishing booking itinerary that, now covering the entire French-speaking world, once involved a show in Quebec one evening, and one in an Alpine town the next - arranged, presumably, by an agent who thought that a thousand miles was a few inches on a map. *Plus ça change.*

Despite a restless existence of travel, music, women and booze, Brel was the vehicle of no flow chart of *paparazzi* titbits that would yet splash vivid and scandalous hues on his personal life. To his devotees, the depths of depravity for Jacques were chain-smoking and a fondness for *boules*, a ball game that was as much part of his touring luggage as a change of socks. Zizou and other more fleeting paramours with whom he was never photographed, were not brought to notice by a press who'd judged any besmirching of his public persona as untimely now that he was esteemed as a national hero whose every record and concert was an unmissable cultural event.

As far as outsiders were concerned, he endured a cruel separation from his family in Brussels for the sake of Art and his fans. His arrivals at Avenue du Duc Jean weren't far removed from those of Santa Claus with his presents for the children and a kiss for the self-reliant, infinitely patient and presumably contented Miche. To his ailing mother, however, Jacky was still regarded as a black sheep who should have made the most of his chances with the firm - more so now that Romain could no longer wash, shave or dress himself.

Few say what they really mean about close relatives to strangers - especially journalists. Therefore, who can guess the true feelings of Pierre and the cousins about Jacky's popularity and wealth? Just because he'd made some gramophone records, the child they'd known all their lives had become such a legend throughout Europe that it would be strange if they didn't catch 'Au Printemps' on the wireless at some hour every 21st of March.

Jacky looked as if he still worked at Vanneste and Brel on the evidence of the nondescript garments he wore on a stage of Brechtian bareness - even when, untroubled by any rival attraction like Phillipe Clay, he head-lined at the Olympia - which, in parenthesis, was to be the site of two *en public* Brel albums (in 1961 and 1964). The core of the accompaniment on each would be Brel's small combo, supplemented by an orchestra.

In its full flowering, Jacques's act was worth seeing. After the curtains part in dream-like slow motion, a *diminuendo* of animated chatter swells to unacknowledged acclamation as the cynosure of all eyes - who most likely had vomited with nerves seconds before - seizes instant possession of all with the first of a preordained fifteen *chansons* - one or two of them new and unrecorded. Of his hits, even specific couplets provoke sponta-neous salvos of applause as he sings 'Quand On N'A Que L'Amour' with-out embroidering its in-built elegance - or extemporizes like a jazz vo-calist by maybe dragging out the vowels of the hook-lines of 'Les Bich-es' over Jouannest's descending piano figure, every dredged-up nuance like a brush-stroke on a painting. Backing off until the microphone was at arm's length, just a sandpapery quiver can be as loaded as a roar with it halfway down his throat.

Between each item, he scarcely gives himself time to draw breath - though he may relinguish his guitar to an aide, manage a buck-toothed grin of baffled wistfulness as he wipes his face with an outsize hanker-chief or, depending on how steamed up he was, remove his jacket. Un-like placid Brassens, Brel would sweat away up to two pounds in weight up there, facial blemishes rising through the stage make-up and turn-ing red as he goaded himself, the band and, vicariously, his onlookers to near-collapse with the exhibitionism of a Johnnie Ray, North America's 'Prince of Wails', who could break down in tears on cue.

In like manner, Brel never sacrificed impassioned content for technical virtuosity when, from an arsenal of facial expression, flickering hand-ballets and other physical gyrations, he bombarded the audience with the characters in his songs. In a pencil spotlight, he'd cover every waterfront from the riled 'La Colombe' soldier to the embodiment of self-abasement in 'Ne Me Quitte Pas' to the simpering ninny of 'Les Bonbons'.

While endeavouring to remain true to his strange star, the swiftest showbusiness lesson that Jacques Brel had learned and would pass on was that 'it's easier to be someone else than to be yourself.'

Chapter Four

'Au Suivant'

One of Europe's highest-paid cabaret artistes, Jacques Brel was now a *French* showbusiness treasure - and, having reached that plateau, any more entries in the Top 20 were mere sideshows. Let someone else have their turn. Besides, Brel was never cut out to be the darling of *le yé-yé* a relatively new Frankish species of pop fanatic prone to outbreaks of barracking at concerts, and treading warily amidst official disapproval at government level.

The first homogenous try at rock 'n' roll had been a 1958 adaptation of the nursery rhyme 'Billy Boy' (in French) by Danyel Gerard, a vocalist under the aegis of Lucien Morisse, a Parisian equivalent of UK pop svengali, Larry Parnes. During Gerard's two year absence on National Service, he was overtaken by fresher sensations - notably Johnny Hallyday. Of Belgian parentage, Johnny's singing and passable mastery of the guitar had earned him a virtual residency at Le Golf Drouot, a *yé-yé* shrine in Paris. He sounded so like the genuine US articles that monopolized its jukebox that a 1960 radio broadcast caused Vogue to hasten him into the studio for an immediate single.

Pathe-Marconi, seeking to provision itself with some sort of 'answer' to Hallyday, grabbed a refridgerator salesman named Richard Anthony to sing principally renderings of US smashes for home consumers; among them Buddy Holly's 'Peggy Sue' and Lloyd Price's 'Personality'. Likewise, Les Chausettes Noires had a stab at 'Eddie Sois Bon' ('Johnny B Goode' by Chuck Berry) and 'Be Bop A Lula' - and Les Chats Sauvages, 'Est-Ce Que Tu Le Sais' (Ray Charles' 'What'd I Say').

Treading a smoother musical path, Belgium-bred Adamo's story reads like a microcosm of Brel's: local radio then a Philips recording deal, and a modicom of success in the Netherlands before relocating to Paris where a favourable *France-Soir* notice for an appearance at the Olympia provoked a string of self-composed hits.

Pascal Danel was in much the same bag - though his gift for melody was belied by the erratic quality of his lyrics. Nevertheless, his chart placings were a firm basis for a continued life as a travelling entertainer - as were those of Serge Gainsbourg. However, an unlikely-looking pop star with his heavy-lidded homeliness, he still preferred to compose for others such as Sacha Distel whose limited but tuneful vocal range was heard on items that, if no incisive insights into the human condition, did not pretend to be more than well-crafted, harmless pop.

Distel-as-vocalist's role-model, Sinatra was to release a Twist single in 1962. This 'most vulgar dance ever invented' (according to *Melody Maker*) was a world-wide sensation in the early 1960s - nowhere more so than in continental Europe where a Les Chakakas, a Belgian septet, even contrived to sneak into insular Britain's Top 50 with opportunist 'Twist Twist' - and a demobbed Danyel Gerard regained lost ground with 'La Leçon De Twist'. Yet it was Johnny Hallyday's million-selling bi-lingual cover of Chubby Checker's 'Let's Twist Again' in 1961 that had convinced most folk that this blond youth was to France what Elvis Presley was to the States.

Others who came into their own too with the Twist and its spin-offs included Sylvie Vartan, Les Playboys, Les Twisters, Les Chausettes Noires - and a certain Eddie Barclay. Through 'J'Irai Twister Le Blues' and an untranslated 'Let's Twist Again', Richard Anthony finally proved a sound investment for Pathe-Marconi - as did Claude François (whose records Chantal and France Brel then liked more than those of their own father) for Philips. François had drummed in a Monte Carlo jazz combo before ambition drove him to Paris where, demonstrating the Twist in a city centre club, he was 'discovered' and groomed for the hit parade via the expected native reproductions of such as 'Venus In Blue-Jeans', 'The Hully Gully' and an 'If I Had A Hammer' that was in the shops a mere week after Trini Lopez's US blueprint.

The daughter of a confectioner, Sheila's musical meat had been British. Backed by Les Guitars Brothers in Le Golf Drouot, the girl born plain Anna Chancel's speciality was hollering the hits of Petula Clark, a UK star who, on marrying into her French record outlet's promotion department, had become as well-known *sur le continent* as she was at home. Yet it was a shrewd translation of Tommy Roe's 'Sheila' that established the ordinary-looking Sheila as an enduring star of lass-next-door stamp with a central role in many vacuous movies that attended an astonishing run of domestic chart-toppers. Swiftly numbering tens of thousands, her fan club consisted mainly of schoolgirls like herself who aped her beehive hairstyle and wore a brand of Sheila attire bespoken by a chain of Sheila boutiques.

Where did Jacques Brel belong in all this? Though he was to press spare songs on Distel and, of the same intrinsic stamp, Mirielle Mathieu, Brel did not succumb to a bemused one-shot go at the Twist like Sinatra, just as he'd never cottoned on to rock 'n' roll - though the pandemonium at some of his shows had come close to its atmosphere. Jacques, see, had gone beyond all but the most serious-minded teenager. He'd become a 'quality' entertainer, singing as much to thirty-something faces tanned on the ski-slopes as those young and disenchanted by wage-slavery: parents with adolescent children as much as the adolescents themselves.

Like Sinatra, Tony Bennett, Matt Monro *et al* - as well as Brassens and Aznavour, who had 'arrived' with his first major hit ('Viens Au Creux De Mon Épaule') in 1954 - Brel's disenfranchisement from mainsteam pop had long been on the cards anyway, partly through his rejection of that style of presentation that encourages audiences to join in *omnes fortissimo* (though 'Les Singes' may be a borderline case). As far back as 1956, he said as much in the opening verse of 'S'Il Te Faut'. Preferring not to mime to his records on television anymore, he carried true handbiting excitement before millions by taking on and resolving risky ad-libbing, giving each performance of the same *chanson* an explicitly different texture.

At times, this backfired, and left viewers with an impression of someone so bound up in himself that everything that happened to him, no matter how trivial, was worth telling the whole world about in song. Furthermore, with the advent of rock 'n' roll, his melodramas seemed as *passe* as those of Johnnie Ray to pop's most vital consumer group. Thus, to Philips, Brel singles had become loss leaders, excused as 'too good for the charts', and an incentive for adults to buy an LP.

In one of the bilious cliches of music journalism, Jacques had Grown Old With His Audience - if only because of the issues he tackled and the more matter-of-fact conversational flow he'd developed since shedding the poesy of yore. Mortality and marital strife, for instance, were each filtered through 'Le Moribund' which, incorporating a jaw-dropping arrangement (like the soundtrack to a Bulgarian cartoon), concerns a dying man's amused reconciliation to his wife's serial adulteries. The subject is less passive but essentially as free-and-easy in 'Les Femmes Et Les Chiens' and 'L'Ivrogne', a nostalgic tribute to both women he's wounded, and ones who have done the same to him.

He's less of a man-of-the-world in 'Marieke'. One of Jouannest's most poignant melodies is complemented by a pining for times past that is expressed in French when dealing with the plainer present, and Flemish for the lost mellow sunshine of a holiday romance along the expanse of coast from Bruges to Ghent.

'Marieke' drank from the same pool as the contemporary cabaret standard, 'When The World Was Young (All The Apple Trees)' - and so would 'Les Bergers' in its nostalgia for an unattainable childhood if not for its bucolic detail. As 'Les Bergers' was arrayed in the set couplets that were common in old French tragic verse with its alternate masculine-feminine rhymes, then 'Le Prochain Amour', slow and string-drenched, resorted to mediaeval lyricism to forge connections between love, the revolution of the Earth's seasons and the transience of the individual; the first verse's 'dead leaf that was the short day' paralleling 'but soon must come the hour/when fades the fairest flower' from the anonymous 'Ballad Of Robin And Marion'.

As inevitable as death, says clear-headed Brel in 'Le Prochain Amour', is that, as it was with Marieke, 'the next love won't last beyond the next summer'. Nevertheless, he'll undergo the same pain again and again - despite forewarnings - whenever logic can't cool the fever of emotion. He's down to an actual case with a beguiled victim of a Spanish wanton in the midst of the carnival levity of 'Clara'.

From 1961 too, social criticism rears up 'Les Bourgeois'-like in maddeningly catchy 'Les Singes' - from a slang word for 'bosses' - who, in the blunt language that was now Brel's uptempo trademark, are the mysterious and avaricious 'they', responsible for modern civilization's desecration of a child-like arcady governed by nature, non-conformity and love - in other words, noble savagery (which was to slop from the postpunk cauldron brewed by Adam and the Ants twenty years on). With a nod towards Brassens' 'La Route Aux Quatre Chansons', Brel regrets that 'the flower is in the pot, the bird is in a cage and we are given numbers'. 'We' are also subject to imprisonment, censorship, torture, capital punishment and war - and Jacques couldn't let 'Les Singes' go without sticking a pin into religion for good measure.

A vintage year for the quality if not quantity of his *chansons*, it also marked the beginning of Brel's defection from Philips to a new and eponymous firm launched by Eddie Barclay who had recouped more than golden memories from the Twist craze. Sniffing round Brel, he'd lent a sympathetic ear to doleful tales of Philips' royalty rate; its tending more readily to the needs of Brassens - still its flagship act (and still Brel's favourite *chansonier*, confound him) - and its overall lack of understanding. As the expiry date of the contract crept closer, Brel's unease with Philips darkened to thinking aloud about forming his own record label, and then, after some heart-searching arithmetic, to a certainty that, hot property for any European company, he'd be an even better proposition on independent, committed Barclay. Everyone there was hungry to succeed, and - so Brel and Charley Marouani had been led to believe - monetary killings deferred to artistic freedom.

In an age when negotiations between entrepreneurs and artists could be mapped out on a serviette over lunch, Brel melted into Barclay's contractual caress in March 1962. As well as increasing financial incentives, Jacques preferred the back-slapping joviality round Eddie's desk to the corporate mumbo-jumbo of a Philips board meeting - for the relationship between him and Eddie, if blowing hot and cold at times, were to be almost the same as that Jacques had with Charley, and it would surprise no-one when he re-signed with Barclay in 1967, and again in 1973 (for thirty years).

Under the new regime, Brel was able that October to found his own production enterprise, eventually named Éditions Pouchenel - Polichinelle in Belgium, where, as Isabelle was the only daughter not at school, Miche had time on her hands to extend her role as administrative Aaron to his *in absentia* Moses, and take on all manner of responsibilities from press agent to financial director of the new firm.

Leaving the day-to-day mundanities of business to his missus, Brel reaped unexpected dividends from his years as a professional entertainer. In the first instance, offers of non-singing projects would include stints as narrator of Prokofiev's *Peter And The Wolf,* and presenter of *Rendez-Vous De La Musique Europe*, a radio programme of classical music in April 1963. Yet, parroting link dialogue written by someone else, it was a task for which he proved ill-equipped in spite of the crash-course in the classics he'd undergone in Rauber's car.

The teenage Jacky's Thursday afternoons gawking at Hollywood in Le Cinema Pax appeared to have been wasted too. As early as 1956, he'd undergone a screen test at the request of director Paul Deliens, who considered that, though even loyal Jojo expressed doubts, Brel might be up to carrying a short, *La Grande Père De Monsieur Clement*. Deliens' judgement proved incorrect; Brel was wooden, and the venture lost money.

More rewarding was a liaison with Ernst Van Altena, the first to render Brel's lyrics into Flemish. Brel was so delighted with the results that he released a Holland-only EP that included an all-Dutch 'Marieke'.

Van Altena was a frequent visitor to both the Brels' Brussels home and their seaside cabin at Roquebrune Cap Martin, a workshop for many Brel *chansons* including 'Les Paumes Du Petit Matin' - and desolate 'Le Plat Pays' (which subsequently found its way into music handbooks in Belgian schools). This and 'Les Bourgeois' were among selections for Brel's first LP on Barclay. While retaining François Rauber, the production criteria was now less concerned with inflating songs with heavy-handed orchestration and gratuitous frills. The abundance of old was stripped away in favour of a sparser ensemble from which a one-finger electric organ would provide a haunting counterpoint in 'Le Plat Pays' that, had it been recorded in an earlier year, might have been saturated in massed strings. Rather than banks of brass and woodwinds, a solitary trumping euphonium would enliven a 'Le Caporal Casse-Pompom' all the better for not being buried in grandiloquence. The strident zest of Brel's singing and, in the leakage of other participants' laughter, the premeditated carelessness in 'Le Caporal Casse-Pompom' was the most conspicuous example of a hitherto unprededented audacity whereby margin of error and the exhilaration of the impromptu was prized more than treacly slickness.

An antithesis of nonchalant 'Le Colonel' of 1958, German 'Le Caporal Casse-Pompom' aches to 'see Paris in spring again/parading once more at the front of my platoon'. As if it was on a late 1960s concept album, this track is followed by another inverse - 'La Statue', an opus carried musically by co-writer Rauber's mood-heightening tempo changes. A young wastrel on the winning side enlists because he's been stirred by spicy imagery of fancy-free *frauleins*. He leads an evil off-duty life, even confessing to having 'prayed to Satan', seen as a sort of diabolical pimp. After his death in battle, his exploits are overestimated in his home town where a statue is erected in his honour. His soul enters the statue, and he's condemned to spend eternity in its fixed pose, gazing unblinkingly at pigeons and children.

From the same rich harvest of *chansons*, 'Une Île' works sensually rather than intellectually, conjuring up an ambience (and, as you will read, self-fulfilling prophecy for its author) of warm latitudes, dreamy sighs, pattering bongos, and an ocean dawn from the quarterdeck: a slow boat on a final voyage to a Far West.

As surely as 'La Statue' was hot on the heels of 'Casse-Pompom' so the calm of 'Une Île' is shattered by the up-tempo agitation of 'Madeleine', a soliloquy by a guileless boy metaphorically rubbing his hands at the prospect of his weekly date with gorgeous Madeleine, but doomed to be stood up. He waits interminably at the tram stop with a bunch of lilacs to escort her to eat at Chez Eugene, and on to the flicks where he intends to fill her ears with his usual deadly serious blandishments - as unrestrained in their way as those in 'Ne Me Quitte Pas'.

Madeleine's complacency is nowhere as glacial as that of the fascinating creature in 'Ne Me Quitte Pas'; she enjoys her admirer's attentions despite - or because of - family objections ('She is far too good for me/so says her cousin Gaspard'). Perhaps she's been ordered to terminate their meetings - because she's too late for first the meal and then the cinema. Wet and shivering in the rain, he can't tear himself away - and the infatuated fool will be back at his post tomorrow evening. As it had been in 'Clara', experience is recognising mistakes when they recur.

That the feast planned at Chez Eugene is something-with-chips (drowned in mayonaisse no doubt) means that the scenario of 'Madeleine' could only be Belgium - probably Brussels where Jacques billeted himself with his Miche and the girls on aggregate for four or five days each month. Then would come his talismanic 'Over to you!' to the wife, and the hand-squeezing departure in an increasingly more splendid automobile for another distant stage, studio or she knew not what.

Like Lord Palmerston, the Victorian statesman, Brel was liberal abroad and conservative at home. His love-hate of family values unsettled, he still donned his own father's mantle as head of the household. As most of Miche's scoldings would end with 'We'll have to speak to your father about this!' like the chorus of a *chanson*, Chantal, France and Isabelle (yet too young to know of Papa's renown) were inclined to be conscientiously 'good' to stockpile ammunition for the defence when their cases came up shortly after Jacques was heard outside, fiddling for his door key.

Commanding terrified wonderment, he'd ease into his customary armchair, and, like deified Caesar come to mete out justice among the Gallic peasants, permit business to proceed. In the name of the family, Miche would review each girl's conduct over the weeks since his last visit. Now and then, the embers of long-running feuds and resentments would be fanned: Chantal enraged at France for appropriating her collection of chewing-gum cards; France displaying the now non-existent mark on her arm where Chantal had pinched her; Isabelle suspecting that one or other of them had snapped a limb off one of her dolls. Some accusations would cancel each other out as Papa got answers to his probing questions, and delivered judgement.

Brel was particularly minatory about bad table manners and poor school reports, but threats to send France to a convent rebounded with her delight at the notion of fleeing from both the tension-charged home and the French academy that all three daughters attended because Papa didn't want them to grow up with a Brussels accent.

France and Isabelle were in their more mercurial eldest sister's shadow, especially as Maman relied on Chantal to shoulder some of the loads that would otherwise be those of a less extraordinary Papa. Nevertheless, now well into adolescence, Chantal no longer had the enthusiasm a child often has for the onerous chores on the rota its mother might draw up. Though an absent father nurtured self-resolve, Chantal's childhood was shorter than it needed to have been. Moreover, very much her father's girl, she was frequently in trouble at school. The insulting 'politeness' to teachers, the red-herring tactics to waste time in class, the copied homework, the orders to spit sweets into the litter bin amassed to such a disturbing degree that Maman rang Papa - who never bothered otherwise to chat to his daughters on the telephone - requesting him to confront Chantal with her infamy (*'You* talk to her!').

The outcome was Miche bundling Chantal on the next flight to the south of France where Jacques was 'resting'. A high spot of her four day trip was accompanying him to a concert by Gilbert Becaud. Less tangibly, she became privy to a side of Papa of whom she and the other two had previously been unaware, owing to his sub-dividing his lifestyle into compartments labelled 'Belgium' and 'France'. After the novelty of fatherhood had worn off, and his work and nature had rendered the Brels even more of what was virtually a one-parent family, he and Chantal had never been chummy, but now, instead of the sermonizing monologist of home, Papa was all affability, the ice-breaking instigator of two-sided conversations with one with whom he'd had little truly intimate contact.

As far as Jacques had a favourite child, it was probably Chantal. Perhaps he recognised in her the aspects of both his former and present self. In the Cote d'Azur, he laughed with her, hugged her, gave his florid vocabulary its head in her presence, introduced her proudly to other grown-ups (including Becaud) as if she was a grown-up herself, and let her stay up past her bedtime. He even spoke about her going on the Pill as soon as she was sixteen, and put on hold his dislike of the Belgian fashion of calling parents by their forenames. Chantal was flattered but wondered - privately at first - how such a man was capable of creating *chansons* of such sensitivity. Nonetheless, by the last evening, she was gorging herself with food and drink, and shouting raucously across the bistro with the best of them.

Back in Brussels, however, Brel backslid into his role as unbending ruler of children whom he'd lecture on their shortcomings; gravely recommend Camus, Rostand and like authors for them to read, and, on a impulse, desire them to take up the harp, a fittingly feminine instrument. As Chantal's attitude towards school hadn't improved, he put her to work in a hospital throughout the next summer holiday (just as he himself had been compelled to do a baker's round by Romain). How satisfactory to him was Chantal's subsequent decision to train as a nurse - though he was to frown when France, testing the water, mentioned a hitherto unspoken fancy to make her way in the world as a dancer. There was room for only one tortured artist in this family.

When Papa was at large, it was incumbent upon the girls to maintain tip-toed, whispering silence until he rose for a dressing-gowned breakfast at eleven. His habit of flicking cigarette ash into a saucer was annoying, but like everyone else in the house except him, Miche - more the wife of her husband than mother of her daughters - had learnt to keep her feelings in check. As the breadwinner - and for the way he won it - Jacques was the only one allowed to flare up, sink into depressions, have neuroses, be unreasonable.

When asked in an interview who was the most important person in his life, he replied, 'To be honest, it's me'. The callow lad who'd showed off at Hector Bruyndonckx's party had become a past master at not making it too obvious that he wallowed in the admiration of old pals - most of them still leading run-of-the-mill lives - at restaurant dinners and evenings at home. He'd dress down, and would seem unchanged by the accelerating adulation. He couldn't help being famous, could he?

He'd reserve a *soupçon* of charm for everyone in his circle; enquiring after relations, noticing whether they'd sprouted a beard or lost weight, and bring them up to date with, say, the new car or, if he'd noticed, Isabelle's reading. Yet, for all this hail-fellow-well-met familiarity, he was quite used to sudden lulls in the conversation, and that look that mingled awe and scepticism - as if he wasn't altogether real. No-one told him why to his face or repeated any of the stories they'd heard about what he got up to when he was away, but he'd turned into an awful fellow if truth be told. Nevertheless, they stuck by him for those moments when the devious tempest of his ego dropped, and the old, less selectively amiable Jacques peeped out.

Recently, he'd scraped acquaintance with Jean-Pierre Grafe, a lawyer who was soon to be Belgium's Minister of Culture. Many were surprised later that they even knew each other, let alone become the best of mates. They didn't agree on anything except which strange club to dignify with their presence whenever Brel was benighted in Grafe's abode in Liège - though Jacques would make no direct reference to such activities in 1965's 'Il Neige Sur Liège'.

Yet, if hardly Mr. Normal, Brel's private life was often how it may have been imagined by fans who wouldn't hear a word against him - though others might have been dismayed at how ordinary, even boring, he was sometimes. A pipe-and-slippers type, he watched sport on television, attended soccer matches - and, once in a blue moon, Mass. He was also present at his father's eightieth birthday party. With the same observed exhibition of reverence, he'd listen to classical albums. His eyes would glaze over too when Miche talked him through domestic and Editions-Pouchenel accounts, her explanations rich with phrases like 'tax concession', 'convertible debenture' and 'capital expenditure'.

Whenever people came round, he enjoyed fireside palavers that could last till daybreak. Discussions for the sake of discussions about, say, euthanasia, the existence of God or the transmutation of souls would drift off on tangents of character assassinations, free association poetry and Brel asides about a ballet, a novel, a television play he was going to write. Nobody was sure whether to believe him or not.

He'd take the family out for self-conscious meals where every diner would gape as the Brels were conducted by the *maître d'* to the best table; the women envious of Miche for hooking such a well-heeled showbiz star of a man.

They didn't have to live with him - not that Miche did most of the time. Yet she'd long come to terms with it. Stable, practical and persevering, she seldom complained about him as he did about her behind her back.

She lacked imagination, he said - and, like the maudlin drunk's lament to the barmaid, My Wife Doesn't Understand Me. Outsiders were perplexed by Miche's submissiveness to his caprices, once cooking pancakes at midnight for fifteen guests he'd brought home with him.

Optimistically, she assumed that somehow they'd be a proper family again one day. He still shared her bed, and now that they could afford a succession of French, Irish or English *au pairs*, she could join him in Paris on a regular basis. His rooms there had a temporary air about them. There was scant furniture, and if he wasn't in the mood to cook, food could be summoned by telephone from a nearby café - for it was a rare day now if he could finish a meal in a roadside eatery without having to autograph a napkin whilst perhaps masticating a sausage.

A target for graffiti and marathon vigils by fans, Brel's flat was, in Swinging Sixties parlance, a 'crash pad' where he spent little time, often storming in from an engagement at five in the morning, and leaving again at noon. On tour, he'd roam from hotel to rootless hotel where the switchboard would relay fawning without friendship to one whose every action was worth a half-page in *France-Soir*.

Some editors had been itching to break the distressing news that, since ditching Zizou in 1960, he'd been carrying on with Sylvie Rivet, a record company publicist. Indeed, she'd gone from bed companion to full-time girlfriend, nearly a second wife. Green-eyed, beautiful, cultivated - and discreet, she'd met him via Serge Gainsbourg, a mutual friend.

It didn't take long for scum newspapers to flesh out this latest development, but when prodded about his love life, Jacques either fogged, changed the subject or stared back with curiosity, dragging enigmatically on a cigarette. Yet the archivist in him dictated the accumulation of the most scurrilous cuttings. Headlined 'JACQUES BREL AS HIS WIFE SEES HIM', one syndicated interview with Miche was far from the scoop of the century. Briefly, she made light of his philanderings. No, they didn't upset her - and no, there was no question of annulment.

As she was as morally generous as Mistress Quickly towards Falstaff, what about the lad himself? Brel was even more evasive and defensive - but once his tormentors' persistence drew from him a cornered 'I don't care what you say. Who are you to tell me I've abandoned my family? I've got the telephone, the train - I can get in touch with them anytime I like'. 'I'VE ONLY ONE MISTRESS: MY GUITAR!' loomed over the consequent article.

However, when playground gossip brought this or that *affaire de coeur* to the children's hearing, Brel ordered the distribution of photographs of him with Miche and the girls, all arms draped affectionately round each other, as the prototypical *famille Bonvoisin*. Next, he requested Charley Marouani to grant no more interviews for either Miche or himself in the immediate future - though he'd volunteer the occasional chat to left-wing newspapers and to those journalists who bothered to discuss his work.

Brel's disdain for the press was compounded when they massed around the lychgate of the churchyard at Romain's funeral in January 1964. Are you going on to the the show in Lille tonight after the wake, Jacques? Haven't you cancelled it out of respect? Can you and your mother stand a bit closer for a quick snap?

Lisette had the removed look of a dying woman - which she was. Prior to her passing two months later, her youngest son had composed both 'Vielle' and 'Les Vieux'. The former might have applied as much to him and Miche as his parents in that it dissected the tenderness that grows between twosomes after lust lies limp. To music by Jouannest and Corti, 'Les Vieux' was, however, the more enduring. Its accompaniment had the twinkle of an old-tyme music box commensurate with a retired and aged couple of no more earthly use to anyone, waiting for the end, quietly apprehensive, bereft of dreams but pensive at windows. Theirs is a simple round between breakfast and sleeping side-by-wrinkled-side. Now devoted friends who used to be lovers, they are stranded in time, lacking the incentive to get the piano tuned or adopt another pet. Hobbies and pastimes are just as pointless. Subconsciously, they are both disturbed by the ticking of a gold clock (the 'time that passes' of 'La Mort') that embodies an unspoken promise to each other, 'I'll wait for you' - as the first to go will until, more bent and wizened, the other totters up to the threshold of paradise too.

If 'Les Vieux' is among the spookiest songs ever recorded, one of the most embittered is 'Les Toros' - goaded and snorting half-tons of heaving muscle who on Sundays suffer and die 'for us'. 'Us' means grocery clerks (with 'horns of cuckolds') as personifications of every miserable little bloke who, as escapism from the working week, pretends to be Garcia Lorca, Don Juan or Nero, making life-or-death decisions with his thumb about this or that tormented bull who, with a feathered spear dangling from its neck in the swimming heat of a Spanish summer, might dream scathingly of a hell where men (especially worn-out matadors) will burn - and conclude (with Carthage, Waterloo and Verdun as examples) that a bullfight is just one of multitudinous man-made hells.

A cry and a laugh are never far apart with Brel. Present at a far lesser hell than that in 'Les Toros' is the ambitious lieutenant of 'Zangra' who, over an arrangement that flits between two radically different musical sections, longs for a giant leap through the ranks by a single act of heroism rather than crawling upwards with leaden steps to become a bungling 'too old general', routed from his fort by the enemy. Zandra's women 'speak of love, and me of my horses'. They are also capricious and cheating, but where would we be without 'em? Jacques had made the same point in the chief lyrical thrust of languorous 'Les Biches': every female is a ruthless, manipulative foe, regardless of background, but a male still pursues one until she catches him.

'Les Biches' was one of Brel's eternal favourites, but he'd look back in anger at another from the same cache of *chansons*, 'Quand Maman Reviendra', that he'd never attempt on stage because 'I don't like that number very much. A lot of unfortunate things happened to it. Initially, I penned it with different music, but then I had to redo it completely - not in the way in which I had envisaged it originally. The scene was set in the outskirts of a town in the United States. I wanted to project myself as a proletarian - which I'm not - and a twenty-year-old man, some sort of imbecile - and I'm neither of them either. Yet I convinced myself that I was twenty and sitting on a pavement in a working city. I wasn't being honest with myself, and, therefore, spoilt the whole song.'

He was as mindful as his investors that the interpretation of his *chansons* was a matter of perspective, and that many identified him with the personalities in them: 'I didn't want it to happen, but I accept that it has. Indeed, I'm almost happy when someone tells me that they think such-and-such of my songs is a love song. If they want to believe that, so be it. There is a book by Daninos[i] in which a tourist arrives in Venice, and exclaims with great pleasure that it's like Bruges. If that likeness between the two cities brings him joy, that's fine.'

Like an animal rights campaigner, forthright Jacques was the voice of the voiceless - those he considered 'as unhappy and as bored as I sometimes am. They feel better that somebody knows and tells them what he knows.' Nonetheless, because he couldn't quite dull the sheen of his privileged breeding, it was more difficult for John Citizen to imagine himself as Jacques Brel than as Charles Aznavour - now on terms of fluctuating equality with Brel as heir apparent to Brassens. With his school janitor looks and rather undersized height, 'everything about me is common,' admitted Charles, 'I am ordinary like real people. The romantic Frenchman's image is a problem for me. I am not a heart-throb. I am the man next door. The public may see me with Brigitte Bardot in my arms for a TV show, and that is good, because if I can make it, so can they.'

Yet from the amateur psychologist viewpoint of the *chansonier*, it was Brel who was the most accomplished at probing the desolation of those chewed upon and spat out by life. This is nowhere more apparent than in harrowing 'Jef', a portrait of a jilted down-and-out, weeping openly and feeling no shame, on a city pavement. A confidant is trying to console him - 'No, Jef, you're not alone' - by denigrating the 'fake blonde' responsible for Jef making such a boo-hooing spectacle of himself ('This has become like a picture-house/Where people come to watch you'). He offers to blow his last three sous on a cheap dinner (with chips and *vin ordinaire*) for them, and then on to booze and roister some more in Chez Françoise, and afterwards be as dissolute as they please with the tear-sheets in 'the house of Madame Andrée'. Sounds marvellous, eh? Jef doesn't think so, but, drained of his tears, he finishes up on a park bench with his mate, plunging into an orgy of maudlin reminiscences and pathetic fantasies.

Few live happily ever after with Brel as raconteur. 'Failure is almost inevitable,' he shook his head sorrowfully, 'We create goals but we're not strong enough. Our goals are not sufficiently feasible to justify the route on which we travel towards them. We aim for a destination somewhere along a road, but the road doesn't exist either.'

'Jef' might not have been a barrel of laughs, but 'Mathilde' has a kind of grievous elation to it through its cantering propulsion and mixture of hatred and irrational longing for worthless, ravishing 'Mathilde' returning to her shocked and forsaken lover. To him, she's 'confounded', 'blessed' and, by the final line, 'my beautiful Mathilde' in whose arms he will heedlessly 'go back to hell'.

Just as false-hearted is 'La Fanette', but, on a deserted beach, her victim reacts more in understated sadness than trumpeted anger. This - with 1963's 'La Toison D'Or' - is another transmission of Brel's mistrustful attitude towards women: 'If we play their game, we find ourselves in the final count, poor, diminished, empty.' Yet he wasn't yet so jaded that he couldn't relive teenage lovesickness in 'J'Aimais'.

A young man of like sensitive stamp is dispirited by the hurried loss of his virginity in the routine and robust caress of a diseased bawd in the mobile army bordello of 'Au Suivant'. To the Chinese water-torture chink of a glockenspeil, he feels obliged to take everyone else's path of least resistance through life. For all its sordid imagery, 'Au Suivant' got past the universal aunt that was the Gallic media as, because it was Jacques Brel and not, say, Les Chausettes Noires singing, it was not the musical equivalent of some distasteful movie. It might even have been Art.

Jacques Brel didn't care what he said, did he? To the tom-tom beat of 'Le Dernier Repas', he came right out with it: 'I have insulted the bourgeoisie/without fear and without remorse'. In another sense, there was worst to come in 'Amsterdam' - a canticle to an unconscious existentialism that vies with 'Au Suivant' as the third best-known Brel *chanson*. Creaking into a reluctant but quickening lilt like someone recovering from a hangover, it maps out the life cycle of a hard-drinking, whoring seaman who expires clownishly during a tavern brawl, 'full of ale, full of drama', because, essentially no different from the pleasanter chap in 'Au Suivant, he knew of no other way out.

In the last verse, he drinks a toast to 'the whores of Amsterdam, Hamburg or elsewhere' who sell 'their pretty bodies' for 'a lump of gold' - as do the more refined gold-diggers in 'Les Jardins Du Casino', on the lookout for either a young rake or a sugar-daddy.

While these ladies might have come from the pages of Zola's *Nana*, 'Le Tango Funèbre' had been anticipated unwittingly by nothing so sophisticated. Fusing song and dialogue, the prolific British comedy actor and singer Stanley Holloway left us with 'Ain't It Grand To Be Blooming Well Dead', a serenade from a coffin *en route* to a cemetary that might have been in London's East End. Decades later, Brel's *chanson* has the stiff in question guffawing mirthlessly at the hollow emotions and crocodile tears of 'friends' and uncaring relations who have costed him down to his socks during a nosy grubbing through his belongings. With an inheriting gleam in their eyes, they put on a solemn front when 'following...my costume of wood' on a bleak journey that terminates in a 'bony meadow'.

'Les Timides' covers the same ground with less humour, not only in some of its emotive phraseology ('and when they slide into the depths, I can tell when they die') but also in its exposure of humbug. This is less studied in 'Les Bonbons' where an *ostinato* pinged on a xylophone enhances the drivelings of one who does not query a received ritual of presenting girls with chocolates (rather than Madeleine's more perishable flowers) as a form of hire-purchase of a desired result - which, in this case, is honourable. His wooing of flame-headed Germaine, therefore, meets with her mother's benevolent neutrality if not approval. However, Germaine uses him as an excuse to get out of the house to meet someone of less chivalrous intent. Her behaviour provokes sympathy not censure because the official lover is the sort who, with the cruel puncturing of his romantic idealism, regresses to ungallant if ineffectual slyness.

'Les Bonbons' takes place in a rural province where the 1950s didn't really end until about 1966. Even Paris was several steps behind trend-setting London, now the world's prime purveyor of pop music, thanks to the beat groups who were deluging overseas Top Tens in a large scale re-run of the hysteria known at home. A new Philips signing, the fated Singing Nun from a Domenican convent near Brussels, was the most overt sign of Gallic resistance to Britain's domination of world pop, but out of the sub-cultural woodwork too had crawled legion outfits like Triangle, Les Sunlights and Les Cyclones who'd had their quiffs sculpted into moptops, and seized upon whatever attributes of the new cross-channel idioms with which they felt most comfortable.

From Gerry and the Pacemakers' portfolio alone had come respective translated xeroxes in 1964 by Claude François and Richard Anthony of 'How Do You Do It' and 'You'll Never Walk Alone'. Sheila cashed in with Manfred Mann's 'Do Wah Diddy Diddy', and nineteen-year-old Françoise Hardy, visualized by lazy columnists as a 'new Greco', with an EP entitled *C'Est Fab*.

A support spot to The Kinks at the Olympia would evoke screams for another newcomer, Michel Berger, for his own stylized songs, while Danyel Gerard's 'Les Vendages De L'Amour' was film thespian Marie Laforet's first single - and *the* hit song in France in 1964. Her parallel career as a *chanteuse* continued with records of mostly folk and Latin material from North America. She was also a fan of Bob Dylan - as was Hugues Aufray who had jumped from skiffle to bandwagons new - such as the album *Aufray Chante Dylan*. Others were also dipping into Dylan's songbook, and quoting his lyrics as if they were proverbs - particularly since he was now singing through his nose about myriad less doe-eyed topics than before.

The less fashionable Brel too had revealed infinitely greater possibilities in pop composition beyond 'protest' and unrealistic boy-girl spoonings. In 1965, he endeavoured once more to leave the orbit of pop altogether by grafting a libretto - slightly reminiscent of that in 'Amsterdam' - onto *'Les Trois Histoires De Jean De Bruges*, the 'symphonic poem' that was François Rauber's entry for a competition overseen by the Parisian National Conservatory of Music. Lasting no more than fifteen ordained minutes, each contribution was to be performed by the same orchestra, though there was a free choice of vocalist.

The text was apportioned between the warblings of baritone Jean Christophe Benoit - and recitations by Brel, despite his reservations that 'it isn't very interesting. *Jean De Bruges* concerns a sailor who would have lived a few hundred years ago. He'd tell tales to anyone who'd buy him a drink. We use three of these stories. The first tells how he fell in love with the little mermaid of Copenhagen. The second how a storm made England into an island by separating it from Belgium. The third is centred on a monstrous whale which bled to death and formed the Red Sea.'

He'd insist that 'We did it for a laugh,' after this harbinger of *Tubular Bells* failed to bridge any gap between *chanson* and anything deemed as more 'highbrow'. Nevertheless, Brel consulted a disinclined Rauber about further such 'works' before deciding not to try again just yet to free himself from the stylistic straitjacket fastened to him by those who liked 'Ne Me Quitte Pas', packed out his concerts, and bought the collection of his lyrics - the first of many - published in Paris in 1964.

Net income from these was either tied up in budgetary receptacles or ploughed back into Éditions Pouchenel - and Brel's wallet would often hold hardly any hard cash. He'd become unaccustomed to paying for things that way as he never had to prove his identity to sign bills for large amounts. Small change too was as unnecessary to him as eyesight to a monkfish because road managers and other menials took care of minor purchases. Yet, if not the most provident of men, there were no hand-tooled diamond rings, guitar-shaped swimming pools or pyjamas of monogrammed silk. However, he'd dine where no waiter's eyebrows would rise if he ordered mussels-and-chips with beer in Montparnesse restaurants where only the likes of Dali, Fellini, Hemingway and Bardot could afford to clatter cutlery on plate. With the ease of a daily rail commuter, he'd jet first class from Cayenne to Cannes - the bulk of his retinue cramped in the main tourist body of the craft.

A fascination with aviation that would last for as long as he lived had started with a display of aerobatics during an internal flight across France from one booking to the next in 1964. The buffeting and plummeting had sickened Jouannest, but Jacques was enthralled by the element of risk, and the disciplined freedom of a pilot. Purchasing a wooden-framed bi-plane, the first of several successive crafts, he hired an instructor to be on hand at a moment's notice for irregular tutorial flights whenever there was a gap in his tour-album-tour sandwiches. He would manage his first long haul in June 1966 with an aerial safari of ancient monuments in Italy, Germany, Greece, Crete and the Near East.

He also had the wherewithal to move Miche and the girls to a five-room apartment on the eighth floor of a modern block in a smarter district in Brussels - and himself to the same Parisian building where Brassens used to live in a thoroughfare in a village-like suburb of boating lakes and golf courses. Here, as in his previous dwelling, he liked to fix his own breakfast like the confirmed bachelor he should have been. Moreover, however demonstrative Sylvie's yearnings were to redecorate the place or have his babies, he wouldn't countenance her having the same degree of control over domestic arrangements as the *bona fide* Mme. Brel - though when he was on tour, it was Sylvie who received the telephone call every evening, and Miche the intermittent postcard.

Miche may have feigned aloofness at Jacques' increasing attachment to Sylvie, but one night, he made a flippant remark about admitting adultery if she wanted a divorce. He was so astonished by her reply that he asked her to repeat it. Before he came home to Brussels again, she said, she'd discuss the ways and means with a solicitor. However, hours of noisome home truths later, there was an abrupt and inexplicably tearful reconciliation.

NOTES

1. Creator of the humorous 'Major Thompson', an English expatriate in France.

Chapter Five

Music For The Millions

The only direction should have been down. Jacques Brel could live quite cosily into old age on the consolidated fruits of his success if, now in his mid-thirties, he retired as a travelling entertainer. Indeed, he was already speaking of it. Yet Brel was about to be sucked into a vortex of events, places and situations that hadn't belonged even to speculation even when he first played the Olympia. After a while, he was past resistance to circumstances that seemed to make it impossible to either go back to the old life or make long term plans. If his itinerary had included a show in Siberia - which it would - it mightn't have seemed all that strange.

Closer to home, no Gallic pop star, except Chevalier, had made sustained headway in Britain before the mid-1960s. By proxy, Serge Gainsbourg had entered both the UK and US chart as provider of potboilers for Dionne Warwick, Petula Clark, Twinkle and others, and Richard Anthony had crept into the UK Top Twenty in 1964 - though concentration on overseas markets affected his domestic standing until 1966's 'Fille Sauvage' (the Rolling Stones' 'Ruby Tuesday') brought him back in from the cold. However, a like preponderance of English language material - not all of it translated - in Johnny Hallyday's concert sets, and well-received British TV appearances did not belittle him in the eyes of his countless grassroots fans, proving, therefore, that it was feasible to broaden your spectrum without necessarily alienating your old following.

Whilst likewise keeping a weather eye on France with scrupulous media plugs of his latest single, Sacha Distel would amass sufficient global popularity to star in his own US television spectacular. Yet this clean-cut smiler was fighting the same intrinsic battle as the crassest pop act that wished to get off the Gallic treadmill and rake in the dollars. Grasping too that North America was the market that counted most, one of Johnny Hallyday's former managers would be sparing no expense in grooming Parisian teenager Mirielle Mathieu as a second Piaf. Though less *outré* than that little madam, Mirielle sported a similar 'urchin' haircut, and her domestic hits (on Barclay Records) were a dry run for the States -

though her repertoire would remain invulnerably French no matter what tongue the actual lyrics she sang.

A minor territory like France or Belgium would cease to matter financially if, like Mathieu and Distel, you were on a winning streak in this hugest sales area of all. Though he'd chosen eventually to consolidate his standing in Europe, Bobbejaan Schoepen had been performing since 1953 on the hallowed boards of Nashville's weekly Grand Ole Opry - which is to the country-and-western artist the same as Everest to a mountaineer - and had made nationally-networked guest appearances on *The Ed Sullivan Show* as well as Britain's *Royal Command Performance*. Moreover, Nicole Croisille, a jill-of-all-trades on the Parisian stage, landed a cabaret residency at Chicago's Playboy Club where she was bruited as being in the same league as Judy Garland. She then proceeded to take Uncle Sam's fair land for every cent she could get for the rest of a career that touched its apogee in 1966 with her hand in the first French film soundtrack album (*Un Homme Et Une Femme*) to climb into the US *Hot 100*.

Nicole's Playboy spot had incorporated Brel *chansons*, but Jacques himself was relatively unconcerned about distant syndication or that pop had developed into a predominantly English-language music and would remain so for all time. He was becoming as peculiar to his own patch as Freddy Quinn, a vocalist unknown internationally, but selling millions in West Germany. Yet, despite himself, Brel had impinged upon Anglo-Saxon regions almost by stealth after US recording manager Nat Shapiro had become evangelical about this singing wordsmith from Belgium to his CBS superiors. 'I don't know. What do you think?' was the spirit that had pervaded the company's unleashing of 1957's *American Debut* LP on the congested wavelengths of the United States. Nevertheless, by 1964, when *Music For The Millions (À L'Olympia)* was cobbled together by Philips for Britain as well as North America, a substantial Brel cult had snowballed from a target group consisting largely of the very people Brel vilified for their compounding of mediocrity. 'The bourgeoisie are a form of materialism,' he'd tell London's *Melody Maker*, 'All that kills a dream. For me, that's the bourgeoisie - that's security. It's a non-commitment of heart. That's what makes people old before their time.'

He might have appealed to the great unwashed in Paris - demonstrating to the illuminati that multitudes could be right - but in London, Washington, Leningrad and Toronto, Brel devotees were more likely to browse in bookshops, and drag along to his concerts those for whom the main purpose of the evening was to see and be seen during the intermission. To them, exposure to Brel was like watching a film by Cocteau or Warhol, or listening to some minimalist composer: a cultural duty first, and *divertissement* frequently a poor second. Such snobs would think privately that it was like an antedote to pleasure on the principal that the more arduous the effort needed to appraise something, the more 'artistic' it is.

Nonetheless, quite a few bought a Brel album simply because they liked it. For whatever reason, there had been enough potential native customers - and Gallic expatriates - for Jacques to be cajoled into exploratory performances at New York's Carnegie Hall in February 1963. Rather than deliver a final encore, he'd asked the crowds if they'd comprehended the lyrics. All responded with a shouted unison 'No!' and a lengthy continuation of applause in appreciation of what they'd *felt* he was singing about, the spell he'd cast. 'He only sings in French, and he says nothing in between his songs,' noted folky Carnegie Hall stage veteran Tom Paxton, 'You would think the language barrier would be *"formidable"* but the communication was tremendous. He was animated and passionate and comical and cynical.'

This was all most gratifying. Furthermore, financial outlay had been recouped, and it had been considered a worthwhile exercise to make reservations for further Brel shows at the place whenever a sufficient gap appeared in a touring schedule that stretched, theoretically, as far ahead as 1967.

He returned to Carnegie Hall for two sell-out appearances in December 1965 to an audience that included a slew of powerful critics who had finally got to hear of him. Without exception, their opinions were favourable. 'It was possible for a member of the audience who did not understand a word of French to understand emotionally and to be swept along by what Mr. Brel had to say,' noticed Robert Alden of *The New York Times*, 'Using his large hands, supple body, expressive arms, strong voice and even mischievously humorous legs, he becomes the bitter sailor drinking in the port of Amsterdam, the old person who is waiting for death, the timid suitor, even the bull dying under a hot Spanish sun.'

The latter example referred to a 'Les Toros' updated to embrace Iwo Jima, Hiroshima, Saigon - and Stalingrad, a name he did not omit when the troupe had dared a visit to Russia for five weeks from October 1965, taking in Leningrad, Moscow, Georgia - whose decidedly non-bourgeois populace, decided Jacques, 'rely more on dreams than reality' - and outposts (some within the Arctic circle) that could only be reached by helicopter, and where electricity turbines were so underpowered that there was often no hot running water. Even in bigger towns, the last restaurants closed at 10.30 p.m. - not that the food was much to Brel's taste, apart from the caviar and vodka.

Onerous too were the shows that started as early as eleven in the morning. Worse, all proceeds had to be donated to charity because the rouble was not then an exchangeable currency. Moreover, at the Moscow stop, the audience (including the French and British diplomatic corps) were treated to an official translator stopping Brel every fifth number or so to explain the lyrics - but that, as they often say, is showbusiness, and the artist's valediction was kindly. The Soviets, he said, had shown 'affection and generosity.'

The following year was busy too with an agenda covering a youth festival for peace in Helsinki and full-scale tours in Lebanon, Poland, Egypt, Greece, Israel and Madagascar. That November, it was standing-room-only at London's Royal Albert Hall - though the English were then less rapturous about him than their colonial cousins. Guests at a reception afterwards included the Duchess of Bedford - and Charles Aznavour who was making more headway than Brel outside France in the wake of 1965's *His Love Songs In English* LP. This, reckoned Jacques, epitomised an emasculation of the *chansonnier*'s craft.

Brel would be mentioned only in passing in Aznavour's first autobiography[1], but, before the fond smiles of the public, there was an outward display of matey abuse and coded bonhomie between the two. 'When are you going to be in Las Vegas?' read a fraternal telegram from Aznavour to Carnegie Hall - to which Brel cracked back that Charles was the only person he knew who could stand up in a Rolls-Royce.

Catching this diminutive *chansonier* at the London Palladium ten years later, I have to agree with Bob Dylan's view that 'Aznavour just blew my brains out. I saw him in sixty-something at Carnegie Hall. I went there with somebody who was French, not knowing what I was getting into.'

Unlike wide-haired, twenty-five-year-old Dylan (who'd managed a maiden Albert Hall showcase in 1965), both Brel and Aznavour were regarded as too maturely showbiz - too Frank Sinatra - for the teenagers, though cool young marrieds might have put Brel on the turntable during dinner parties. Therefore, bereft too of the in-person publicity blitz expected of a Maurice Chevalier, Brel's presence in London in 1966 had been worth only a brief feature in *Melody Maker* and less than that in the UK's other music journals.

His name might have been unknown to the man-in-the-street in Andover, Augusta or Alice Springs, but support from a trendy minority might have bound Brel to fulfilling decades as one of Gaul's leading musical ambassadors. In that boat already were Les Compagnons De La Chanson and Jan Rosol, a French folk singer forever on BBC radio schools programmes. With persistence, Brel might have achieved then the renown of, if not Chevalier or Aznavour, then the Swingle Singers, a choir that had been assembled in 1963 by Ward Lamar Swingle, former conductor of Les Ballets De Paris. Addressing themselves to jazzy arrangements of the classics - particularly Bach - their wordless style had the novel effect of predetermined mass scat-singing.

Brel was as respected - or, at least, as patronized - by those foreigners aware of him. He was, therefore, well placed, had he desired, to represent the *chansonier* as contributory to the rich tapestry of continental Europe's performing arts. Instead, he chose to work to rule. He was often absent from the venue minutes before showtime. Encores were rarer than albino blackbirds, and, before the audience realized that there wasn't going to be one, he'd be *en route* to the hotel in the limousine that had been ticking over in a rear alley. Flanked by retainers, he'd stonewall fans and other riff-raff hovering in the lobby, and retreat to his suite, fastening a 'Do Not Disturb' sign on the door-knob and drawing the curtains. As it was with Dylan and Sinatra, the self-defensive ban on nearly all interviews was still very much in force too. 'The last journalist who tried to see him was thrown downstairs for his pains,' the promoter of the Albert Hall bash had warned, 'I don't even know if I'll be seeing him myself.'

After much fuss, Karl Dallas of *Melody Maker* had gained admission to a nicotine-clouded room where Jacques was not especially gregarious during the short time he'd granted that most reputable of British pop music newspapers. Exhaling smoke with a sigh, his features would pinch in thought at each question put to him. He didn't say anything very significant, but his surrounding *cortège* hushed when he answered, exchanged knowing smirks, laughed when he laughed and fetched him drinks by the tumblerful. He denied that his mob were his equivalent of the 'Memphis Mafia', Elvis Presley's inward-looking cabal, qualifying this with 'I feel for them like youngsters feel for their pals. I am happy when I tour around for a couple of months with people I like. I like to hang around with them, and they leave me feeling completely unrestrained.'

They'd learned to leave him alone and field all outside interference when he was in a creative mood, pacing up and down the carpet, guitar and notebook within reach, initially a one-man composer, librettist and arranger possessed by an impulse that might have manifested itself at an inconvenient moment in, say, a lift, backstage passage or during an airline lunch. 'La Valse De Mille Temps' had revealed itself when Brel was hurtling round hair-pins bends in the mountains towards Tangiers. Then the river of imagination had so burst its banks that he lurched into a lay-by to quell it with a biro.

Sometimes, he would write at the speed of a train, while on more pedantic occasions, he'd draw Rauber, Corti or, most often, Jouannest into the process, standing over one of them at the piano, perhaps teasing a chanson from little more than a riff and a few half-finished rhymes. Listening intently as it ripened, Brel would sling in chord changes and other ideas as enough of a discernable melody was pieced together to beget in Brel twists to the plot and facilitate the expansion and nagging redrafting of the commensurate lyrics, usually in seclusion.

If anything, songwriting was more difficult nowadays. He'd try to stimulate his muse by drugging himself with challenging books - Camus, Valery, Saint-John Perse, Henry Miller - often several at a time, but, as soon as he got stuck, he'd throw in the towel, and fish Rider Haggard, Jack London or something else as comfortingly over-familiar from the shelf. Once, he'd had non-stop inspiration, but now, if he wasn't careful, he'd hear himself going through the motions with detached efficiency, exploring formula themes and buzz-words over and over again like an alchemist of old repeating the same experiment, week in, week out, in vain hopes of making gold.

Now and then, however, Jacques Brel succeeded. With Jouannest, he came up with 'La Chanson De Jacky', even if it was a blurry retread of 'Les Bergers' and 'Marieke', albeit from a radically different viewpoint in its romping portrayal - set in Belgium - of a shady specimen's lost innocence and his desire for just a brief return to the era prior to his corruption to get his nerve back for whatever lies ahead. Likewise, there was an indistinct but existing connection between 'Le Prochain Amour', 'La Mort' and the new 'Fernand' in the intimation of mortality. A lachrymose friend stands self-consciously alone in the silence of eternity at Fernand's grave. 'Ne Me Quitte Pas'-esque flights of fancy (e.g. 'I will invent for you a family/Just for your burial') and repetition of key phrases convey disquiet and a tragi-comic surreality ('and now, Good Lord, You must be very amused/And now, Good Lord, now I come to cry').

If nothing like it in form, 'Fernand' has the same contradictory aftertaste of enjoyable depression as Gregorian chant, having been penned after Jacques and Miche's excursion to a Benedictine monastery near Bruges in 1964. Flattered that one of the monks, Thierry Maertens, was no stranger to his records, Jacques kept in touch, eventually persuading Maertens - shortly to leave the priesthood - to attend a concert, and, during the drive back to the abbey, engaging him in profound discourse about the connection between sex and spirituality in the newly-concocted 'Les Amants De Coeur'; Brel paying lip service to orthodoxy in having his children baptised and confirmed, and, as the speedometer touched 100 m.p.h., death or 'the gate to the underworld' as the intelligent rather than intellectual Brel put it. 'Death is justice, real justice,' he said with the splendid certainty that now seemed to permeate everything he said and did, 'If I use it in my songs, it's because it's the most absurd idea, accessible to all. 'He broke off before adding, 'It's very impolite of God not to inform us of the hour of our death.'

'La Mort' - and 'Les Singes' - rear up in 'L'Âge Idiot' in the sense that modern man as he ages feels progressively safer in a series of institutions - 'barracks' - that lead to 'his last barracks', the tomb. Brel's verse structure hangs on the effect of each passing decade ('un âge idiot') on the eyes and the stomach as we seek increasingly more transient gratifications, especially after 'the countdown begins' at thirty. By the age of sixty, we live, Brel reckons, only to fill our bellies, and our eyes 'cry no more tears' as we head irreversibly towards 'the stomach of the earth'.

Precedents were more covert in 'Ces Gens-Là', a well-crafted melancholia of one telling somebody of the same social rank of his love for Frida, the daughter of a household that survives by perpetual mental arithmetic, ekeing out a low income. His ardour seems liable to fade owing to the family's acquiescent resignation to its plight, and his own inborn contempt for 'these people here', who are put to the back of his mind as soon as he makes his excuses and leaves.

Brel made less general observations - and may have drawn from direct experience - in 'Grand-Mère' (a puffed-up business woman with a two-timing husband) and 'Un Enfant' (yet to be disillusioned about his parents' love affairs with other parties).

Naturally, these new items were disadvantaged by better-known *chansons*' head start of up to twelve years of availability on disc. Cognisant of this, Brel, when venturing into the non-Gallic unknown, would adhere mostly to 'Quand On N'A Que L'Amour', 'Ne Me Quitte Pas', all the old stand-bys - as he did at Carnegie Hall - where, in 1965, a certain Mort Shuman had vanished into the night afterwards, lost in wonder. He was to become to Brel as Boswell to Dr. Johnson.

A New Yorker in his late twenties, Shuman had formed, with Jerome 'Doc' Pomus, debatably, the most popular songwriting team in America. 'They were the most unlikely couple you could meet,' affirmed British singing guitarist Joe Brown, 'Mort was a big redneck American - that was the way he looked, he wasn't a redneck politically - while Doc was a hunched, crippled guy. They should have been on *What's My Line*. No-one would have guessed that they wrote teenage love songs.'

Mort - who thumped the eighty-eights in a sub-Jerry Lee Lewis fashion - and Doc had supplied sound chart-making goods for such diverse hitmakers as Elvis Presley, Ray Charles, Fabian, The Drifters, Andy Williams and Dion and the Belmonts before going separate ways - Mort, in the first instance, to a less profitable alliance with Philadelphia producer Jerry Ragavoy, but 'I was completely disillusioned with the crass commerciality of the whole thing,' Shuman would admit to Radio Merseyside presenter Spencer Leigh[2], 'I stayed at university because I thought it was best to have an education. I also had wanderlust. I went to England, to Paris, to Mexico, to Spain, to Israel and to the Caribbean. Around 1964, I was dying to chuck it all in, pick up a guitar and go on the road - just like Jack Kerouac.'

For most of what remained of the 1960s, he settled in London, making ends meet with hits for The Hollies, The Small Faces and others inescapably identified with the country's beat group explosion. 'I wrote with Kenny Lynch and Clive Westlake,' he recalled, 'who were wonderful mates of mine. "Sha La La La Lee" [a 1966 Top 10 entry for The Small Faces] was the result of a direct challenge. Someone bet me that I couldn't write another rock 'n' roll song again.' A middle-of-the-road ballad, Cilla Black's 'Love's Just A Broken Heart', however, would be attributed to Mort, Kenny - and Michelle Vendome, composer of the original French version, picked up by Shuman in a publishing office during the same trip to Paris that he stumbled upon Jacques Brel.

'Of course, I knew the work of French artistes like Georges Brassens and Charles Trenet,' affirmed Mort, 'but someone who worked for Barclay played me some records by artists that I'd never heard of. One of the albums was by Jacques Brel, and I thought it was super. The only time I'd heard such virility in a voice was in black singers. I just had to find out what he was singing about. Then I had to translate it. Brel wrote about things that you didn't normally hear people singing. He sang of things that you normally only found in philosophy or in novels. His songs were unbelievable. They were such personal songs. By that time, Dylan and the Beatles were doing interesting things, but I was much more impressed with Brel. I showed his songs to my publisher in the States, and he told me that people didn't want to hear that sort of thing on record. That only made me more determined.'

A lyricist bitten as hard as Shuman by the Brel bug was the self-styled 'most popular poet in the world', Rod McKuen. Among his first interpretations was a 1964 rendition of 'Le Moribund' as 'Seasons In The Sun' by The Kingston Trio (on which fellow Californian McKuen's gravelly husk of a voice was, allegedly, heard). With their smooth harmonies and dazzling smiles, these acoustic collegians had first encroached upon national consciousness with a million-selling dilution of the nineteenth century murder ballad 'Tom Dooley'. The way the Trio told it, judicial hanging was no more terrifying to the condemned Dooley than having to report to the headteacher's study for the cane.

'Seasons In The Sun' was similarly anodyne. Instead of 'I want them to dance when it's me they're putting in the hole' as the opening line of the chorus, Rod made it 'We had joy, we had fun, we had seasons in the sun.' With all further what's-the-use-of-it-all ugliness removed (not to mention the sex), it was to change hands yet again to emerge by the mid-1970s as a sentimental lay about some old idiot's happy memories - with ascending key changes to pep it up - and as harmless as 'Tie A Yellow Ribbon Round The Old Oak Tree' or 'Stand By Your Man'.

McKuen had been so satisfied with his result in 1964 that he sang it himself on a forthcoming LP - 'but I didn't know that it had been sent to Jacques. When I went on holiday in France in 1964, I asked a publisher - Phillipe Boutet - if he had any new songs that I might adapt for the American market. He played me a rough demo of a number that had been written by Jacques Brel for Jean Sablon. It was called "Les Amants De Coeur", and it was only towards the end that I realized that it was my own song, "The Lovers". I subsequently learned that Brel had received my recording of "Seasons In The Sun" and was so pleased that, after a long and tiring tour of France, he'd adapted another song on the record, "The Lovers", into French.'

If slushy with violins, 'The Lovers' was actually stronger lyrically than 'Les Amants De Coeur' - not a masterpiece of song anyway. Nevertheless, a rendezvous between the two protagonists was set up when Boutet rang round there and then, reaching Jacques at a dentist's appointment. A restaurant feed and back to Brel's for coffee that night unharnessed both a common sense of humour and a ratification of future reciprocal arrangements, summarised by Rod: 'We think of our songs as collaborations and not translations because I wanted to retain the feel of Brel's words while translating them as freely as I wished.'

An unauthorized 'La Colombe' had been recorded - along with 'Marieke' - by Judy Collins, who ran in the same pack as Tom Paxton, who'd come into his own when the civil rights movement fused with folk to be labelled 'protest'. Left-wing and far removed from mainstream showbusiness, it was rooted in ethnic material and self-composed items in which, significantly, the words also mattered at least as much as the music. On hearing Judy's 'La Colombe', Paxton was to become a lifelong convert: 'I thought it was very beautiful, and then I heard a few more of his songs, also by Judy, and next I saw the man himself at Carnegie Hall. It was a spectacular appearance, and so I started a romance with Brel's music. His songs really had a big infuence on me. "Annie's Going To Sing Her Song" was directly inspired by "Mathilde". His music had guts to it, and I thought that there were real possibilities in a cabaret, Left Bank approach. It meant you didn't have to have a traditional folk music approach to say something, to make a statement.'

Brel was also infiltrating British mainstream pop. Traces of him could be heard, for example, in the work of Mancunian songwriter Graham Gouldman whose 'For Your Love', a 1965 Number One in the UK for the Yardbirds, contained 'I'd give the moon if it were mine to give' and other lines that might have come from a listen to 'Ne Me Quitte Pas'. Simplified Brel-type scenarios cropped up the following year in Gouldman's 'Bus Stop' for The Hollies and Herman's Hermits' 'No Milk Today'.

Acknowledgement of Brel's influence would be less unconscious after he was unearthed by one Noel Scott Engel, after he'd adopted the stage alias 'Scott Walker'. After several flop singles and a spell as bass player with the Routers, a Californian instrumental outfit, Ohio-born Engel had teamed up with singing guitarist John Maus and drummer Gary Leeds. As The Walker Brothers, they'd tried their luck in Britain where a second 45, 'Love Her', breached the Top Twenty in 1965. Next up were bigger chart strikes with 'Make It Easy On Yourself', 'My Ship Is Coming In' and like slowish outings framed in heavy-handed orchestration, all emoted by Scott in the golden-brown richness of a coltish Sinatra. All three Brothers were elevated to pin-ups in *Fabulous*, *Mirabelle*, *Rave!* and like periodicals aimed at teenage girls. However, with a disturbing hat-trick of comparative misses as well as bickering between Engel and Maus, disbandment was on the horizon by late 1966.

During these traumatic months, Scott was to experience 'one of the happiest days of my life when a German girlfriend gave me the first English translation I'd seen of Brel's lyrics. She would translate more of his songs for me'. He was to be bitterly disappointed that a date on what was perceived as his final tour with The Walker Brothers was to clash with the Belgian's Albert Hall show. Nevertheless, if Mort Shuman was Brel's most credible backroom interpreter in the English-speaking world then, Scott Walker was about to become his most public mouthpiece.

NOTES

1. Yesterday When I Was Young *(W.H. Allen, 1979)*
2. *Most Shuman quotes in this book are from the same source.*

Chapter Six

'Like Taking A Picasso
And Changing It Around A Bit'

In 1966, Jacques Brel was at the apogee of his sectarian popularity as a performer in alien realms. As a composer, however, his impact was more by insinuation to an immeasurably wider world. The songs rather than the shows were of more advantage to Brel - and his estate - in the long term. In the process, however, certain of his more acerbic lyrics would, like 'Le Moribund', be emasculated, truncated and, in some cases, so warped that they bore as much resemblance to the originals as a Marx Brothers film to its screenplay. Rather than burden the listener with tracts about anything too disagreeable, many of Brel's foreign interpreters were inclined to approach his *chansons* with the argument that the music should blend with words in which meaning did not necessarily have to take precedence over phonetics.

Mosaic-like though his lyrics were in construction, the fastidious Brel was, perhaps surprisingly, untroubled about havoc wrought on them by others as long as the assorted and incoming monies settled into the complicated but fixed financial channels leading to his bank account. No corporation marionette, Brel on his home turf maintained an intense and often unwelcome interest in every link of the chain from studio to pressing plant to marketplace, but elsewhere, 'really he couldn't care less,' believed Mort Shuman, 'He was not interested in appealing to the English-speaking world.'

He had no need of us - and maybe he felt too that the battle wasn't worth fighting as no direct decoding would seem credible anyway because he was so unEnglish. 'There's (a Brel) song ["Je Suis Un Soir D'Été"] where the title in English would be "I Am The Sun Of The Night" [*sic*],'continued Shuman, 'Now that's an utterly impossible title for an English song and, at present, I can see no way of translating it. Again, what would an English audience make of a line like "The commissionaire is commissionairing"?' Cor blimey, me plates of meat don't 'alf 'urt. Must be these daisy roots I'm wearin'.

Brel's unconcern was mirrored by that of Gilbert Becaud, whose 'Le Jour Où La Pluie Viendra' gave Jane Morgan a British Number One in 1958 when rendered as 'The Day That The Rains Came Down'. Two years later, his 'Je T'Appariens' became The Everly Brothers' 'Let It Be Me' as 1962's 'Et Maintenant' provided Shirley Bassey with a hit in 'What Now My Love'. Much-revived too would be Vikki Carr-via-Becaud's 'It Must Be Him' ('Seul Sur Son Étoile').

Boris Vian didn't mind either when 'Le Déserteur' was warped to Peter, Paul and Mary's own devices. Claude François's attitude was the same in the more negotiable matter of his own co-written 'Comme D'Habitude'. Adored as 'Clo-Clo' by teenagers, François had next addressed himself to their parents with a greater proportion of largely self-composed ballads. His deepest penetration into markets beyond France would be oblique but lucrative when the reflective 'Comme D'Habitude' was superimposed upon wily Canadian pop singer Paul Anka's lyrical grid to become 'My Way', a set-work for every third-rate Sinatra after it became Ol' Blue Eyes' signature tune - and holder of the record for the longest stay in the British chart. It also drummed up further royalties for its creators via revivals by artistes as diverse as Elvis Presley and The Sex Pistols.

Jacques Brel's gains in this sphere came from not one multi-million seller, but many items that spread themselves thinly enough over years of cover versions to accrue a comparable amount of hard cash - even if the motives behind them were suspect. 'In English, the people who've dabbled in Brel have done it in a slightly dilettante way,' summised Duncan Browne, a musical colleague of Mort Shuman, 'using it perhaps as a cool thing to have in their repertoire. At one stage, it was very hip to know something about Brel and maybe do one of his songs on one of your albums.'

Brel's Big Three were 'Seasons In The Sun', 'Amsterdam' and 'If You Go Away' ('Ne Me Quitte Pas'). After the Kingston Trio version faded away, 'Seasons In The Sun' stuck its head above the parapet again as an album filler for Nana Mouskouri, a bespectacled Greek vocalist popular in France, and as a flop 45 by The Fortunes, a combo from Birmingham. From this modest resurgence, it would finish as the brightest diamond in Brel's treasure chest.

1. *June 1st, 1950: just married - with Thérèse Michielsen - 'Miche'.*
2. *With daughters Chantal, Isabelle and France.*
3.-4. *Suzanne 'Zizou' Gabriello.*
5. *Maddly Bamy.*
6. *With Maddly Bamy in Hiva-Oa.*

1. With Lino Ventura and Claude Lelouch' 'L'aventure c'est l'aventure', 1972.
2.-3. 'Emmerdeur', 1973.
4. Cannes Film Festival, 1973, Brel far right.
5. 'In L'Homme De La Mancha' at the Théâtre de la Monnaie, Brussels, 1968.

1. Captain Jacques Brel and his aircraft 'Jojo".
2. Learning for pilot's exam.
3. With Maddly Bamy in Hiva-Oa.
4. 'L'Askoy II', the boat that took Brel to Hiva-Oa.
5. Plate commemorating Brel's years on the island.
6. Jacques Brel's gravestone in Atuona.

Yet the adulterated *chanson* - by *any* Gallic composer - most likely to trip off John Citizen's tongue is 'If You Go Away'. Its evolution as a 'My Way'-'Send In The Clowns' cabaret warhorse was aided by its discovery by 'quality' artistes of the 1960s such as Sinatra - jackpot of all songwriters - Tony Bennett, Perry Como, Jack Jones - all the Las Vegas shower - as well as Shirley Bassey, Nina Simone, Glen Campbell, Ray Charles, Dusty Springfield, Neil Diamond, you name 'em.

Such endorsement was, however, both a *salaam* to and a travesty of Brel as it had been with 'Le Moribund' after the attentions of Rod McKuen. The irrepressible bard had then set to work on 'Ne Me Quitte Pas', turning lines like 'Don't leave me. You must forget. Everyone can forget what has already gone' into 'If you go away on this summer day, then you might as well take the sun away'. However, Rod retained 'I'd have been the shadow of your dog/If I'd thought it might keep me by your side' when he recorded it himself in London in 1968. 'Only Frank Sinatra and I have ever sung that song right,' he commented, 'Everybody else invariably sings "I'd have been the shadow of your shadow" - which is wrong.'

With 'Amsterdam', however, McKuen did not keep North American radio in the same tasteful focus. He also got hold of the wrong end of the lyrical stick - though the stick still existed. 'The lyric was about a man who was so sad that all he could do was piss in the ocean,' he'd reckoned, 'I wanted to show that these sailors had been alone all their lives. So I wrote "In the bellies of whores they have spilled out their youth/ On the long run to nowhere in search of the truth." That was much better!' Thanks in part to right-on Rod, just as evenings in some British folk clubs pass but rarely without some seated twerp with a six-string having a go at Ralph McTell's 'Streets Of London', so it is today with Brel festivals in the Netherlands - especially in the city itself - and 'Amsterdam', both in French and however it had been rendered by McKuen (and other wordsmiths) in English.

Other Brel-McKuen collaborations include 'The Statue', 'The Women' ('Les Biches') - recorded by a Glenn Yarborough - 'Zangra', 'Come Jef' ('Jef') and the neo-monologue 'Song Without Words' (1963's 'Chanson Sans Paroles'), each party allowing whatever *cartes blanches* were required. 'Jacques condensed "The Lovers" by eliminating the bridges in my music,' noticed Rod - whose *Seasons In The Sun* album would include '"Come Jef", a song I particularly like. It's about a young boy who tries to commit suicide as he stands on a bridge over a river. Sometimes my lyrics are totally different to what Brel wrote in French. "I'm Not Afraid" [another covered by Sinatra] has nothing to do with Brel's own lyric ["Fils De"].' While Mort Shuman gave up after trying 'on and off for years to do it justice in English', 'Le Plat Pays' presented the more businesslike McKuen with no problems whatsoever: 'I moved it to America.'

Though the French and English words of Brel and McKuen were frequently alike, of all Brel's Anglo-Saxon exponents, Shuman remained the most faithful to the spirit if not precise text of the original Brel. A rather ga-ga discussion with the composer in a Saint Maxime bar had spurred the disciple into more pragmatic action than merely reworking the *chansons* and registering them with a publisher. 'Brel wrote about things you didn't normally hear people singing. Here was a man who combined raw force with the most meaningful lyrics I had heard in songs,' exclaimed Shuman, 'a deep understanding of the human condition. This is what I wanted to bring back to America: no more "Yummy Yummy Yummy/ I've got love in my tummy".'

The wheels of Mort's Brel-fixated universe began coming together when playwright Eric Blau incorporated 'Ne Me Quitte Pas', 'La Valse De Mille Temps' and, later, 'Marieke' into 'O, Oysters!', a production that opened in early 1967 at the Village Gate, a small cafe-theatre in Greenwich Village, New York's vibrant bohemian district. These were sung by the show's female lead, Elly Stone, a folk singer on the college circuit before becoming the Gate's resident entertainer.

This was the first phase of Blau and Nat Shapiro's plan to present Brel's work in theatrical form. Knowing that Shuman was a victim of the same passion, it made sense to bring him into the ongoing discussions, initially to liaise with Éditions Pouchenel and Miche - though it would have been insulting not to have invited the co-writer of 'Sha La La La Lee' to assist Eric with the words. 'We tried to translate as many as we could,' said Mort, 'Blau was much more poetically-minded than I was. I had no talent so far as writing poetry was concerned, so I concentrated on being a craftsman. I tried to capture literally what Brel had said. I translated while Blau adapted.'

Before progressing any further, however, a concordat had to be established with Rod McKuen. 'There were certain songs that Rod had done before us,' noted Shuman, 'We came to an arrangement over two or three songs, and Blau and I gave them new translations. It was no great problem as McKuen hadn't stuck to the originals. He wrote his version of "Amsterdam" *after* ours, but what he wrote had nothing to do with what Brel had written'.

There was also the matter of Scott Walker, who had settled in London after the sundering of The Walker Brothers. He would recall that 'one day I went to have a drink with Andrew Loog Oldham (The Rolling Stones' manager) and, as we tend to have similar tastes, I mentioned Jacques Brel. He told me he'd just got some Brel songs which Mort Shuman had translated, and played me some really rough demos that Shuman had done. After sorting through some more, I began recording them, and it worked'

Walker's first post-Brothers A-side had been 1967's 'Jackie', the Blau-Shuman reading of 'La Chanson De Jacky'. This incorporated phrases that no schoolgirl who'd adored the John, Scott and Gary trio in 1966 would have imagined any of them using, despite Scott's warning that 'In a song, I now look for what I consider to be the truth. The people following me don't want sugar-coated rubbish.' The very opening line of 'Jackie' was 'And if by chance I should become/A singer with a Spanish bum' - which, expounded Mort, referred to 'a flamenco dancer - because the way they dress means that their bums stick out. They are the charmers and, of course, the ladies fall into their laps. Brel is saying in that song that even if he were like that, he would still want to be like a little boy, cute and dumb.'

It was the business about 'authentic queers and phoney virgins' that ensured that the BBC would wash their hands of 'Jackie'. Scott's pre-taped insert for *Top Of The Pops* was cancelled, and disc-jockey Simon Dee told those who tuned in his *Midday Spin* on Radio One that he was forbidden to play it although there had been requests. A Radio Two listeners survey branded it 'a nasty song' despite Walker's outcry that 'I put "Jackie" out because it was so refined and beautiful, even if it stands a good chance of being banned and crushed. I'm not deliberately going out to shock with "Jackie". I don't want it banned. I want it to be looked at, even though I do not think it will be a big hit.'

The controversy hoisted it to a grudging Number 22 in Britain's winter chart, and stirred up interest in the eponymous Walker LP for which had been selected 'Mathilde', 'Amsterdam' and 'My Death' ('La Mort'). The latter, promised Scott, was 'an important song, a strangely aching song, and people come away itchy after hearing it.' If not greatly recognised as such at the time, it was something of a breakthrough that Scott was able to plug 'My Death', as wordy and profound as its 'La Mort' template, on *Dee Time* - the lightest of BBC television's light entertainment shows - and *The Billy Cotton Band Show*, a variety programme that, by tradition, commenced with elderly bandleader Cotton bellowing his 'Wakey Wakey!' catchphrase and then high-stepping with a line of choreographed dancing girls. Walker's 'My Death' followed a spot by Mrs. Mills, the programme's resident solo pianist, whose beefy mitts had pounded out 'When You're Smiling', 'Bill Bailey', 'Lassie From Lancashire' and others in the same singalong style.

How the opening verse of 'My Death' begins depends upon the sexual leanings of the singer. According to Shuman and Blau, death can wait either like 'an old *roue*' or 'a patient girl who knows the score' (to rhyme with 'swinging door'). David Bowie was to give in to the man while Walker chose the more socially acceptable partner in 1967 after Brel, on receiving a copy of the *Scott* LP, and seeing the artist promote it on television in the Netherlands and France, instructed Shuman to place all his *chansons* at Walker's disposal.

This mandate was described as 'like taking a Picasso and changing it around a bit' by an awed Scott. Though theirs was not quite the same as the relationship between Nadezhda von Meck and Tchaikovsky, Walker elected to have no personal contact with his hero: 'I don't know why, but I think of him as being a certain type of person, and I want to keep all the illusions I have of him'.

Instead, to concomitant banter about passwords and spy novels, Kenny Lynch, Shuman's sometime collaborator, would pass the latest Brel interpretions from Mort and Eric - who, laughed Kenny, 'looked just like Groucho Marx' - to Walker at a special meeting place in London's Hyde Park. After sifting through the manuscript paper, lyric sheets and demonstration tapes he'd given, Scott would issue renderings of 'Next' ('Au Suivant'), 'Sons Of' ('Fils De'), 'Funeral Tango' ('Le Tango Funèbre') and, as inevitable as Valentino's recording of 'Kashmiri Song', 'If You Go Away'.

Walker would release no more Brel after 1969's *Scott 3*, favouring rather his own sturdy compositions. As all writers do, Scott borrowed from others, trying to cover up sources of inspiration so that nothing would remain infuriatingly familiar. Yet, though never guilty of plagiarizing either melody or lyrics, Walker came up with many songs, both before and after *Scott 3*, that remained not so much affected by Brel as taken over by him - as if Jacques was roosting in Scott's mind. 'Old Folks' appropriated a Brel-via-Shuman title - while 'Archangel' (for the Walker Brothers) had lifted the overall musical drift of 'Voici' and 'La Lumière Jaillira'. Walker also tended to employ orchestras under the batons of Wally Stott, Johnny Franz and like conductors as efficiently middle-of-the-road as Andre Popp and Michel Legrand - and Billy Cotton - to bring forth a sub-Rauber effect.

On the same wavelength - even the same station - as any quantity of Brel *chansons* were 'Rosemary' - aging spinster looking after her widowed mother, fondly recalling a fling with a travelling salesman - 'Two Ragged Soldiers' (resounding echoes of 'Jef'), and 'Hero Of The War' - in which 'Mrs. Reilly', widowed in the previous conflict, shows off her mutilated soldier son's medals to the neighbours. Then there's 'Joe', 'Big Louise', 'Montague Terrace In Blue', 'Little Things (That Keep Us Together') and, possibly the most prime example of all, 'The Girls In The Street', castigated - unfairly (and peculiarly) - in the rock journal *Hot Press* as 'a concrete backdrop for his own self-conscious attempt to write concrete poetry.' Of Scott's post-Walker Brothers period, it would be kinder - but far from entirely accurate - to say that Brel and he then bore the same similarity to each other as Dylan and his gentler British 'answer', Donovan. However, Scott was to escape from his particular ruling passion to pursue a style that would almost-but-not-quite rebuff any easy comparison to Brel.

A more important London-based composer, Ray Davies, had become, by 1966, a British *chansonier* or its closest equivalent. After 'You Really Got Me' and several more smashes with his Kinks that adhered to the same riff-based format, he forged a new, intrinsically English - and frequently unfashionable - pop form. Its first manifestation had been 1965's 'A Well-Respected Man'. Further satires - such as 'Dedicated Follower Of Fashion', 'House In The Country', 'Harry Rag', 'End Of The Season', 'Mr. Pleasant' - and other commentaries - 'Waterloo Sunset', 'Two

Sisters', 'Wonderboy', 'Shangri-La' *et al* - were as potent and as idiosyncratic as anything by Brel, and borrowed as freely as he did from outmoded musical genres. Davies was certainly aware of, if not Brel in particular, then both the *chansonier* tradition and whatever was pop's current state of play. 'Mr. Pleasant' had been conceived as a reconstruction of an item that Piaf might have chosen, and there was also talk of Ray releasing a 1967 arrangement of 'Et Moi Et Moi Et Moi'[1], a French Number One for Jacques Dutronc, ex-guitarist of Les Cyclones, who had scored a solo Top 10 entry with 'Le Vagabond' before taking the Gainsbourg route then of composing for others.

A similar pattern to Ray Davies can be traced in Ken Howard and Alan Blaikley's work for Dave Dee, Dozy, Beaky, Mick and Tich - via a shift from glorious rows like 'Hold Tight' and 'Save Me' to augmenting the guitars-bass-drums group with all manner of orchestrations for themed epics set in ruined haciendas ('The Legend Of Xanadu'), the high seas ('The Wreck Of The *Antoinette*') and, of most relevance to this discourse, the heart of London's organised crime network ('Last Night In Soho'). Po-faced critics dismissed Alan and Ken as peddlers of superficiality, but there would be a shock in store from this most unlikely duo to have been influenced by Jacques Brel.

Another beat group composer, Denny Laine of The Moody Blues, had, like Scott Walker, become a Brel convert in 1966 - when the outfit's 'Boulevard De La Madeleine' had faltered outside the Top Fifty while weaving the tango into the rich tapestry of post-Merseybeat pop. John Entwistle of The Who, had the mark of a Brel-esque *chansonier* too in ditties concerning a hallucinating alcoholic ('Whisky Man') condemned to a padded cell; voyeurism ('The Window Shopper'); a deserted husband threatening suicide from a skyscraper ledge ('Thinkin' It Over'), and the repercussions of mistaking an ordinary woman for a prostitute ('I Was Just Being Friendly').

Longer and more harrowing were Van Morrison's 'TB Sheets' - about the bleak resignation of an intimate beyond recovery from tuberculosis - and any given morosity by Canadian rhymer-turned-singer Leonard Cohen. As it had been with Brel, the dirge-like tunes of 'Laughing Len' were often suspended beneath worthier if lugubriously 'poetic' lyrics. With a similarly lugubrious baritone, but of more jocular stamp as a songwriter, Jake Thackray, Yorkshire born and bred, seemed destined for a career as a teacher of modern languages. However, knowing some basic guitar, he began composing and performing songs as audio aids for his classes, and when working as such in Lille and then Algeria, he absorbed the music of the *chansoniers*, particularly Brassens and Brel, becoming friends and forming a sporadic songwriting partnership with the former.

On returning to his home city of Leeds, he moonlighted on regional radio, notably BBC's *Look North*, which led to a spot on *The Good Old Days*, a long-running BBC TV wallow in music hall nostalgia from the City Varieties in Leeds; residencies on nationally-networked television magazine series - where he was required to turn out one new topical ditty per programme - and, at the age of twenty-eight, a 1967 debut album, *The Last Will And Testament Of Jake Thackray*, containing 'Jumble Sale', 'The Statues', 'Personal Column' and other staples from his stage repertoire. Like his later releases - and a book of his lyrics, *Jake's Progress* - it sold steadily if unremarkably to a committed following - though there were lucrative cover versions by such as The Barron Knights, Jasper Carrott and Fred Wedlock, and he irritated the lower reaches of the singles chart in 1968 with 'Lah-Di-Dah' - about his behaviour towards boring in-laws at the 'fancy pantomime' of his wedding reception - which was to be re-arranged as a duet by Petula Clark and none other than Rod McKuen.

In his markedly different manner, Thackray - who was to die in 2002 - may be seen from a distance of years as being as much of a champion of English language *chanson* as Scott Walker. Yet, with sufficient nit-picking vigilance, evidence can be found of debts owed by virtually any significant English-speaking songwriter to Jacques Brel, whether Bob Dylan, Ralph McTell (introduced to Brel's music by Thackray) or - a known admirer of Scott Walker - Reg Presley, mainstay of The Troggs (though it was drummer Ronnie Bond who penned 'It's Too Late', the most Brelesque selection on 1967's *Trogglodynamite*)). However, food for thought is that so few are mentioned in Olivier Todd's *Jacques Brel: Un Vie* the nearest you'll get to an authorized biography. Rod McKuen and Scott Walker warrant not a single entry apiece in the index, and Mort Shuman has only one - with the mis-spelling of his surname adding insult to injury.

NOTES

1. In 1973, 'Et Moi Et Moi Et Moi' was adapted with English lyrics by Ray Dorset. As 'Alright Alright Alright', it reached the UK Top Ten for his group, Mungo Jerry.

Chapter Seven
'What Is Sickness To The Body Of A Knight-Errant?

He'd pride himself on knowing an oft-visited country's geography better than most of its inhabitants. Finding himself back at the same venues time and time again, Jacques Brel at least had chances to form genuine friendships rather than play backstage host to starstruck fans. He'd take up conversations begun the previous year with waiters, bar staff, stage hands, bell hops - and night spot managers such as Clairette Oddera, proprietor of an eponymous watering-hole in Quebec where Brel and his roaring boys repaired after finishing at the city's Comedie-Canadienne theatre.

A blonde and usually rather jolly former actress, Clairette had the same big-hearted, cherishing quality as Suzy Lebrun, back at the Club L'Échelle . She was also very keen on Brel's music, and remained so even after a first visit to her club when the man of the moment had been talking shop continually whilst holding dogmatic court. An instant pundit with no time for tact, he'd dismissed Pierre Calvert, Jacques Blanchet and other Canadian songwriters within hearing distance with 'They need a kick up the arse. They're too lazy. They write some extraordinary lines, but the rest of it is crap' - though this did not include Félix Leclerc, on whom Brel intended to pay his respects the following afternoon before proceeding to his next port of call.

He spent the grey of morning, however, installed in the lounge bar in the company of a bottle of whiskey and Clairette who was in need of consolation after the recent murder of her boyfriend. Inviting him back for breakfast, she changed the subject to Canadian internal policy which she attempted to explain to Jacques but without much success.

As well as shielding his private life, the persisting cut-back on press interviews served to smokescreen Brel's pedestrian political views - though in other respects, he was good copy: plain speaking delivered in thickened Belgian as he countered inane and impertinent enquiries as reiterant as a stuck record. Yet, while he was turning over an idea for a novel about a gullible revolutionary who dies for a cause about which he is ignorant, Brel was cautious about revealing his own ignorance, even naivety. Allusions to current affairs were rare in his *chansons*. Besides, the difficulty with topical ditties is this: what becomes of them when they are no longer topical or the topic gets tedious?

In interview, however, he'd let slip statements such as this one during the 'Les Flamandes' ferment: 'If I were king, I'd send all the French-speakers to live with Flemish-speaking families for six months and *vice-versa* - like military service. That would solve all our ethnic and linguistic problems very quickly - because everyone's tooth aches in the same way, everyone loves or hates spinach. Those are the things that really count.' Following his heart rather than his reason, Brel also spoke vaguely on other occasions about, say, 'the unemployed' without going into economic ramifications, and, unless you count the one-word utterance in 'Les Toros', would never make any doctrinal statement about Vietnam, even in the light of genuinely violent anti-war demonstrations, student sit-ins and 1968's left-wing *événements* in France, stoked up by Daniel Cohn-Bendit ('Danny the Red'). Even Philippe Clay had penned a lyrical riposte in his latest single, 'Mes Universités'.

Yet, while terrorism on the television news was now widespread enough to horrify Brel as much as a shoot-out in a gangster movie, he was active after a dispassionate, pop-starrish fashion in publically supporting pacifism and left-wing popular opinion - and he, Jouannest and Jojo were present at one such rally in Paris which drew from him the charitable comment: 'It's going to fail. It's all stupid. It won't serve any purpose.'

Soviet Russia was a police state, granted Brel, but he wondered whether the Communists might not have been right about building the Berlin Wall. The better-informed Jojo would cringe at Jacques' elbow, and see ahead of him the task of calming friction by filtering through to the masses damage limitation verbiage ascribable, however indirectly, to his renowned friend and paymaster - particularly after gala receptions at embassies (French more often than Belgian) where Jacques had been presented to dignitaries and their hoity-toity children.

Just before 1962's general coup in Algeria, a performance at the Hotel Aletti in Algiers had been punctuated by a loyalist heckler bawling 'French Algeria!' during a hush - to which Brel had retaliated, 'I don't care. I'm Belgian.' Afterwards, he felt uncomfortable when waylayed by extremist factions who wanted him to join with them. Superficially affable, he'd catch the eye of Jojo or Charley, questioning by frightened telepathy whether it was OK to exchange anything beyond a side-stepping smile before being shepherded away - though, on a radio chat-show during the visit, he'd voiced the - admittedly, commonly-held - belief that decolonization was inevitable. He also mentioned that he was unlikely to perform in Algeria again.

On stage at the Hotel Aletti, he'd affected his customary exuberance during a set no worse than any other dished out for ticket-holders that year. It was already dawning on Brel that, more and more often, the highlight of the day wasn't the actual concert, but the building-up and the winding down as he circled a globe less and less eye-stretching. By 1966, a Holiday Inn in Dijon was just like one in Beirut. The Coca-Cola tasted exactly the same. Everywhere was the same. If it's Thursday, it must be Antwerp. He came and went by night. When asked what such-and-such a city had been like, he was damned if he could even find it on a map. What's more, in the distorted days before on-stage monitors, vocal balance was achieved by simply moving back and forth on the microphone. Sometimes the backing musicians would be too loud, and he'd be virtually gulping it.

There was always the money to think about as he weighed up the cash benefits of churning out 'Ne Me Quitte Pas', 'Les Biches', 'Madeleine' and all the rest of the good old good ones night after night against his self-image as an artist. 'I couldn't care less about money,' he'd protest, 'If you told me that I was going to be poor one day, I wouldn't complain.' He'd never have the opportunity to prove it. Even so, while box-office receipts remained astronomical, there was a danger of attendances falling off through over-exposure and years of unbroken newspaper visibility. Though a half-full house for what turned out to be his final show in New York would be down to a blizzard, Jacques Brel was becoming as too familiar in France, Belgium and their colonies as he'd been in the Parisian clubs, *circa* 1955. Like a Metro train, if you missed one Brel recital, there'd be another along if you waited.

What was left to enjoy about such a shallow and pointless job in which, like it had been at Vanneste and Brel, he couldn't wait until clocking-off time? Even then, he couldn't be unphotographed stepping from a lift or unrecognised in a bar - though a grin and autographs might settle the matter if his car was pulled over by *les gendarmes* for speeding. 'Windows follow me,' he'd sung in 1963's 'Les Fenêtres', 'All to the bottom of my sheets (!).'

As early as the post-Albert Hall knees-up, he'd discussed with Aznavour the possibility of downing tools as a working *chansonier*, arguing that 'I'm not de Gaulle, and it isn't the end of the world', suggesting that the older Charles ought to stop too. 'I'm fed-up with working with musicians,' Jacques declared, 'I don't want to end up as a has-been.' Among names mentioned in the sentence that followed were Philippe Clay, Richard Anthony and Gilbert Becaud.

The Raubers, Charley and Jojo were told of what became Brel's irrevocable decision to quit one stormy summer night in some hotel or other on tour. The rest of the crew were kept in the dark - apart from the pragmatic Jouannest who lined up a post in Juliette Greco's employ. While he would recall the whispered confirmation, 'We're not going to do this again', between songs during one concert, Jacques would proffer journalists nothing so absolute: 'I would never be able to do without writing, but I promise you that I will stop singing one day, but I'd go back to it if I were starving. I no longer wish to be hungry - no more days with just Camembert. If I have to sing for another month at the Lido, in Paris in order to live for another year, then I will do it without hesitation, believe me. Apart from that, I won't miss stagework in the slightest.'

He cropped up rather more in the papers as the first date of his most public journey approached. No longer was he ploughing so much energy into keeping away from the *paparazzi*. Instead, nicotine-stained fingers were scribbling down the quotable leaderettes he was firing off, explaining his withdrawal. *Le Monde* would comprehend that 'I'm giving up touring after fifteen years, having written four hundred songs and recorded about two hundred of them. With habit, you become skilful. I'm at saturation point. I need to go elsewhere.' Others seized upon 'The only luxury in life is being able to make mistakes. What irritates me most is being sensible'; 'People of fifty make love better than people of twenty, but they can't make love every day'; 'It's not normal to sing to the public. It's normal to sing in the bath when you're happy'; 'To write a song is a man's work, to sing it is the work of an animal, and lately I have become too much of an animal and too little of a man.'

Of the few foreign journals to pick up the story, North America's *Saturday Review* put it down to Brel's resentment at being cast as more than a pop star. Like Bob Dylan, he was seen as some sort of spokesman for not so much the lumpen proletariat as the bohemian minority. 'Brel's humanity consists of not exempting himself from the charges he levels at the world,' it ran, adding that 'his work conveys a sense of shared concern about universal experiences.'

As well as reporting that some of his fans had threatened suicide, more lurid chronicles made more concrete speculations about Jacques' behaviour. It was surely a publicity stunt like Maurice Chevalier's 'retirement' announcement a few years back. Even before it was published, he'd be planning the comeback. No, it wasn't that. Brel's liver was in a bad state, see, too much boozing, and the doctors told him to take it easy, otherwise it'd be curtains in the most absolute sense. They say that he's still lively enough to visit brothels, though.

Whatever the quality of coverage, it ensured an overflowing turn-out at his farewell to the Olympia - the first concert of the season - on 6 October 1966. Because the customers were participating, however passively, in a historical event, all the lavish and over-priced programmes sold out well before the doors to the auditorium opened. Containing no debasing advertisements, the main text was by Georges Brassens who had volunteered to compere on that night-of-nights. In his citation with its obligatory paragraph about Jacques' charity work - like his hand in a publicity film for UNICEF - and the touching modesty about it, Brassens wrote 'Jacques Brel has changed a lot since he began. He's become more inward looking. I was exactly the same when success came. I believe that, despite what he says, Jacques Brel likes those that he criticizes the most. He's full of generosity, but does everything to hide it. He criticizes the Belgians in abstraction, but he cares obsessively for them.'

One Belgian conspicuously absent was Miche, though she sent a congratulatory telegram to join the rest of the good-luck messages papering the walls of her husband's dressing room. These represented nearly every phase of his fourteen years on the boards, whether Greco, Clairette Oddera - or Suzy Lebrun with her 'I am with you with all my heart. I shall not be with you this evening because there'll be too many people around you.' More impersonal were missives from such as Petula Clark - as much a celebrity in France as her native England - Johnny Halliday, Adamo, Mirielle Mathieu and more common-or-garden devotees. The most disturbing pause in Brel's backstage pacing was to answer a call from Zizou, who wanted to meet him after the show - alone.

An almost palpable wave of goodwill washed over Jacques when, dead on time as usual, he entered the spotlight for a succinct forty-five minutes. There was no need, but he couldn't resist a couple of new compositions like cantering and self-referential 'Le Cheval' ('And every night/ When I sing "Ne me quitte pas"/I miss my stable/And the tranquillity of yesterday') from his imminent *Jacques Brel '67* album.

He was a triumph because everyone wanted him to be. They all had a glimmer of how much Jacques had on his plate, and worried when he showed signs of strain, glowed when he got second wind, and were still giving vent to an barrage of clapping, whistling, cheering and stamping a full twenty minutes after the last chord of the band's play-out had reverberated. As expected, he chose not to plunge into an encore. Nevertheless, he deigned to reappear in slippers and dressing gown for a brief speech thanking his public for 'fifteen years of love'.

Some old pals were allowed past security afterwards to a backstage area where backs were slapped as the champagne flowed - though Jacques stuck exclusively to beer while sparing time for everyone who entered his circulating orbit, and doling out a few minutes of chat each to both witnesses and participants in some of the stirring exploits of yore, and those pressing for a stake in his future. He went missing for a while for a quiet drink with Zizou in nearby La Cloche d'Or, a natter centred on the escalating collapse of his 'marriage' to Sylvie.

He was able to put this at arm's length during the six months it took to fulfil existing contracts; the idea being to rake in the most loot with the least effort by accommodating thousands in one go. With a support bill embracing acrobats, dancers and a young vocalist called Michel Delpech, typical of the overall scheme was sixteen appearances at the same theatre in Quebec between 25 March and 9 April 1967.

He waved into the baying blackness and vanished from the concert platform forever on 16 May 1967 in Roubaix near the French-Belgium frontier. Exhaustion and a feeling of anti-climax scattered the troupe afterwards with only Jacques and the Delta Rhythm Boys, a jazz band, choosing to paint the town red. Pouring a huge quantity of alcohol into himself, Brel's chatter got steadily louder, his eyes brighter and his rampaging more manic in what amounted to an unspoken wake for all he'd just left behind.

In a feature that read like an obituary, *France-Soir* conjectured that 'he has too much talent for there to be a successor. After him, you can't say "Next!"'. Agreeing with this, Brel named no heirs, but mentioned Adamo out of politeness - though he went as far as confessing mild dislike for the music of newcomers like Michel Polnareff, hirsute Antoine - modelled on Bob Dylan - and Marie-Paule Belle, but could understand their commercial appeal. Yet, flopping onto a chair next to French comedian Robert Delieu in a music hall green room, he launched into a withering attack on the present state of pop affairs, concluding with 'I tell you one thing, Delieu; after me, the *chanson* won't have anybody.'

Admittedly, there was Aznavour who, earlier in 1967, had completed a record-breaking run of almost seventy standing-room-only engagements at the Olympia - and Adamo had, in 1966, notched up three chart smashes in succession. Like Distel, Adamo's clean, conservative image garnered a large middle-of-the-road audience but, with a shy smile that belied personal tragedies known to his fans, his allure also antedated that of the US school of singer-songwriters of the early 1970s - especially when, after a 1967 trip to the Middle East, he penned 'Inch Allah' and 'On Se Bat Toujours Quelque Part', thoughtful anti-war singles that earned Adamo the approbation of the blossoming hippy sub-culture.

Other fresh arrivals tended to be in a *different* rather than *lower* league to elder statesmen like Aznavour and Brel. The principal personal characteristic that Jacques Dutronc shared with the Belgian was that he was a heavy smoker too - and his name would be dropped by Brel in the 1968 *chanson*, 'Vesoul'. Dutronc's main clients as an assembly-line songwriter had been Zou-Zou (a former Twist exponent who became a French oppo-site number to mini-skirted British models Jean Shrimpton and Twiggy) and Françoise Hardy. He may have been contented with his lot had not he and Jacques Lanzmann, editor of *Lui* magazine, chortled at the same jokes. Setting simple melodies and clever hook-lines to Lanzmann's rap-id-fire lyrics - specifically designed to be funny - a career as a kind of Frankish Benny Hill hit its stride with 'Et Moi Et Moi Et Moi' - which became a national catch phrase. Later efforts like 'Mini Mini Mini' - the skirt not the car - were better known beyond France but LP tracks such as 'Hippy Hippy Hourrah' and 'Cactus' (with a nonsensical chorus) were more characteristic Dutronc-Lanzmann fare.

For Dutronc to cut the cackle invited professional suicide. Because he didn't mind making a monkey of himself on stage, he was unlikely to steal female fans from Danyel Gerard, even if the latter's drawing pow-er had palled after he got engaged. Nevertheless, Gerard had ploughed back his earnings into a lucrative production company, and had forged a second career as a commissioned songwriter with Marie Laforet's 'Les Vendanges De L'Amour' and Herve Villand's 'Mourir Ou Vivre' among his hits.

Of those Gallic pop luminaries for whom songwriting was more inci-dental, Johnny Hallyday had checkmated old rival Richard Anthony at every turn, especially in South America where a 25,000 attendance at a Hallyday show in Argentina was not untypical. Neither was it unusual to hear Johnny keeping fervidly abreast of whatever was happening in more vital markets as exemplified by the selections on his *Olympia '67* LP like 'If I Were A Carpenter', 'Hey Joe', 'In The Midnight Hour' and Los Bra-vos' 'Black Is Black'. Meanwhile, Sheila's rags-to-riches story was being serialised in *France-Soir*, and tit-bits about her amorous entanglements were to become more rivetting to her followers than her latest record.

To most adolescent consumers, Brel was famous rather than popular. Certainly, neither he nor Brassens had been considered worthy of an en-try in *Spécial Pop*[1], a work of reference for teenagers, but perhaps be-ing placed in between Spanish one-hit-wonders Los Bravos and Billy Bridge, a Danyel Gerard protégé, among other more overtly pop acts that festooned such tomes, may have been detrimental to Brel's position as a 'songwriter's songwriter', held in awe by such discerning musicians as Greco, Paxton, Thackray and Walker. Yet how much more appropriate was it to happen upon Jacques Brel somewhere between Brahms and Bruch in *Groves Encyclopaedia Of Music And Musicians*[2]?

Brel didn't quite fit anywhere in that watershed year of 1967. He didn't cut much ice with a young audience dazzled by flower-power and psychedelia[3]. In reprisal, though he was seen in hippy gear at a fancy dress party in Paris around this time, not for defiantly short-haired Jacques were the sitars, backwards-running tapes and self-conscious symbollism that cloaked many fundamentally vapid perceptions.

Paradoxically, 1967 was also a boom year for schmaltz as Petula Clark, Tom Jones, Engelbert Humperdinck and others of similar kidney all racked up huge European best-sellers. Yet, if items on *Jacques Brel '67* were awash with cinema intermission strings, its content had as little to do with Humperdinck's 'The Last Waltz' as The Pink Floyd's 'See Emily Play'. The very sleeve had him neither in kaftan and beads nor bowtied tuxedo. On the front it was roll-neck pullover and sports jacket; on the back, in jeans and sockless sandals and the jacket removed. He was puffing a customary cigarette and, reflective of the flying lessons he was taking, sitting on the wing of a two-seater aeroplane.

The disc itself got under way with the trilling piano figure of 'Mon Enfance', the longest number at just under six minutes. Bound as he'd been to see through adult posturing, he addresses his own childhood and glorified adolescence when 'I had the eye of a shepherd but the heart of a lamb'. Piano also leads Brel's most moving piece in years, 'La Chanson Des Vieux Amants', musical fell-walking rather than mountaineering in the low dynamics that are in keeping with the air of tiredness and repressed misery of an elderly couple, at ease about each other's amatory peccadillos as they step closer to that bourne from which no traveller returns.

Just as 'La Chanson Des Vieux Amants' is a prequel to 'Les Vieux', so the sleazy shuffle that constitutes 'À Jeun' is an inversion of 'Le Moribund', when a husband learns of his wife's extra-marital larks on the day of her burial. The basic notions of both *Jacques Brel '67* songs would resurface on a later album in 'Comment Tuer L'Amant De Ma Femme' in which a deceived spouse avenges himself on his wife's boyfriend by ensuring that, via the lady, he catches the cuckold's syphilis.

Charmed, I'm sure. To oscillating flamenco-style guitar, 'Mon Père Disait' puts the boot into the poor old Belgians again - as does 'La La La' which encloses both a hardly credible 'Long live Belgians!/Crap on the *Flamingants!*' couplet and perhaps the quaintest arrangement of Brel's entire recorded catalogue: funereal tempo, stabbing organ chords and a cacaphony of *glissando* trombones and busked muted trumpet - and, as the first verse reaches its climax, a horrible exaggerated vocal vibrato repeated regularly enough to convince me that it was deliberate.

To the same tune and xylophone chimes of the 1964 prototype, 'Les Bonbons '67' has our lad, now a cross between Walter Mitty and Billy Liar, still sniffing round Germaine. Her scornful peals of laughter punctuate his claims that he dwells in the *chic* George Cinq hotel in Paris, and has lost his 'Brussels accent' ('nobody else has that accent/Except Brel on the TV'). He also comes across as an aging trendy who, like the uncertain agitator in Brel's proposed novel, is possessed by false liberalism, following protesters to this demonstration and that without quite understanding the purpose.

Had the preceeding *Brel '67* opus, 'Fils De', belonged to an optimum moment of Jacques' performing career, it might have become a 'standard' *à la* 'Ne Me Quitte Pas'. In translation, the lyrics mutated into even more of a 'shopping list', but this lullaby-*cum-accelerando* waltz, growing from co-writer Jouannest's plaintive chinking to full orchestra, is an up-tempo conveyance of Brel's trademark pleasurable regret.

Similar in tone was the album's valedictory 'Le Gaz' - and the recycling was to continue. The heroine of 'Je Suis Bien' (also recorded by Juliette Greco) is no longer young, comparing the greyness of the present to times past. Again, we're back in Belgium for 'La Bière': lusty drinkers drawn into happy vocal unison, ostensibly in praise of beautiful, foaming beer; the satiric words overlooked as much as those of The Strawbs' mickey-taking 'Part Of The Union' would be in 1973 by British trade unionists wishing to adopt it as an anthem. Six years on, the US admiralty would be as blind to the inherent campness of Village People's 'In The Navy'.

While the same old themes developed new properties and thus steered clear of actual stagnation, Brel suspected that he'd bitten his composing talent down to the quick. 'Animals sense a storm coming,' he gloomed,

'Men too. I'm not interested in becoming an industrialist of song.' More and more nowadays he'd suffer writer's blocks and ante-start agonies as he knuckled down to another album. After he'd strummed for a bit, the 'phone might ring. If not, dinner would be getting cold or an interesting programme just beginning on television. Maybe he'd try again tomorrow.

Days would trudge by without a trace of a melody or lyric. The spirit was willing, but he lacked both financial motive and the hunger to create. All the particles of song would sound the same, infantile vibrations hanging in the air. Languor would set in, and Brel's mind, bathed in tedium, would drift off once more to the refrigerator, the TV, the drinks cabinet. If sundown brought on a need for merriment, it was sad to sink it into a sofa when it cried out to be shared with others. Therefore, if moderated, there was no immediate let-up in the roistering that had once post-scripted his concerts.

What he could barely enunciate, even to himself, was that he missed the limelight. Certainly, he did not retreat from public life on the evidence of television appearances such as an affectionate send-up of Jean Sablon on a New Year special in 1969, *Le Château Des Chansons*. Even in the hiatus between the Olympia and Roubaix, he'd contradicted the title of *Adieu Aux Foules* ('farewell to the crowds'), a lengthy interview in October 1966 with himself and runner Michel Jazy, who, having broken the record for the mile in 1965, had just retired from championship sport.

Off-camera too, he was seldom forgoing opportunities to be the focal point of eyes grateful to him for just existing. At showbiz *soirées* where guests sipped posed cocktails like melted crayons, a murmur would reach a crescendo that Jacques Brel had entered the building. This wasn't television or a picture in *Paris-Match*. Jacques Brel was actually within, asserting his old magnetism in abundance as newer stars and their acolytes droned round him like a halo of flies.

For a while, they spoke of him as if an old nag put out to grass. However, a pampered but empty semi-retirement was not to be Jacques Brel's way. With an inner ear cocked to the far-off roar of the crowd, he pored over offers that, falling daily onto his doormat, lay beyond pop music, and chiefly in the theatre and the cinema. He hadn't a clue how to go about most of those he was to take on. Nonetheless, with commendable application, he'd learn what he could *in situ*, get a clearer picture from the confusion, and, unknowingly, banish many preconceptions and introduce new ones.

As if it was the most natural thing in the world, he'd be 'spotting' uncut film sequences with a stop-watch, arguing with a stage manager about scenery, fretting about character development or deliberating about camera angles. A surprising number of critiques of the end results, if condescending at times, vouched for the presence of more than might have been expected of an entertainer from an industry where sales figures and bums-on-seats were arbiters of excellence.

Brel seemed keenest on extending himself through acting roles. Even before he'd put the final seal on his concert career, Miche had fallen on a venture that would be, she felt, tailor-made for one who had been called the 'Don Quichotte de la chanson' by *Le Figaro*. When in New York on behalf of Éditions Pouchenel in February 1967, she had mixed business with pleasure by alighting on *Man Of La Mancha*, a Broadway musical based on the novel upon which Miguel de Cervantes' reputation will always rest.

After the dimming of the house lights, out of the gloom had appeared 'Cervantes', incarcerated in an Inquisition dungeon in 1605, and keeping himself sane by projecting himself into the personality of Don Quixote, a country squire whose mind is so addled by romances of mediaeval chivalry that he takes it upon himself to devote the last chapter of his life to a foolish but noble quest to redress the wrongs of a world where 'evil brings profit, and virtue nothing at all'. Blind to reality throughout his consequent adventures, he only sees 'life as it should be, not life as it is': an idealist frustrated and ridiculed by materialism. He carries this illusion to a closing scene centred round his death bed - from which he leaps with an exultant yell of 'What is sickness to the body of a knight errant?!'

Knowing that her husband's adolescent imagination had been captured by the *Quixote* sagas, Miche couldn't wait to let him hear the album of the show. As the play-out groove whirled on the stereo during one of his flying visits to the family home, Jacques could see that he might have *been* Cervantes/Quixote in a previous existence. Who else could get under the skin of the *non compos mentis* paladin as Brel could? He wouldn't even have to act, simply be himself, as Sinatra had as 'Private Maggio' in *From Here To Eternity*.

Nothing else would do but he must fly over and see *Man Of La Mancha* for himself. He sat through it five times in all and wept. Of the songs, he identified strongest with the now much-covered 'The Impossible Dream ('The Quest)', and, in so far as he could comprehend English, could hear elements of his sardonic side in the hypocrisy of 'I'm Only Thinking Of Him' and the humouring of the deranged Don in 'Golden Helmet Of Mambrino'. He also caught facets of Germaine from 'Les Bonbons' in the female lead, Dulcinea.

Fastening a thoughtful seat-belt prior to take-off from Kennedy Airport, Jacques was already visualizing that night in Europe when the overture heralded the recreation of the cell scene with himself as Cervantes. For the moment, however, he couldn't go beyond fantasy - though he already had the shadow of a moustache and scrappy beard to at least *look* the part, and was intending to approach Jean-Jacques Vital, a producer with a respectable track record in legitimate theatre, to oversee it. He had also sewn seeds in the mind of the musical's originator, Dale Wassermann, who was to become better known when his 1961 play, *One Flew Over The Cuckoo's Nest*, was transformed into an award-winning movie fourteen years later.

Man Of La Mancha had started life as a television drama, directed by Albert Marre, husband of mezzo-soprano Joan Diener. Mentally earmarking a leading role for herself, Joan had goaded her husband into suggesting that Wasserman turn it into a musical. As he lacked the necessary musical ability, Wasserman contacted Joe Darion, composer of oratorio and opera, and - more of a jazz buff - Mitch Leigh to help him make the idea tenable.

It materialized into what Jacques was to refer to as a 'tragédie musicale' during turgid deliberations between Wasserman *et al* and Éditions Pouchenel, either over transatlantic telephone or face-to-face, usually in New York. For all his renown, Brel hadn't been given the go-ahead straightaway because Wasserman and his team were after an actor who could sing rather than a singer whose acting style might prove to be 'economic' at most. Having not seen him in all his Carnegie Hall glory, he was to them merely some *French* pop star.

A supplicant once again, it was a measure of Brel's determination to win the role that he agreed to go to Los Angeles to audition, salving his wounded dignity to Miche with 'They know their jobs. They don't take anything for granted.' On the day, it was clear that he had dramatic possibilities - and, yes, he'd certainly fill auditoriums in Belgium and France. However, the high command, wringing their hands over cost, and the statistical fact that Anglo-Saxon musicals hadn't been all that well-received in France, wanted Jacques next to submit a sample interpretation of one of the songs. He put forward 'La Quête', which, after adjustments by Mitch Leigh, was virtually a verbatim translation of showstopping 'The Impossible Dream'.

After the manager of Brussels' Théâtre de la Monnaie, Maurice Huysmans - who had also caught the musical in New York - was sincerely loud in his praise for both it and Brel, the backers caved in with the proviso that Albert Marre should direct. Initially, this met with the approval of Brel who, sticking to his belief in US 'professionalism', was a model of co-operation, accepting criticism and advice gladly, completing the French lyrics, being punctual at rehearsals, and learning all his lines by the first of these.

He was not, however, so humble that he could not push his luck by proposing François Rauber as orchestra conductor; old touring comrade Dario Moreno, now portly and very middle-aged, as peasant sidekick Sancho Panza, and pulchritudinous French actress Françoise Giret as Dulcinea. After a few weeks, he lost the latter battle, and Marre's wife - who'd been Dulcinea on Broadway - was signed up instead in spite of Brel's suspicion that she was less known outside the States than she made out. From then on, rehearsals became sour with fraught tempers, stand-up rows and walk-outs, but, mastering the chaos, Marre kneaded the show into smooth enough shape for the premiere.

Because the Théâtre de la Monnaie pit, unlike that in New York,was too small to accommodate the musicians, they were placed in the balconies (eighteen one side, seven the other) with no space for a grand piano. It was murder for Rauber, and, what with the off-stage confrontations and various technical problems too, *L'Homme De La Mancha* in theory should have been disasterous.

Shaking with fright as the curtains rolled back, Jacques in his new guise was too aware of the chasm into which even he might plunge in front of the home crowd. Yet, if not permitted to forget his genesis - as Brel made no attempt to temper his local accent - the more clear-headed critics, if not over-enthusiastic, were surprised at how able he was as a 'proper' actor - as well as being in astoundingly good voice.

Brussels was, to all intents and purposes, an out-of-town try-out for the Théâtre des Champs-Elysées in Paris where the show had been booked in the first instance from January to May 1969. A small army of Brel's famous friends - including Chevalier - as well as Miche and the daughters were out in force for the grand opening. If anything, the star was more crippled with nerves than ever: 'I feel like I am back at the Trois Baudets in 1953.' Nevertheless, he gave as admirable an account of himself as he had in Belgium.

While this was recognised in the press, a doleful mood mounting backstage put a wet blanket on euphoria. *L'Homme De La Mancha*, so it appeared, was jinxed. Jean-Jacques Vital had suffered a heart attack, and, before the Paris opening, one had actually finished off Dario Moreno during a holiday in Istanbul. At Brel's instigation, Robert Manuel from the Comedie-Français was reeled in to be Sancho, but, because he couldn't hold a tune, entire songs had to be replaced with recitative.

Brel himself was feeling rather off-colour too. Neither a hypochondriac nor a malingerer by nature, he was more fatigued than he expected to be, albeit after over one hundred and fifty performances. He had also lost four stones in weight. Those closest to him had noticed with more than a little concern his pallor when the greasepaint was removed, and a habit of half closing his eyes as if in pain. He couldn't say specifically where it hurt most; it seemed to hover all over. Searching for plausible causes of this general malaise, he informed himself as much as waiting newshounds that 'officially, I'm suffering from gastro-enteritis,' when the show was stopped for a revenue-draining fortnight to allow him to recuperate.

He recommended, but was set to bow out before midsummer to start work on a film, *Mont-Dragon* - about which the show's investors had not yet been informed. He would also be unavailable when *L'Homme De La Mancha* was taken to Quebec that autumn. Into the bargain, while it had played to nearly two hundred thousand, the Champs-Elysées season had not broken even, and, owing to contractual difficulties, it hadn't been feasible to issue in time the soundtrack album that might have saved it. A meeting was called to decide what night *Homme De La Mancha* would finish and be written off as a loss.

By the final evening, *luvvie* affection was in short supply. So intense was the atmosphere of misunderstandings, sly machinations and depressed forebearance that Vital, Marre and Diener absented themselves from the farewell dinner where Jacques wisecracked nastily at their expense before everyone slunk away; Jojo, Brel's real life Sancho Panza, with a face like an Ostend winter. It would be pleasant to think that the musical's put-upon executive body recouped its outlay from the 1972 motion picture version starring Peter O' Toole and Raquel Welch.

It was Brel who'd be obliged to fork out for the time and trouble involved when his next venture came to grief. To Rauber's music, he had composed *chansons* that followed the text of *Le Voyage Dans La Lune*, a children's story by Jean-Marc Landier. With a sizeable budget at his disposal, it was to be presented at the Théâtre de la Monnaie in 1970, possibly as a ballet. A date - 29 January - was pencilled in for the premiere, and tickets were sold. Untold profit dangled in front of him, but still Jacques dithered. Monetary killings, he surmised, were secondary to art - which is why he washed his hands of *Le Voyage Dans La Lune* during a conference with Rauber and Huysmans two days prior to a subsequently cancelled opening.

Why waste time and effort generating debts when all you had to do was sit back and let the royalties that others were earning for you roll in? As well as income from the shoals of cover versions of his *chansons*, there had come in 1968 a three year Broadway run of *Jacques Brel Is Alive And Well And Living In Paris*, a musical that, like *Man Of La Mancha*, was to become a film.

This highly practical evidence of its musical director, Mort Shuman's dedication to the Brel *oeuvre* consisted of twenty-five *chansons* reconstructed by Shuman and Eric Blau as a theatrical experience for English speakers. Sweating over Jacques' French librettos, they'd had to take certain McKuen-esque liberties, but what the hell? The bloodthirsty onlookers of 'Les Toros', for example, were supplemented with plain girls with bare midriffs and roses in their teeth. One flash of inspiration was Eric or Mort's discovery that 'marathon' mirrored the phonetics of 'les flamandes' - and, lest we forget, the story goes that the composer himself was going to call it 'Les Bretons' at first before concluding that 'Les Flamandes' scanned better.

'We thought of doing it in sections with Brel's songs grouped in some way,' recollected Shuman, 'but in the end, we decided to let the songs slip and slide through. We put the show on in one of those places smelling of stale beer - what you'd call the typical setting for jazz artists.' There had been a precedent of sorts in the *Brecht On Brecht* revue at the Circle In The Square, only a short walk from the Village Gate, the too apt saloon bar-cum-cafe-theatre setting of *O Oysters!* and now *Jacques Brel Is Alive And Well And Living In Paris*[4].

During the casting, Mort Shuman wound up preparing for his debut on the professional stage in an apparently unlooked-for starring role; his burly physical presence and workman's voice deemed perfect for the 'Amsterdam'- 'Next' strata of songs. 'I hadn't intended to be in it myself,' he professed, 'but as I auditioned people for the show, I found that I was singing the songs as well as anyone.' The other three principals were the Mirielle Mathieu-like Elly Stone from *O Oysters!*, Alice Whitfield - voiceover in numerous radio and television commercials -and a *bona fide* pop singer in Shawn Elliott, who'd scrambled into the *Hot 100* in 1965 with the quasi-calypso, 'Shame And Scandal In The Family'.

With its after-hours essence of disinfectant and a flat echo of the day's booze and tobacco intake, the first performance attracted mostly those who'd seen Brel himself at Carnegie Hall, plus later converts and curiosity-seekers with only the foggiest notion of what they'd paid to see. Judging by audience reaction, the evening was wonderful, but reviewers didn't think so - and, in the light of their rubbishings, *Alive And Well* began haemorrhaging serious money.

'They destroyed the show,' sighed Mort, 'and it was a horrible situation - but, by a strange coincidence, Clive Barnes, the theatre critic of *The New York Times* [who had covered Brel at Carnegie Hall in 1966], lived in the same block of flats as I did. I slipped a note under his door, saying that I knew he didn't usually see shows in venues like ours, but if he could find the time to come one Saturday afternoon, we'd be glad to see him. He came and he loved it. He had a radio programme and he gave us the text so that we could quote him. Then a few weeks later, he wrote a feature about us in *The New York Times*, and that helped the show a lot'.

Sparked off by Barnes' approval, the enterprise was in a profit position within weeks. Some customers - among them Tom Paxton - went so many times that they could parrot the continuity. While the Village Gate residency was ongoing, understudies were brought in so that the troupe could hit the road, coast to coast. At Palm Beach, there was an outburst of heckling - 'you dirty bastards!' - over the substance of 'Next', 'Jackie' *et al*, but, other than that, it was rave notices all the way, whether the *Kansas City Star* ('a refreshing show well worth seeing') or the *Sacramento Bulletin* ('terrific'). One in *Billboard* singled out the deserving Shuman as 'a virtuoso performer. He's funny and sad, and dominates the proceedings completely'. *Time* preambled weightily with 'The wounds and balms of the human condition are so commonplace that men eventually experience them without noticing. It is only when art magnifies truth that audiences become aware of it - and of themselves' before rounding up with 'the *Brel* show is one of the most powerful magnifiers currently in use'.

The rest of the world - well, most of it - followed gushing suit. From Johannesburg to Stockholm, it was packed houses everywhere as Jacques Brel spread beyond the intellectual fringe and bohemia to the frontiers of the commonweal. Only a king's ransom would lure *Alive And Well* outside the biggest cities, so unsought cheaper alternatives were flung together. Even today in a Transvaal township or fjordic bailiwick, you'll come across provincial repertory companies approximating *Alive And Well*; a sole upright piano banging out as best it could music scored for the polished session players heard on the original cast recording, packaged - by Columbia Masterworks no less - as if it was classical music or a Shakespeare play. The less volatile of Brel's translated *chansons* were heard too in synagogues, churches and on peace marches; the Bible Society adopting 'If We Only Have Love' ('Quand On N'A Que L'Amour') as a secular hymn - like 'Le Plat Pays' had been already in Belgium schools.

Few countries were subdued in their hailing of *Alive And Well*. Among these, not surprisingly, were France, Belgium and connected territories that liked their Brel medicine neat and considered it futile to attend something in which familiar songs were presented in another language. Moreover, some felt uneasy about certain of Brel's more masculine *chansons* like 'Jef' (as 'You're Not Alone') being sung by women.

Though touched that Shuman *et al* cared enough about his music to pay such indefatigable homage, Brel himself hadn't been especially enthused when brought over to see *Alive And Well* in Greenwich Village. 'I went to see Brel after the show opened,' said Mort, 'He let us go ahead, but he didn't co-operate.' Nevertheless, when it returned to New York for a fifth anniversary performance - at Carnegie Hall of blessed memory - Jacques showed willing by coming on stage at the end to take a bow and utter a perfunctory 'thank you'. He was, if anything, embarrassed by the jubilee atmosphere, imagining that everyone was astonished that he wasn't either in deep old age like Stravinsky or long dead like Shakespeare.

He, Miche and Jojo made a holiday of it by taking in other theatrical events, notable the Broadway production of the *Jesus Christ Superstar* rock opera. That Jacques enjoyed it was praise indeed - because on the *Man Of La Mancha* jaunt, he'd gone to see *Cabaret* at the same venue but shuffled out during an interval.

To far less acclaim than *Cabaret* and *Jesus Christ Superstar*, *Alive And Well* was recreated - via French Canadian producer Denis Héroux - for the silver screen, only to fade from general circulation soon after its release in 1976. As it had been front-of-cloth at Carnegie Hall, Jacques would accede to a fleeting cameo.

Since the *La Grande Père De Monsieur Clement* episode in 1956, Brel had suspended dreams of impending ascent to film stardom to concentrate on what was then seen as the possible; his only involvement in movies being interviews and stage performances for grainy *cinema-vérité* documentaries about himself - one by *Grande Père* director Paul Deliens.

Bobbejaan Schoepen and Phillipe Clay had each been in films since the early 1950s, and Serge Gainsbourg had made a deceptively small beginning with a blink-and-you'll-miss-him bit part in 1959, but, by the middle of the subsequent decade, hardly a week would go without an announcement that some Gallic singing icon or other was about to go before the film cameras. Just as Marie Laforet plugged gaps between her celluloid ventures by flirting with pop, so Charles Aznavour, Johnny Hallyday, Françoise Hardy and Sheila were among Gallic chart names used expediently to spice up the credits and guarantee a flick some additional interest. Yet Brel's relatively brief but intensive resumption of his movie career would testify to more intrinsic virtues. After eleven years of acting out his *chansons* on the boards, he would impregnate the new genre with much the same sensations, having thus taught himself - as Aznavour had - 'to other be' more effectively than most.

The first of the ten movies that he'd make in almost as many years was 1967's *Les Risques Du Métier* - 'the risks of the job' - based on a novel by Simone and Jean Cornec concerning 'Jean Doucet', a diffident primary schoolmaster falsely accused of indecently assaulting girl pupils. It was co-written by director Andre Cayatte - who'd also worked with Aznavour. When Brel's increasingly more butterfly concentration alighted on both the screenplay and the main character, they grabbed his undivided attention - for, beneath the bouts of gossip-column exhibitionism, he was, like Doucet, quite a timid person.

'This teacher was just me,' he'd insist just as he had about Cervantes/Quixote, 'and for that reason, I accepted straight away. I was pleased to do it. Don't get the impression that I am just an actor playing any sort of part. I *am* that man: a shy fellow who does not dare to rebel, and is precipitated into a nasty situation.' Permitted a say in the evolution of the plot, the lyricist responsible for 'Les Bourgeois' and 'Les Singes' revelled in former lawyer Cayatte's undermining of both police tactics and the judiciary - but the film Brel saw at the premiere in Brussels was not the taut drama he'd once thought it might be. 'It's a great Belgian film,' he snarled sardonically afterwards, but the general verdict was that, if not as natural an actor as Aznavour, Jacques had coped well with a fair-to-middling vehicle.

Phillipe Fourastié's *La Bande À Bonnet* did not extend the limits of the avant-garde either. Dashed off in about two months, it was on at a cinema near your continental pen-pal in late 1968 with Brel as 'Raymond la Science' in a dull account of a French anarchist movement at the turn of the century.

Over several *La Bande À Bonnet* shoots, Brel had struck up a friendship with lensman Alain Levent, who was promoted to photo supervisor for *Mon Oncle Benjamin*, directed more painstakingly than the previous Brel efforts by Edouard Molinaro, the Donald McGill of French movies.

With no highbrow or sociological pretensions, it was also the best known of Jacques Brel's films. Originally, Molinaro had Jacques in mind for a thriller, but both were happier with an adaptation of the *Mon Oncle Benjamin* play by Claude Tillier.

In the title role of a rakish country doctor, Jacques cut a boisterously coarse figure in the Gallic farce tradition. An evocation of eighteenth century France prior to the Revolution, it was knockabout, virtually *Carry On*, in its structure. Though it sank beneath the weight of visual silliness, the story line was Benjamin, resentful at being made to - literally - kiss the arse of the lord of the manor, getting his own back - with a subplot in which he trifles with an innkeeper's innocent daughter.

Brel seemed to have fun making *Mon Oncle Benjamin*, having endorsed it further by assisting with the script during a stay at Molinaro's house near the forest of Rambouillet. Furthermore, when Molinaro's wife, a pilot, was killed in a 'plane crash during the filming, Brel even had temporary responsibility for scrutinizing each reel, frame by frame, astounding technicians with his recommendations about rhythm and pacing - deduced from his comprehensive shadowing of Deliens, Cayatte and Fourastié.

Next, because he admired Jean Valère, its director, Brel took a back seat and re-grew a moustache to be a demoted army officer angrily in charge of his colonel's stables in 1970's *Mont-Dragon*. He didn't mind either about being kept in ignorance about the flimsy thread of what turned out to be a finished product as disappointing as *Les Risques Du Métier*.

The following year, Jacques was the trapper Van Horst, Canadian hero of *Le Bar De La Fourche*, new *amigo* Alain Levant's overreaching and, unhappily for him, most memorable essay as a director. The Breton countryside functioned as wind-chilled rural Quebec, the setting for a story line that interested Brel for about a week before he decided that he'd had his fill of the delays caused by the unseasonable rain, the juvenile lead, the learner-director and the repetitive song he'd put into his own mouth for a film that just about walked the line with critics and customers alike who, nevertheless, recalled how much more attuned Jacques had been that spring as a divorced judge in one of then-unfashionable

Marcel Carne's last flicks, *Assassins De L'Ordre* - in which justice triumphs over a brutal *gendarmerie*.

However, for *L'Aventure C'Est L'Aventure*, a 1972 Cannes festival nomination, Jacques was supervised by Claude Lelouch, who, at thirty-five, was still regarded as something of an *enfant terrible* of French cinema. Younger and flashier than any of Brel's previous directors, he was buoyant with a huge commercial success for *Un Homme Et Une Femme* - acclaimed mostly for its spectacular effects. The inferior *L'Aventure C'Est L'Aventure* also featured Johnny Hallyday - with Jacques as one of a gang of hooligans. This was a smaller role than usual, but it was to have an important bearing on Brel's personal life.

It was on a *L'Aventure C'Est L'Aventure* location in Antigua that he had embarked on an off-camera affair with twenty-eight-year-old Maddly Bamy, briefly one of Les Claudettes, the formation dancers in Claude François's stage show. The attraction had been mutual from their first conversation - 'our eyes met,' Maddly would recall, 'and, from that moment, we were inseparable' - with each consequent day cementing them more securely in the same flow of feeling; Maddly on discovering the sensitivity contained within this Fascinating Older Man's brash outer shell, while sending frissons through Jacques' being was her dusky beauty - wasp-waist, firm breasts, flawless complexion - and the disarming directness that put him on his mettle. Part of the fascination too was her refusal to be an adjunct to him, unlike other of his women who were lost in his shadow.

Born in the French West Indies where her father was an agent for a sugar plantation, Maddly had grown up in Paris where she first saw Brel on television. After Johnny Hallyday recorded some songs written by her elder brother, the schoolgirl acquired *entrées* into the music business and, through this, the cinema, and it raised no eyebrows when she entered the world of work as a production assistant for a film company. It wasn't long before her timorously pretty but deceptively commanding face was noticed by trade moguls, and bit-parts led to bigger roles on both small and big screens. The fees were invested wisely, and, by 1971, when she met Brel, she'd was head of her own Maddly Productions corporation.

Jacques was nonplussed by Maddly's self-possession that would not allow her - anymore than it would have Catherine Sauvage - to be bothered
by either his wife or a more recent complication when he'd left Sylvie
very suddenly to continue an *amour*, started secretly a year earlier, with
her married best friend, Marianne. The seduction had taken place when
Marianne and a queasy Sylvie had both accompanied him on a sea cruise
that also excited in him a long-dormant passion for the rolling waves, and
he would apply himself to sailing with almost the same zest as he had already to flying - which Sylvie had loathed too.

Digesting technicalities from studying aircraft instruction manuals
was anathema to Jacques, but he had progressed in leaps and bounds by
having an alert expert show him what to do. Learning from first-hand
experience, he was ready to fly solo in seven hours instead of the usual
twelve. Thus he gained a private licence, and then an advanced diploma.
When not needed on a film set, he'd wing off somewhere within reach
by radio; the risk of his death or injury in high altitude misadventure in-
sured by Lloyds of London.

He was coming to know every airstrip in France and its environs. For
the world to become an even bigger oyster, the next step had been to
join an aeroplane club near Hyères on the Cote D'Azur and then a flying
school in Geneva in 1969. With commendable effort, Brel passed the the-
oretical examination in March 1970 and, after a test that involved nav-
igating through Alpine mountains, had been accepted by the Swiss authorities as a fully-fledged pilot. That he was to become an authorized instructor two years later argues a talent well above the ordinary. Had he
not been so fully occupied with songwriting, acting and other pursuits,
Jacques Brel might have gone down in history as a truly great aviator.

To Maddly, provided Jacques didn't mind her having distractions too,
flying, sailing, whatever he did - as well as Marianne, Miche, whoever
would have him - could stay in the picture for as long as he liked. However, art was not to imitate happy-go-lucky life when Jacques reunited with
Molinaro for 1973's *L'Emmerdeur*[5], remarkable for a scene with Brel,
like someone out of one of his own *chansons*, being most compellingly
clumsy and pitiable as he grovels before his bride on horseback, begging
her to leave her lover and come back to him.

He'd compose to rigid order to complement particular passages or when soundtracks demanded it - jogalong 'Les Coeurs Tendres', a solitary *chanson* commissioned for 1967's *Un Idiot À Paris*, for example, or incidental music with François Rauber for *Mon Oncle Benjamin* - but otherwise his songwriting had become sporadic with only twenty new *chansons* in copyright between the last hurrah in Roubaix and *L'Emmerdeur*. Nothing much was coming by the turn of the decade. In August 1972 - a slow moment in a busy filming agenda - he would add words that he could have written in his sleep to a Rod McKuen melody that would translate as 'To You' on the North American's next album. This closed a five year hiatus from Brel's last published effort, 'Regarde Bien Petit' (describing a man and a boy on guard duty wondering about a portentious shape in the distance).

Yet more Brel records were sold after he'd forsaken concerts than before. These included repackagings, compiled of necessity with a pronounced pre-1967 bias. The most common choices from latter day material were 'La Quête' - and 1968's 'J'Arrive'.

Founded on a curiously circular *staccato* riff and the repeated title phrase, 'J'Arrive' harked back to to Brel's old preoccupation with both the passage of time and man's inescapably involvement with the Earth's seasons. A mordant 'Seasons In The Sun', it is fixed firmly in late autumn when gold begins to turn to marble, thus aligning with that point in life where time is marked by the first deaths of members of one's own over-the-hill generation: rain and tears, and the imagery of the chrysanthemum, a late bloom often placed on Belgium graves. Brel ruminates on lost opportunities, achieving goals ('arriving') too near the end, and a desire to last 'until dawn, until summer, until spring, until tomorrow', long enough to revisit the changeless and changed haunts of his youth like the anti-hero of George Orwell's *Coming Up For Air*.

As cheerless in its way, 'Je Suis Un Soir D'Été' personifies its embittered singer as an urban night so humid that it covers every complexion with beads of sweat; a metaphor for nature's effortless incursion upon twentieth century humanity, whether the 'Les Vieux' couple's reappearance with one tooth left between them or, in the same verse, girls who dance 'to the death of spring'.

In as much as this might be an allusion to Stravinsky's *Rite Of Spring*, so 'L'Éclusier' may have something to do with L'Écluse, the cabaret club in Paris where, for all his objections about its small size, Brel had been glad to work when first he touched the brittle fabric of fame. Was it a hollow endeavour to get back to some kind of womb as 'Les Bergers' and 'Marieke' had been? Yet, if you take this *chanson* at face value, it explores the same contrast as 'J'Arrive' and 'Je Suis Un Soir D'Été', i.e. between the cycle of growth, death and rebirth and the fate of the individual. It's seen through the eyes of an ancient lock keeper who thinks of spring only as the time when his own father drowned.

What was the matter with Brel? Why were his ebbing reserve of *chansons* so oppressively long-faced? It went deeper than artistic weariness and disillusion. At thirty-nine (past the 'countdown' of 'L'Âge Idiot'), he was experiencing respiratory problems - shuddering gasps and cold sweat - and groggy awakenings that these days were unconnected with alcoholic hangovers. A puffy, parchment visage stared vacantly back at him from the bathroom mirror, and weight loss was increasingly more noticeable on the scales. With hair as long as it'd ever be - on a sleeker par with Mick Jagger's, *circa* 1964 - he looked just like the tormented, highly-strung Left Bank hand-to-mouther that he'd let the press believe him to have been.

As yet, no doctor could diagnose anything that could be named. All Jacques could do was slow down, relax and let time do the rest. Nevertheless, expecting the worst, he couldn't help the foreboding that afflicted itself on him as he built up a damning picture of his state of health before placid denial that there was anything to worry about. Maybe he was panicking unduly.

NOTES

1. Albin Michel, 1967
2. Macmillan, 1996
3. Though there were isolated cells of appreciation like Feathers,
a London trio, fronted by David Bowie, that slipped Brel items into
its repertoire.
4. A paraphrase of the prototypical alarmist post-war newspaper
headline ADOLF HITLER IS ALIVE AND WELL AND LIVING IN
BUENOS AIRES!!!
5. This was remade in Hollywood as Buddy Buddy *in 1981.*

Chapter Eight

'Drawers Full Of Scenarios'

In February 1971, Chantal and France, now very grown up, were out of favour - as they often were nowadays - and, therefore, did not accompany their parents and Isabelle on a holiday in Guadeloupe (where, incidentally, Maddly had family and owned property). It was a deserved convalescence for Jacques who could not be coaxed from his bed before ten for the day's sightseeing, sunbathing or wary swimming. Yet, though there physically, his mind was generally elsewhere - and, before returning to Europe, he had mapped out a detailed outline of the first of two melancholy films devoted to the glory of failure that he would direct himself.

With the working title of *Les Moules*, it was delivered without revision to an initially excited producer, Michel Ardan, the 'angel' for *Assasins De L'Ordre* - though the writer had to put some of his own money into its low budget. Brel's draft was a thirty-page annotation of one scene after another - like the verses of a very long *chanson*. Though Ardan found this unorthodox presentation refreshing, he wasn't happy with calling it *Les Moules* - 'The Mussels', but also construed as an offensive colloquialism - and during consequent discussions, it would become *Léon* (also, the role Jacques had plainly staked out for himself) and then *Franz* - after Franz Jacobs, the proprietor of a bar in Knokke. He was famous for looking very well on an apparent daily consumption of fifty shots of whiskey and one hundred cigarettes.

The bare bones of *Franz* was the tragi-comic love of an unglamorous couple in their forties, leading the kind of life Jacques might have led had he stayed at Vanneste and Brel. It began with some petty bureaucrats being sent to a seaside sanatorium to recover from various complaints attributable to the stress of work. The joker of the pack is pigeon-fancier Leon, liverish, clumsy, and the unretaliating victim of the others' cruel pranks. Unmarried, he is dominated from afar by his mother to whom he writes every day by pigeon post.

One day, two women arrive unexpectedly - dowdy Léonie (played by the *chansoniere* Barbara, once a contender for Sheila's pop crown) and her antithesis, glitzy-sluttish Catherine (Daniele Évenou). It is the former who fascinates Léon. Desperate for affection, he lies to Léonie (as she does to him) about the circumstances that brought him there. He had been, he brags, a mercenary in Zaire, the Guevara to a long-dead Franz's Castro. A combination of wounds and keeping pace with the off-duty roisterings of Franz - the hero Léon would have liked to have been - had probably led, says he, to his present state of health. A shy courtship is nipped in the bud when Léon's self-preserving Maman takes him home, appalled that, as it had read in his latest letter, a turn of events like proposing marriage to Léonie had even occurred to her son.

Throughout the shooting that summer (mostly along the familiar waterfront between Ostend and Knokke) Jacques - while muttering his lines over and over again - kept trepidations about his hitherto untried skills as a director so in check that he blocked an attempt by Ardan to summon the seasoned Edouard Molinaro for the technological donkey-work - and to guide and temper Brel's more preposterous (and expensive) ideas, some of which are now standard procedure. He didn't have to be told to employ helicopter for long shots, but Brel was one of the first European film-makers to videotape the 'rushes' - uncut demonstration scenes - thereby bypassing the false economy of holding up proceedings for the laborious development of cheaper cine-film.

Ardan had no reason to wring his hands over Brel's music for *Franz*. During the opening credits, the fittingly forlorn 'Les Despèreres', composed in 1965, was sung by up-and-coming Dutch singer, Lisbeth List (a protégé of Aznavour, recommended to Jacques by Ernst Van Altena). With the sound at any given moment mattering more than individual items, the remainder encompassed waltzes by Wagner and François Rauber plus Belgian accordion tunes, elongated where necessary to complement particular sequences. As in all of Brel's pictures, little was designed to divert attention from the action.

The actual filming of *Franz* was completed one week ahead of the two month deadline. To celebrate, the director threw a party that spanned a local restaurant and, more publically, Franz Jacobs' bar. Buried in the uneuphonious uproar were the strains of 'Les Flamandes'. Its life-and-soul, Brel was as free with his uncouth language as his wallet. Smiling indulgently at his frolics were peripheral guests such as the Italian actor

Lino Ventura - star of *L'Aventure C'Est L'Aventure* - and Claude Lelouch, whose laudatory remarks[1] about what he'd seen of *Franz* would blaze from posters in cinema foyers.

Before that came post-production chores that were riven with avoidable obstacles. Firstly, the well-meaning Dutch printers transformed the North Sea's uncompromising grey-green to travelogue blue. Mirth, hesitation and ultimate anger chased across Brel's face on seeing it, but after the error was rectified, he yawned though the interminable re-running of each celluloid mile during editing that was nowhere as enjoyably novel as it had been when a dabbling lay advisor for *Mon Oncle Benjamin*. Having thrust total responsibility upon himself, Brel had never been out on a longer limb.

He would hardly be able to contain his inner tension as a *woomph* of flashbulbs floodlit his entrance to the premiere on 6 March 1972 in Paris. The morning papers found much to praise. A poignant episode centred on Léon and Léonie's cycling excursion along a canal was mentioned as outstanding, while Brel-as-director was put on a par with early Alfred Hitchcock by another scribe. Others were more level-headed. It was a sound enough yarn, and Jacques Brel had tried hard, yes, but the dialogue was flawed, and some of the characters - notably Léon - not wholly credible during a slow-moving one-and-three-quarter hours.

Those *au fait* with Brel's past detected much of his customary humour and self-denegrating pessimism. Lines like Catherine's 'talk to my arse; my head is ill' would not have been out of place in one of his *chansons*; some of which were quoted directly by the shabbily likeable Léon - who, when drunk, actually bursts into song - and, if barely audible, states that 'Belgium is a country where minorities argue in the name of two cultures that don't exist.' To musical intimates, there was nothing new either about the mischievous placing of a dead bird in Léon's serviette or a naked Catherine in his bed. Similarly vicious tomfoolery had been a diversion from the monotony of touring.

Franz had got away with enough for Jacques to embark on *Far West*, his most abiding undertaking as a director six months later. Blaming Ardan for the previous foray's shortcomings, he engaged none other than Miche as producer, brushing aside her inexperience by citing the hash that he considered had been made of *Le Bar De La Forche*, and her calm handling of Editions Pouchanel's mind-stultifying monetary and legal mechanics. He and she then raised most of the cash required (much more than for *Franz*) from the coffers of their own company, that of Belgium's Ministry of Culture and - putting his money where his mouth was - Claude Lelouch.

Le Far West was to feature Daniele Évenou, Lino Ventura, Michel Piccoli - and, of course, Jacques as the 'good guy'. Dropping the relaxed mask he'd assumed for *Franz*, he betrayed his wobbling confidence behind the camera with a bossy hauteur, verging on meglomania. Moreover, rather than trust a stuntman, he himself would dangle from an aircraft by a rope. Stinging ears all over the set was the tongue-lashing Brel doled out to Évenou who, contracted to play a strip-teaser, had not informed him of her now-visible pregnancy. With ruthless efficiency, he could turn on the old sweetness-and-light when obliged - as he was to cajole the intransigent manager of a cement firm into letting the crew film its office building. Brel also enlisted the services of various *gendarmerie* and platoons from the Belgian army for the movie's climax.

To outsiders, Brel's methodology appeared slapdash - as if he was making it up as he went along. There was, indeed, much improvization *à la* Lelouch, and many scenes that may have seemed like a good idea at the time. However, as more and more clutter fluttered onto the cutting room floor, direction and outcome shone through with increasing clarity. *Le Far West*, it transpired, was about Belgian adults on an odyssey to fulfil Jacky's lost childhood fantasy.

They were led by 'Jack' (Brel) as a sort of a quixotic Clint Eastwood, who, at one point, actually disguised himself as Don Quixote, complete with lance and charger. Elsewhere, there were a bison race, the conversion of a colliery into a Wild West town, and the discovery of gold bullion that caused the travellers to split into two factions.

Jack and the heroine, a young black paraplegic named Lina, advocate restoring the loot to the King, but the rest disappear with it. In the final reel, the fairy-tale atmosphere dissipates, and Jack and Lina are gunned down in the thick of machine-guns, tanks and other functioning symbols of modern battle.

Originally, Jacques had wanted the dream to become reality with the equestrian rataplans of the happy pair galloping through the vastness of the prairie into the sunset, finally reaching the Far West - as the majority of ticket-buyers would find themselves tacitly urging the two to do. Though Brel also removed some autobiographical elements and the strikes against government, police, army, the Church - all the common targets - one critic, searching for precedents, would evoke 1969's obscure and self-indulgent *Can Heironymus Merkin Ever Forgive Mercy Humppe And Find True Happiness*, the directorial debut of Anthony Newley, an English inverse of Brel in that he was an actor who had become a singing composer. [2]

The *Far West* music, nevertheless, was a triumph of a kind. Pieced together by Jacques in an office adjacent to the editing department, it was a feast of remembrance in its exhuming of 'Le Plat Pays' and, more opaquely, in a new song, 'L'Enfance', with a couplet about 'all the adults are deserters/the bourgeois are the Indians'.

In another respect, however, *Far West* was quite contemporary, given both the popularity in the early 1970s of spaghetti westerns, and that Hollywood cowboy flicks were much in vogue for pop idols wishing to extend themselves. Ringo Starr had donned spurs to be a *bandido*'s sidekick in 1970's *Blindman*, and Bob Dylan's abilities as a thespian were about to be realized as 'Alias' in Sam Peckenpah's *Pat Garrett And Bill The Kid*. Furthermore, all over the world, multitudinous licensed premises had mutated into rootin'-tootin' replicas of Dodge City saloons. Barging through the swinging half-doors of a Dominican bar or a pub in Oxfordshire, you'd bump into Calamity Jane lookalikes and stetsoned quaffers of sour mash whiskey. Belying daytime guises as computer programmers or janitors, conversations would be peppered with Deep South slang - e.g. 'mess of grits' for 'plate of food' - picked up from Merle Haggard albums. On a stage, a band might gild the *yee-hah* exuberance with bluegrass breakdowns and downhome sincerities like 'Okie From Muskogee', 'Crystal Chandelier' and Elvis Presley's 'American Trilogy' medley.

When *Le Far West*, theoretically allied to a current fashion, was chosen to represent Belgium at the Cannes film festival in May 1973, Brel gave it an extra boost by allowing himself to be interviewed on *Radioscopie*, a French television magazine, the evening before the screening. As well as musing that he might not have had a career if he'd been good-looking, he endeavoured to convince those watching - and himself - that he wasn't worried about the verdict of the Cannes jury. He thought, nonetheless, that, as he'd sweated blood over it, *Le Far West* deserved objective judgement.

Almost as an afterthought, Brel's celluloid baby was shown the day after the odds-on favourite, Marco Ferreri's *La Grande Bouffe*. Those who'd seen the curate's egg that was *Franz* agreed that Brel's latest venture was an improvement. Among several startling moments were the scene in which the pseudo-cowfolk walked down a motorway on foot, and another in a Kafka-esque Brussels Palace of Justice with Lina and Jack being received by various doorkeepers then the King all played by the same actor. There was also a Buñuel touch about the monarch's old ministers covered in spiders' webs.

Certain jaded and inattentive pundits who had drawn the short straw for the official unveiling of *Le Far West* were determined not to like it. While exchanging smirks at each other's cleverness, it was the bane of such people's existence that they had to write about an upstart amateur who was doing something they couldn't do. Brel was such an obvious sitting duck that they felt entitled to snipe at his portrayal of Red Indians; claim to lose the thread of the story through scenes they thought should have been rigorously scissored; not laugh at things meant to be funny; snigger during the sexy bits, and play safe by concluding that *Le Far West* was a half-hearted send-up of one of these two-a-penny westerns.

'They didn't understand a thing,' howled Jacques, who vanished to his room in the Hotel Normandie for the next two days. With no glad welcome guaranteed, distressed friends braved his depression to make sympathetic noises as, encircled by leftover food, crumpled bedclothes and overflowing ashtrays, he conquered his vocational desolation by refusing to accept that *Le Far West* was an artistic flop. What the hell did the critics know? As it happened, *Le Far West* drew nearly twice as many customers when on general circulation as the seventy-thousand-odd that had bothered with *Franz*.

Fanning dull embers, Brel proffered the press the faggot of a follow-up to *Far West* as he had, he calculated, 'drawers full of scenarios'. Nevertheless, it was in a mood of despondent forbearance that he weighed up a leading role Lelouch had offered in *Le Mariage* (the sunshine and showers of a couple's forty years together) before deciding that he could make no more long term commitments. Besides, a movie's demanding schedule with its early mornings had became onerous.

Brel also procrastinated too long over Claude's proposal in 1974 that they co-write a screenplay revolving round an aircraft crossing the Atlantic in the pioneering days of aviation. By then, though such a storyline was close to Brel's heart, his active interest in the cinema evaporated as much as his toleration of even his own films ('looking at my features for an hour and a half, that's beyond my powers of endurance').

Towards the end of his movie period, Jacques Brel had discouraged his wife and offspring from visiting his place of work, despite its frequent close proximity to Brussels. This was partly because he wanted to avoid potentially excruciating encounters between family and mistresses. Even so, France had turned up at a *Far West* location, and had detected a friskiness between her father and Maddly even before he introduced them. Until then, none of his daughters - not even twenty-two-year-old Chantal - had spoken knowingly to anyone about his other women.

Naturally, France could not help but inform her siblings about short-skirted Maddly, and dissect her personality and looks with thrilled vigour. While allowing that Maddly was quite jovial and made Papa laugh a lot, France spared no details in recounting how he kept sneaking off to be with Maddly whenever possible, and had gone into rhapsodies about how adventurous Maddly was in bed. Fine words in front of his own flesh-and-blood, you'll agree. Then there was that Marianne, now living far from Paris on the Breton seaboard. In May 1972, Jacques had been named as the third party in her thankfully unpublicized divorce.

The three girls hadn't known how they were expected to take it when, signifying volumes of worldly wisdom, he disclosed that 'all women are tarts - except your mother; she's a saint'. He definitely wasn't one so what did that make them - half-and-half? Women seemed to be either one or the other in his *chansons*. Moreover, what was he on about on Radio Luxembourg with his 'Patience and tenderness are enemies of *le grand amour* - which is itself a social evil. People who are prey to it are destroyed'?

How did Jacques, that most heterosexual of males, prefer his females? On one hand, he confessed that he didn't like 'em too submissive - it was a sign of laziness, he said. Conversely, he couldn't abide those who hen-pecked their husbands. These sentiments were founded less on reasoned argument than the instinctive emotional conviction of one whose reso-lute promiscuity had been born from experiencing too many showbusi-ness gold-diggers who materialize with the promptness of vultures to chew upon and spit out useful men that trust them.

Juliette Greco knew the type well. She'd also been around when there'd been as much calculating lust in Brel back in Montmartre when the world was young. Jacques and Juliette's wanderings since the 1950s had not precluded their keeping in touch, and, though there was less of a twinkle in his eye these days, she could yet perceive in the semi-retired *chanso-nier* and movie mogul - so she'd once remarked - the younger 'man's man who loved women in a desperate, mad way.'

In his forties, the darling of the ladies was still partial to variety. All three members of his present *seraglio* were not, as is often the case, dif-ferent editions of the same character. They were also conveniently far-flung. Maddly was recipient of most attention even if his assignations with outlying Marianne may have been more intense, owing to their brevity. As for Miche, a chief factor that made their espousal work was that they scarcely ever saw each other, and when they did, it was main-ly to discuss business matters. Yet they loved each other sufficiently not to have to prove it as Miche became more of a surrogate mother or elder sister to him than anything else.

He continued to live apart from all his women, passing most of his waking hours in Paris in a newly-purchased studio in Neuilly, a western suburb close to the Seine. Apart from a table and a television he hardly ever switched on, there were few other permanent movables - though, if he'd been closeted there for more than a few hours, the place would unti-dy itself to look as if someone had chucked a hand-grenade into it.

Resident in the same city, Maddly was not as yet a 'wife' as Sylvie had been - though, like her predecessor, she had made up her mind to be, de-spite the disapproval of his children.

The subject of Maddly had come up during one of his chats-cum-ora-tions with France - which took an uglier turn when Jacques started rant-ing in full philistine flood about the younger generation in the stock man-ner of a middle-aged square. Her hackles rising, France expressed her annoyance, and when he ignored it, she had the nerve to storm off, leaving him in shock. He stared after her with a new respect. Who'd have thought it? This was one of his own daughters with an unexampled gesture of contempt towards him instead of the expected cow-eyed obeisance: France standing up for herself; France without her thumb in her mouth.

He'd joke about still sucking his own thumb because he hadn't been given enough love as a child when seeking to dispel the strained atmosphere after Chantal dared to cross him too during the celebration she'd helped organize for her parents' twenty fourth wedding anniversary. Towards the end of the main course, he'd mellowed sufficiently to even apologize for being a neglectful father.

The outcome of an earlier altercation with both Chantal and France had been his refusal to invite them to Guadaloupe (though he made amends by taking them with him alone on a cruise to Italy). Another bone of contention was the eldest daughter's betrothal to a Michel Camerman. As he was an engaging chap who was showing promise as a town planner, Chantal had been perplexed by her father's crabbiness. Jacques - seemingly, with his bohemian hat on - was sure that Michel was very nice, but, speaking from hard-bought experience, he still didn't hold with the reduction of a man-woman relationship to a business contract. It had no relevance, he thought, to what a couple needed to do to remain together. Perhaps it was beyond him to admit to insecurities about his family unit disintegrating - and that Chantal's heart might belong to someone other than Daddy? Perhaps that was why he'd absent himself from the ceremony in Algeria in September 1974.

The door was also starting to close on Jojo Pasquier, but not brutally. The breach was not irreparable, but Jojo seemed to be on the way out in more decisive terms: prostate cancer had precipitated a slow decline. Like Chantal and France, he resented Maddly's descent into their midst, and was happiest when she wasn't around to infringe his laconic affinity with Jacques, the verbal reviling of each other the way old mates do. She was no Dulcinea to his Sancho, and he'd bite his tongue at Jacques' placatory reassurance that she was a lovely girl when you got to know her.

Both Maddly and the ailing Pasquier were among the entourage on a leisurely flight in a Lear jet from Paris to see her folks in Guadeloupe with stops for refuelling in Scotland[3], Iceland and Greenland (where they were delayed by the cold and wind). At the controls throughout was Jacques himself.

Earlier crazes had possessed Brel, and, hanging the expense, he'd had to have all the necessary top-of-the-range equipment, but sometimes he'd lose interest while, say, glancing at the instructions for setting up a newly-delivered gadget. Nevertheless, no pastime had hooked him as endurably as aviation.

The months spent at the Geneva flying school had permitted Jacques to scrape easy acquaintance with other pilots whose blithe dedication to their *métier* was stimulating after the shiftless malcontentment prevalent in certain quarters of the music and film industries. As a Belgian, he was impressed too with Swiss organizational efficiency, manifested most pervasively in the relative concord between the confederation's four language communities.

Back among his own people, Brel's fervour was contagious. Miche was a willing pupil - though Chantal and France volunteered but rarely when Papa wanted someone to take over in the cockpit while he rested his eyes. It was a recreation that only the extremely rich could afford, and, to help it pay for itself, Jacques let out his aeroplane for crew and equipment transportation to Johnny Hallyday and others still twirling on the merry-go-round of pop.

Sailing had also become more than a hobby. Brel had now cultivated a habit of airing his growing knowledge of the sea in a drive to educate those close to him in the art of navigation and the names of an ocean-going craft's components. However, though he sent away for a correspondence course, he only got round to formal training in 1973, and would receive his yachtsman's certificate at Ostend on 1 July 1974.

It was after a roller-coasting month on the Atlantic that he called Éditions Pouchenel for the wherewithal to buy his own wind-driven boat. Without so much as the *phut* of engine to remind him of the twentieth century, he'd be able to escape from a mainland that, he maintained, had disappointed him, and survive by his own skills and courage at the helm of his destiny. Furthermore, now that a new deal with Barclay did not oblige him to deliver albums on a regular basis, he needn't be unduly concerned if he lost touch with an age that prized commodity over creativity. While still able, he was going to lead a full life beyond monied lassitude or trying to stay in public focus. He wished, he said, to circum-navigate the globe, looking in at its most yonder isles - exactly as the fancy took him - and had set aside five years to do so.

France was offered the chance to go with him. This was not so much for her skills as a mariner, but because of all his children, she was at the loosest end; Chantal was about to be married, and fifteen-year-old,
Isabelle had just started at secretarial college.

Brel tied up his own loose ends by appointing Belgian lawyer Jacques Delcroix as executor of his will. He and the sole beneficiary, Miche, next travelled to London for the Earl's Court boat show in January 1974, but it would be in Antwerp the following month that they found for him a suitable luxury yacht. Named after a small island west of Norway, *L'Askoy II* was forty-two tonnes of steel and wood, over twenty feet long - and capacious enough for Jacques' farewell party that ended with Miche lachrymose for the thirty mile journey back to Brussels where, as sleep was impossible, she cleared a chair in her office, and tried to dose herself with ongoing matters to do with Éditions Pouchenel - for, despite her husband's piecemeal delegation of much of its running to others, she still saw herself as its *de jure* patroness.

Faithful Miche was there to collect the car where Jacques had left it in the Antwerp docks after he, France and all hands set sail on a cold and drizzly dawn on 24 July 1974. Miche was then unaware that Maddly was on board too - as France had been until virtually the last minute. Nonetheless, daughter and paramour kept civil tongues in their heads during the three days spent tacking along the North Sea shoreline for everyone to get their sea legs.

Beneath bruised skies, the next week went well too - though the water was aswarm with bigger shipping, requiring careful steering by Brel or whoever else was at the wheel. As the days slipped by, a rota was drawn up whereby the women shopped whenever the vessel dropped anchor, and cooked the meals; France making breakfast, Maddly the rest. Luncheon was to be served on the bridge, and dinner below decks in the saloon.

Aiming for the Azores via the Canary Islands, the *Askoy* funnelled along the southern shores of England without incident - apart from the anchor tangling in telephone cables in Hugh Town bay in the Scilly Isles. Before entering the Atlantic proper, Jacques had written a few letters (signed 'The Ancient Mariner') and, perversely, with the pressure of the next LP no longer looming, he'd even found himself working out chord changes and lyrics for two or three new *chansons*.

Every silver lining has a cloud, and the Great Adventure was to be blighted by so many that it would run aground permanently. While the *Askoy* bore away gently south along the French and Spanish coasts, Jojo's disease took him on 27 August. Brel caught the stark message on the radio receiver in time to drag himself back to Paris for the burial service on 3 September. From his pew, he was at first a detached spectator with no interest or stake in proceedings that might have come from a verse in 'Fernand' or 'J'Arrive'. Amid the sobbing and blowing of noses, he was overheard to murmur 'I'll be next'. Soon, he would no longer not believe it.

Jacques cried his tears; then catharsis and a dull ache signaled a rise from his own half-death. This grew more and more perceptible as the weather got warmer, and the voyage became less like occupational therapy. The odd gruesomely hilarious remark about the funeral hid the downcast and shaken man beneath, feeling his anguish all the more sharply for realizing that there'd never be another like Jojo.

Prior to landfall in Las Palmas in the Canaries came tidings of Miche's imminent flight, with Jojo's widow, Alice, to meet the *Askoy*. There was consternation from France who, not completely cognisant with her mother's open-mindedness, was to be astounded when an unruffled Jacques booked himself and his lover into the presidential suite of the port's Hotel Parador.

With Papa next to her, France would be in the driver's seat of the Volkswagon hired for the few bumpy miles to and from the air terminal. To her mother, the old-young creature walking towards her with his arms out had every appearance of being seriously ill. Several minutes after it occurred to Miche, the thought was acknowledged in a choking screech of 'I am dying!'. France too would always remember that moment because nothing was ever the same afterwards.

A flummoxed split-second later, the vehicle ground to a standstill, and Jacques, devoid of will, was half-led, half-carried out, and laid down on the hard shoulder, his entire body vibrating with eye-crossing coughs that disgorged blood. He perked up enough to apologize for causing so much fuss as, to the agitated clang of an ambulance bell and Spanish-speaking Alice's questions to the paramedics, he was hastened to a hospital founded, by nauseating coincidence, by someone called Jacques Romain.

Smear sampling and other procedures winkled out respiratory problems, and the doctors wondered if the seizure wasn't the beginning of tuberculosis. Brel's condition was not, however, grave enough to warrant admission. As directed, he completed a prescribed course of drugs, stuck to a healthy diet, had a daily nap after lunch, and cut back on cigarettes, but, with every hacking bark still painful, he disclosed his intention to put the sea idyll on ice, and check in straightaway at a medical centre in Switzerland.

From passport control at Cointrin, Jacques, needing to sit every hundred yards or so, was helped along by Maddly to the car that would transport him to a private clinic in the efficaciously clean air of the Alps. Some of the symptoms were stabilized, and Jacques regained strength to face the news that X-rays had revealed malignant cells forming a shadow on the left lung.

Fearing photographers above all, Brel dismissed Miche's suggestion of announcing his lung cancer at a press conference. Then hopeful of a cure, he let brother Pierre - now cursed with grim maladies himself - and few others in on the ghastly secret before returning to the Canaries to ready the boat for a crossing to the Windward Islands. This was thwarted by a swift relapse, and on Guy Fawkes Night 1974, Brel left his daughter in charge while, breathing like a bellows, he repaired to Brussels where he swigged Scotch throughout the sleepless night before an appointment at the Edith Cavell infirmary with Dr. Arthur Gélin, the Brel family consultant since the early 1960s when he performed an appendectomy on France.

Gélin advocated an immediate operation to remove most of the offending lung and thus isolate the believed source of the infection so that the other lung would respond better to treatment. Brel gave grudging consent while putting it on record that, rather than perish by inches as Jojo had done, he'd prefer what remained of his life to be short but active enough to realize his ambition to sail round the world.

During the days before he went under the scalpel on 16 November, he was not a particularly model patient as chief surgeon Dr. Charles Nemry and his team studied and prodded him gingerly as if he were some dead sea mammal stranded on a beach, and spoke to him as if he was a retard. On one lamentable occasion, rage at his state of dependency so overwhelmed Jacques that he hurled slippers as they swished through the double doors of his cubicle to gather round the bed. Nevertheless, because tractability sat ill with restlessness, he was permitted to spend the last evening sipping champagne with Arthur Gélin.

His first visitor after coming round from the anaesthetic was Chantal, clutching a bouquet of flowers. Her father did not see them wilt for, as soon as he was able to pace the corridors of the Edith Cavell without aid, he discharged himself and continued his recuperation at the Brussels Hilton where a Garbo-esque refusal to be interviewed was a provocation to the media. The less trustworthy tabloids were itching to inform readers about whatever was up with the seldom-seen star. *Brel In Booze Hell!* would make a marvellous headline, wouldn't it? Better still, how about *Jacques' Vegetable Existence In Isolation Ward!*? It's a shame nobody can find out precisely what's wrong.

The gentlefolk of the press had disgraced themselves already with stray paragraphs based on conjecture. Even incarceration in the sealed-off executive floor of the Hilton bought no peace as, under the editorial lash, 'creative' journalists disguised themselves as staff, so frantic were they for some sordid scoop.

Advised to avoid stressful situations, Brel fled back to the Canaries a mere six weeks after surgery. He had an air about him that would haunt France down the years. Corpse-grey in the face, his eyes had a burned-out look, accentuated by purple-black blotches under them like mascara that had trickled and dried. Though she was among those in whom he'd chosen not to confide, France's scrutiny of medical books on the shelf rigged up in his cabin had told her enough for an educated guess.

He seemed in turns more irritable and more acquiescent. A former *Askoy* deckhand stoked up trouble with the local police by claiming that he hadn't received any wages. With a withering glance at the deputation on the gangplank, Jacques paid what the visiting Dr. Gélin dubbed 'the price of peace', even stumping up for the wretched fellow's travelling expenses back to Belgium.

Arthur thought it near-suicidal, but Jacques set off from Las Palmas two days before the New Year. One uneventful month later, a sun-dried *Askoy* penetrated the Carribean. Heavy air flopped over the yacht like a wet raincoat, and dark shapes of sharks were sighted slithering through waters like blue crystal. As it approached the spreading panorama of Martinique, France was tested by an apprehension that she'd had all she could stand of both the sea and the sick-making cooing between Maddly and Papa - whose pet-name for her was 'Doo-Doo', for gawd's sake. The veneer of sister-like harmony had rapidly eroded, and France and Doo-Doo were scoring catty points off each other - now not even having the grace to do so behind Jacques' back.

Not belonging any more, France withdrew into an insufferable sullenness towards her father and his omnipresent and increasingly coercive bedmate. After the *Askoy* docked, this came to a head with an ultimatum issued by Jacques: 'Cheer up or leave'. France couldn't so she did. On the day, he handed over some money that he presumed would cover her return to Brussels, but after getting the measure of Martinique, the young woman stayed on, sleeping first in abandoned cars and, at the bitter end, in the house of an Yves Pichard, a gentleman known to Brel, who she'd met on the first day in Martinique. For a while, she kept body and soul together as a temporary bank clerk in Fort de France, the island's capital.

France saw nothing of her bewildering father - though she passed the *Askoy* every morning on the way to work. Letters to him were unanswered, and when once she rowed bravely out to the yacht, she was forbidden to board by the insurmountable Maddly, resplendent in her victory. She, France believed, had cautioned Jacques against seeing any of his nearest-and-dearest in the foreseeable future.

Two months after being cast adrift by him, France had little option but to return to Europe. On the aeroplane, she drifted into the uneasiest of slumbers now that she was more assured of getting home. At Orly, she walked stiffly with her luggage to her waiting mother - who had aged so shockingly that France understood that however deplorable Papa's conduct over the years, he would be mourned genuinely by Miche.

NOTES

1. 'This is a film-maker who takes risks. There hasn't been anything like it for ten years!'
2. Like Brel too, Newley was much esteemed by David Bowie.
3. At Prestwick where, in 1960, Elvis Presley had stood on British soil for the first and only time.

Chapter Nine

Far West?

The majority of the sick are not in bed. Like novelist Guy de Maupassant - with whom he shared thematic and personal characteristics - Brel sought as much pure pleasure as the traffic would allow after a mortal affliction seemed that it would all but extinguish his career. The global circumnavigation was cancelled as Jacques and Maddly lingered in the Caribbean with Arthur Gélin in attendance for his agreeable haze of chatter as much as his medical care. In reciprocation, Jacques was an excellent host with every thought for his guest's comfort; exempting him from nautical chores during a month's island-hopping. However, as it was with France - whose departure had left Brel with long periods of wakefulness at night - Gélin felt that three was a crowd as Doo-Doo and Jacques' canoodling went beyond the bounds of acceptable ickiness.

In conversation with the good doctor, Jacques was inclined to flit from topic to vaguely connected topic. He seemed very much a man in a hurry. The latest plan was to find a new place to dwell, some sort of tropical island paradise - a Far West, if you like. 'It's not a case of wishing for complete solitude,' Brel elucidated, 'but a desire to live in a small house near a town where I could go perhaps once a week. I want to live in retirement, but not as a hermit, and so, in that manner I will be able to put to one side certain misunderstandings which are crushing me little by little; to stop once and for all this idiotic game - which consists of attempting desperately to no longer be playing it.'

Growing to manhood in the hothouse of pop's turbulent and endless adolescence, he'd been treated like a food pigeonhole in a self-service cafeteria. Now that he was not so sure of his tomorrows, it could no longer be taken for granted that Jacques Brel existed just to vend entertainment with a side-serving of cheap insight. His own land wouldn't let him alone, so he'd have to find another.

Guadeloupe was on his short list, mainly because he got on well with most of Maddly's family - especially Madou, her mother. You'd have imagined that Jacques would have had much in common with her songwriting brother Eric, but he, like René Michielsen, was dubious about the new boyfriend's intentions towards his sister. From what he had already ascertained of Brel's dealings with the opposite sex, Eric had premonitions of Jacques serving Maddly likewise in the future.

For Brel, the future, such as it was, did not lie in Guadeloupe: too many people. In its St. Valentine's Day edition of 1976, *Paris-Match* reported that he was 'dans le Pacifique, un navigateur solitaire'. This was old news. With Maddly - and via weeks along the Panama Canal - he had actually glided the *Askoy* into the Pacific the previous summer; an entrance marked by the Grim Reaper coming for Cesare, the couple's pet canary - who was buried at sea with full honours; its keepers clothed in as much respectful black as they had with them. The becalming of the *Askoy* shortly afterwards did not perturb Jacques who was seaman enough to read the weather and predict that a fresh wind was on its way. Neither was this interlude unpleasant to him; the tranquillity even prompted a letter rather than the usual postcard to Miche from 'the end of the world. Since my voyages in Europe, it is, I believe, the first evening of peace.' He was, so it appeared, priming himself for the quiet life he considered he deserved, but, rather than, say, take up golf, he would retreat to perhaps the last bolt-hole his fans and the media would expect to find him.

In November 1975, the *Askoy* had dropped anchor off Hiva-Oa, the largest and most fertile of the one hundred and thirty coral islands known as the Marquesas, one of four archipelagos formed, so myth has it, when the fish hooks of a Polynesian demi-god wrenched up the ocean floor, and scattered across an expanse of ocean wider than western Europe. Under the suzerainty of France, their administrative centre was Tahiti, scarcely more than a speck on the map.

Eight hundred miles to its north-east, two thirds of Hiva-Oa's thousand-odd souls populated Atuana, a colony-within-a-colony that, from the air, was indistinguishable from any other in Polynesia with its roofs of corrugated-iron, trimmed with bands of wooden fretwork which, against the heavy surrounding foliage, looked as fantastic as fairy-tale castles. These lined a few tarmacked streets at the mouth of one of the atoll's nine valleys that fanned out from the misty and soaring twin peaks of Feani and Ootuas. On the topsoil of petrified lava from the vomitings of these and smaller volcanoes - not all of them extinct - sun-softened terrain ranged from lunar-like desert to overgrown jungle.

A sailor's first glimpse of Hiva-Oa was, nevertheless, of precipitous cliff faces and savage aspect. Until 1972, the island could only be reached via one of three cargo boats of mail and essentials. These arrived irregularly and unpredictably after ploughing through high seas that a gale could flay into billows forty feet high.

Sometimes, wind and tide prevented a landing, but Brel's yawl floated like a leaf into the palm-fringed lagoon of Hiva-Oa, initially just another stop for provisions. Indeed, Jacques and Maddly had been mildly exasperated by the community's *mañana* sedateness - that clarified why so few residents possessed a watch. 'It was island life,' shrugged Bamy, 'It might take a whole day to do something'. Yet, peopled by natives - *fares* - and a minority of around one hundred Caucasians (*popaa*), Hiva-Oa could boast a flourishing quantity of horses, goats, cattle, pigs, poultry and domestic pets (mostly cats) - as well as weather that allowed the cultivation of lemon, mango, avocado, mandarin and coconut trees.

After the newcomers ceased behaving as if on another planet, they unwound to such a degree that the *Askoy* was still there in mid-December when Brel requested Alice Pasquier to mail a parcel of couscous, truffles and other foodstuffs not immediately available in the South Pacific. A few days following his arrival, however, he may have treasured hopes of an closer source of supply after a sloop flying Belgian colours in the harbour held his vision like a magnet did iron filings.

Intrigued, Jacques asked a patrolling policeman to hail the craft and request its occupants to join him for a drink on the *Askoy*. Within the hour, the skipper Marc Bastard, his son Paolo and two female companions were sipping whiskey from a magnum with Brel's initials on it, and, after inaugural timidity, the Bastards were chinwagging with their far-famed fellow Gaul on equal terms.

Jacques struck most instant rapport with Bastard the elder, even after Marc confessed that he wasn't Belgian but a Parisian. His journey to his late fifties, he said, hadn't been dull. He'd quit the navy in the 1950s to write crime novels under the pseudonym 'Marc Audran'. Some were completed in Tahiti where his ownership of the isle's first television caused his expulsion in 1964 by an authority that did not encourage any *nouveau riche* smart alec from outstripping old money materially, particularly when even domestic wireless sets were still novel enough there to be regarded by censorious great aunts as meddling with dark forces. Five years on, the mercurial Bastard had gravitated back to France as a government-appointed arms dealer, but the call of the Pacific had him suddenly jump-cutting to Hiva-Oa where, in 1970, he had wed a local lass, and taken up a teaching post at its only secondary school.

For a long time, Bastard would be the only Atuanan with whom Brel could hold an intelligent discussion and sustain the running jokes he bestirred with anyone whose company he enjoyed. Like riders in the Old West, the two parted without ceremonial farewells when the *Askoy* nosed from the concrete jetty to look elsewhere in Polynesia for somewhere for Jacques to hang his hat. An estate agent on Tahiti waxed enthusiastically about Tuamotu - all coconut trees and sandy beaches - in the Low Archipelago, an hour's flight from Tahiti, but the sand was dark, and the client also turned up his nose at the depressing familiarity of its flat countryside.

Out of the question, of course, was Tahiti itself, discovered by Magellan centuries before the arrival of the first French ship. Its commander, Louis-Antoine de Bougainville - after whom a local flower was named - inked on the creamy vellum of his log book that 'I thought I was transported into the Garden of Eden'. That was all very well, but it was not possible for France to seize its place in the Polynesian sun until the advances in communication presented by the Industrial Revolution. Even then, French rule was resisted with diminishing spirit until the High King of all Polynesia, dissolute Pomare V - blood descendant of Tu, the founder of the dynasty (and friend of Captain Cook) - signed away his heritage in 1880 for an annual pension until his unlamented passing eleven years later.

After the first radioactive cloud had mushroomed in the vicinity in 1966 - on Mururoa (where nuclear testing would be resumed thirty years later) - the entrenchment of eight thousand French soldiers and almost half as many civilians in Tahiti accelerated the replacement of fishing by bureaucracy as the economic base of what had mutated from de Bougainville's Eden into a tortured patchwork of high-rise hotels, walled suburban compounds, military encampments, atomic research installations and dirt-poor shanty towns, rife with filth, vermin and undernourished aboriginal children.

Small wonder then that Brel found his way back to Hiva-Oa, comparable in size to the Isle of Wight, and as far from Faaa, Tahiti's international airport, as Heathrow from Kennedy - while, to the east, it was empty ocean all the way to the Americas. After take-off in Faaa, a twenty-seater aircraft took ten hours to reach Hiva-Oa's landing strip and cricket pavilion-like terminal. Then ensued a ride in a jeep to Altuana along a fern-edged and pot-holed gravel track - impassable during the rainy season - on which mongooses were flattened as hedgehogs were on the autobahns of Europe.

Until Jacques Brel's coming to this outpost of empire, its most renowned addressee had been the painter (and former stockbroker) Paul Gauguin who, like Brel, had left his family to live out his final years there. In 1891, he'd written to the Swedish playwright August Strindberg that it was 'civilization that brings you pain. Barbarism is to me rejuvenation.'

Wishing for the same but without having to rough it, Jacques Brel rented an unpretentious wooden house in Atuana from June 1976. It constituted kitchen, sitting room, bedroom, office and bathroom, and was modest for one of his means, but handy for the police station and other public facilities such as the two general stores, hubs of gossip for the island's professional classes with daughters at Parisian finishing schools. It was also within the clang of the Roman Catholic mission bell, and a few minutes dawdle from Calvary Cemetary where Gauguin's cadaver had been mouldering for the past seventy years.

With hairless dome, cavernous eye sockets and other repulsive features, Death The Skeleton was a frequent symbol - as a warning against the sin of pride - in Polynesian places of worship. Given that, physically, he was none too hale, Brel was justified in his aversion to attending church services as well as a more pronounced preoccupation with doom than before in some of the *chansons* he'd got round to finishing.

Devoid of the slightest musical hint of somewhere in Polynesia, 'Les Marquesas' opened lyrically with 'They talk of death the way you talk of what your grocer sells'. Touching too in their admissions of spiritual and personal frailty were 'Vieillir' (which anticipated his end) and 'Jojo' (with the trenchant line 'death to the buggers who are in better health'). However indirectly, each homed in on death's insensateness in preserving the weary old but not the zestful young, and the soul being spared the same deterioration as the body - for, while Jacques still laughed his neighing laugh and grinned askance at the futilities of life, now and then, he seemed faraway. A shadow of unspeakable misery would cross a countenance as woebegone as that he'd simulated to play Quixote. Those in closest contact like Maddly, Marc Bastard and Matira, the home-help, were as uneasily aware as he was that there might be as little as two or three years left. It was understood too that - however much he trivialized it - unless he himself took the initiative, the distasteful topic wasn't to be mentioned outright.

Longer and more discursive than personal concerns were Brel's dissertations about gardening now that he was veering more and more towards the morning of the Earth. Responsible for introducing the plum tomato to the island, Jacques was soothed by working with the soil. At one with nature, all the intolerable adulation his life had embraced, the hit records, the films, the money down the drain, could be transformed to matters of minor importance as he tended the flora and fruit trees that grew round his newly-installed swimming pool.

More than ever, Jacques valued the simple life on Hiva-Oa where naught much was calculated to happened, year in, year out: 'time becomes a boat becalmed, a sail without a breeze/in the Marquesas'. The most exciting daily excursion was the uncomplicated ritual of shopping for groceries as Jacques and Maddly became an everyday sight, hand in hand around Atuona. Sweeter to them than dressing room fug was the salty air laced with the odour of *copra* (coconut oil), Hiva-Oa's principal export.

At first, Brel's hesitant smile had not rested on individuals but had been diffused to the general multitude. He was conscious that his presence in a delicatessen queue was as profoundly disturbing an experience for some as noticing President Mitterrand lathering his hands in an adjacent wash-basin in a public convenience. Yet, if not quite a nobody again, how un-expectedly delightful it was for him to mingle, unmolested by autograph hunters and worse, with the villagers at fêtes , coffee mornings and the like, jawing about rummage sales, the latest hunting expedition for the island's wild boar, and muck-spreading with the best of them.

Hiva-Oa society reminded him vaguely of the Brussels of his youth; nothing more so than an all-pervading religious formalism that turned Sunday into a day of earnest gloom for worshippers under the sway of the incumbent missionaries. Though many *fares* reverted tacitly to pa-gan customs when it suited them, the Bible was often their only reading matter. Cut off from the intellectual and cultural innovations of the out-er world, they were prone to the frequently more bigoted and dogmatic views on the Gospels by appointed preachers than would be tolerated on the mainland.

As he'd been metaphorically yowling about it from the rooftops of Eu-rope since God knows when, the incorrigible Brel could hardly be ex-pected to keep his trap shut about the hypocrisy he perceived in, say, the Polynesian clergyman of Gauguin's day who'd hedged his bets with fire-and-brimstone sermons whilst practicing the polygamy of the Old Reli-gion. Revelling in his own wickedness and professing to be an atheist, Jacques started marinating the air with obscenities whenever the men-of-the-cloth were in hearing distance; once greeting the bishop of the Mar-quesas (and the Atuona postman) with 'Hello, you queers!'. Refusing to address priests as 'Father', he'd mime shooting a revolver at them with his fingers if he came across any in the streets. When one demanded why, he retorted 'I eat priests for breakfast: I am Jacques Brel!'

Some lapped up these childish antics as the prerogative of stardom, though it was noticed that Brel's unmannerly anti-clericalism was not bestowed on the Sisters of Cluny who ran Sainte-Anne, the settlement's main educational establishment for girls, where, willingly, he conduct-ed lectures about composition to the pupils, and Maddly dancing classes, just as Gauguin had given painting lessons in the same building.

Ecclesiastical digits were poked into recreational pies too. The cler-gy censored films shown in either of Hiva-Oa's two 'cinemas': draughty halls with window curtains, hard benches, archaic projectors and no ice-cream during the intermissions. Most customers defected when Brel obtained more sophisticated equipment from Claude Lelouch, and began presenting movies like Cocteau's *La Belle Et Le Bête* after persuading the council to construct a screen wall in the football stadium.

Determined that he and Maddly 'must earn our presence here', Jacques next invested in his own jeep to more conveniently reach outlying hamlets as his intervention in parochial affairs increased. A still-abundant cascade of songwriting royalties brought in more than enough to subsudize his next major acquisition. Christened *Jojo*, his yellow aeroplane was licenced to carry eight persons, and could stay airborne for up to six necessary hours on one tankful in order to cover hundreds of sea miles. It was also sufficiently hardy to cope with the extremes of monsoon and drought, but only a pilot as skilled as Brel was equal to unforeseeable hazards like one Marquesa runway obstructed by a grazing mare indifferent to the flying machine hurtling towards her.

Jacques' reputation in the cockpit had preceded him, and the acceptance by the Tahitian authorities of his Swiss certificate was virtually by pedantic return of post. Brel then took it upon himself to speed up parachuted deliveries within the Marquesas as well as becoming a one-man emergency service. This was exemplified when, assisted by a mere child, the decision faced by an isolated doctor of saving either a woman in agonised labour or the forthcoming baby was lifted from him by Brel who transported all of them from Motu Anakee, rising from the ocean like the tip of an iceberg, to the less primitive medical amenity on Hiva-Oa.

When most inhabitants of the islands contemplated Jacques Brel later, they thought less of the illustrious *chansonier* than a decent if outspoken cove given to such inspiriting acts of humanity. A less celebrated instance of his receptiveness to the wants of his neighbours was when Marie-Henriette, a blind spinster of the parish, pleaded with Marc Bastard for an introduction to Brel, having grown up in Paris with his music. Beyond her wildest dreams, the voice on the radio during her unlit girlhood brought the consequent evening of wine and small talk to a close that time would never erase by tuning his guitar and serenading her for over an hour with *chansons* old and new.

For Marie-Henriette, he may have previewed further items - several co-written with Maddly - that had come to fruition during the millenia that had gone by since he sailed from Antwerp. He threw away more than he kept because, almost without exception, they mined the old seams - 'songs that have been in my head for the last fifteen years'. A case in point was 'La Cathédrale' which, though first committed to paper as the *Askoy* negotiated the Cornish coast, rehashed a pot-pourri of ideas dating from as far back as 'Le Plat Pays'. Shunning the Pacific sun, he'd retire indoors to snatch up his six-string or plug in an imported electronic keyboard with four octaves, chord buttons and an auto-rhythm component that imposed bossa-nova, slow rock, waltz, disco, march and so forth onto whatever he was pressing to create what were, more often than not, just vibrations hanging in the sultry air.

More often than bringing anything as tangible as a *chanson* into being, he peppered his talk with what he was going to do: ten novelettes about incidents in his life under the umbrella title *How To Write A Song*; a comedy musical, and the completion of memoirs that he'd started to dictate to Maddly until it became too much like hard work.

The most visible signs of creativity from him were elaborate repasts prepared with the self-absorption of a witch doctor mumbo-jumboing some magic potion. He'd insist that the eating of them be as correct as the farewell to Cesare. Diners would be subjected, therefore, to a composite of candlelit Belgian army regimental dinner and Polynesian *tamara* ('great meal').

Those welcomed at any given feast were hand-picked from a cast as variegated as that in a disaster movie: a couple of nuns, Marc and Paolo, one of the grocers, the pilot of the 'plane from Tahiti, Matira, Marie-Henriette and Guy Rauzy, Atuona's mayor - all from a circle of those that hadn't tried to insinuate themselves into it solely because Brel was famous. He'd always derived malicious glee from snubbing people like that.

Gauguin had gone a step further by associating almost exclusively with the natives, but Brel - though he liked them, by and large - was leery of their discovery since of a franc's true worth. It wasn't so easy for Europeans to exploit them as it used to be. With intrinsically shoddy indigenous produce prized by naive *popaa* as much as the hand-mirrors, rotgut liquor and like cheap trade goods had been by the Polynesian savages of de Bougainville's day, the *fares* themselves were now instigating much of the exploiting that went on all over Polynesia - particular from those immigrants they presumed had wealth beyond calculation; among them Marlon Brando (who'd fallen in love with Tahiti during the shooting of *Mutiny On The Bounty* in 1961), Dolly Parton, George Harrison and others who holed themselves up in Pacific seclusion.

Brel was inducted into the wiles of the Polynesian by Bastard *père et fils*. For Marc, he penned 'Voir Un Ami Pleurer' - about his friend's wife leaving him. Jacques also displayed a fondness for Paolo in excess of that he'd ever shown any of his children - of whom he spoke so rarely that many islanders didn't realise that he had any.

Chantal, France and Isabelle were, however, all too real to Maddly who may have been justified in seeing them as more of a threat than the wife - as they might have been in thinking that she had taken Papa out of circulation to better poison his mind against them, and that she loved him for his wealth - especially after he transferred the administration of Éditions Pouchenel from Miche to a chartered consultant.

Maddly had hardened his heart against France in Martinque, hadn't she? Why had Isabelle received only one birthday card from him in three years, eh? Yet when Papa remembered their anniversaries, he'd send - in deteriorating handwriting - affectionate greetings with no reference to past unpleasantnesses. A longer letter than usual (from 'your old man') wended over the waves to Chantal and husband Michel in 1976 after the birth of Jacques' first grandchild, Melanie.

A photograph of Melanie stood on the mantelpiece alongside keepsakes like an ivory elephant that had once belonged to Romain Brel. Jacques also remained as in touch with the old country as he was able via the radio and perusal of *Le Point*, *Paris-Match* and other journals that trickled through to the Marquesas.

Still a self-improver - if a less purposeful one now - he'd slip into abstractions as classical music (Schubert of late) effused from the record-player. He also joined the local library and re-read middle-brow books he knew backwards, but, after limbering up with a chapter or two of, say, de

Maupassant, he sometimes meandered into the small hours with Kierke-gaard, Freud - or Nietzsche whose personal credo was that marriage and family were incompatible with a life of constant creativity.

Back home, self-deception, genuine belief and the balm of ignorance were jumbled as Brel's incommunicado enigma deepened with not a new melody or lyric heard from him officially for ages. An unreachable object of fable, he still engrossed countless faithful who expected him to re-emerge from Rip Van Winkle-esque slumber, recovered and contemporary, to debunk the notion of permanent exile nurtured by the likes of *Paris-Match* with its article about 'the strange fate that chose Jacques Brel at the summit of his glory'.

A legend took root, and far-fetched rumours abounded about what had happened to Jacques Brel. Mention of him brought out uncanny and contradictory accounts of what people claimed to have seen or heard, but no-one could cite a precise source of information as he became, according to *Time*, 'an almost fictional figure even to his countrymen'. Nevertheless, like the Loch Ness Monster, there'd been sightings. Someone would swear that Brel had been observed plucking guitar in a cocktail jazz combo as customers chattered in a Hawaiian bar. Someone else would insist that, wild and pathetic, he was prowling an otherwise uninhabited peninsula like some mad Robinson Crusoe. There were even cynics who theorized that his 'cancer' had been a pretext for him to seek refuge from fame - like Bob Dylan's 'motorcycle accident' had been in 1966.

Dylan's broken neck had mended and he'd made his comeback, but Brel could not permit himself the same luxury of hope. Furthermore, mosquitos and the mind-clouding humidity of Hiva-Oa were not suitable for a man with respiratory problems, despite the ventilator system he'd had built in the house. Amid a gathering infirmity that would curtail his driving of jeep and aircraft, he seemed lost without Maddly, more a hospital orderly than passionate inamorata these days. The haplessness of her devotion cut ever more deeply as she ministered to his day-long needs; let him fulminate and bluster home truths without reproach, and talk him through his latest paranoia: that a massive overdraft was besieging Éditions Pouchenel's ledgers.

As if blowing the sparks of optimism, he marshalled enough energy to touch base in Paris in 1976 and, during the same visit, manage two trips to Brussels, mainly to play company director during meetings about finances, and for a residential examination by Edith Cavell's finest. They were impressed at his abstention - with apparent ease - from smoking, and the rounder face and tauter skin that were accentuated by the reappearance of his whiskers. Outward evidence of improving health was at variance with the oscillating pains that kept prostrating Brel, but the cancer, said Dr. Nemry, seemed to have burnt itself out. Nevertheless, he ought to come back for a check-up every six months. Had he considered moving back to Brussels? If not, the nearest clinic to Hiva-Oa was Los Angeles via Tahiti and Hawaii - but specialist treatment there might not be possible on the strength of foreign medical notes.

Before leaving Belgium, he slotted in a conciliatory meal with Miche, and received France at the clinic. She had bought him a cake and a rose, but, not offering her a seat, he dismissed her after a perfunctory exchange as if to a common acquaintance. For her part, France had everything and nothing to say to him as he came to confront the fact that, despite everything the doctors told him, the disease would eat him up. He was trying to alleviate this understanding by presupposing that France hadn't seen the last of him, and that there'd be another day on which to bridge the abyss between them.

To those who knew him less well, Jacques seemed philosophical in a manner peculiar to himself. At a *soirée* in Paris, who should he bump into but Edouard Molinaro. Outside on the boulevard, they were reliving *Mon Oncle Benjamin* when a taxi-driver skidded to a halt and jumped out, leaving an open-mouthed passenger and a line of seething motorists behind him. He panted up to Brel whose conditioned reflex was not to lose a fan by telling him to buzz off, but to listen courteously to a tongue-tied enquiry about when he was going to be to be back on the boards. 'I think that they're preparing different sorts of boards for me,' he replied drily.

As a beehive can function for some time after losing its progenitive queen, so had home-reared pop without Jacques Brel, its Grand Old Man. While his comeback was seen as inevitable by diehard devotees like the cab driver, marginal enthusiasts had drifted away to fresh entrapments. Commercially, he'd been overtaken by old rival Charles Aznavour who was also charging ahead in English-speaking countries with such as a bill-topping season at the London Palladium with Vikki Carr. London recording dates in 1973 had spawned two huge hits, 'The Old Fashioned Way' and, Barclay Records' most lucrative international earner, 'She' - that, if atypical of his *oeuvre*, was to brand Aznavour for years as the saccharine antithesis to truculent Brel.

Charles was the only Gallic solo vocalist to top the UK chart, although 'Je T'Aime...Moi Non Plus', Serge Gainsbourg's duet with English actress Jane Birkin had wrested Creedence Clearwater Revival from Number One in late 1969. The number had been recorded originally by Gainsbourg and Brigitte Bardot, but, uneasy about its mimicking of lingering *carezza*, she had persuaded Barclay to cancel its release. Instead, composer Serge exuding the breathy sentience of one who has been sprinting - recorded it with Birkin, the 'constant companion' he'd met on the set of a 1967 movie. Notoriety procured via a BBC ban caused its abrupt deletion by Philips but, unworried by moral opprobrium, other labels took up the slack, and it zoomed into Top Tens throughout Europe whilst wavering in the lower reaches of the US *Hot 100*. 'Je T'Aime...Moi Non Plus' had enjoyed a further few weeks in the UK hit parade when repromoted in 1974, but chart performances of further Gainsbourg discs were confined to France - though the artist's occasional outrages on its chat-shows were deemed newsworthy in those foreign regions that recalled his and Jane's erotic grunts and moans.

Tittle-tattle about Johnny Hallyday's stormy marriage to Sylvie Vartan and a more recent hip operation kindled headlines too as he evolved into less France's Presley than its 'answer' to Cliff Richard in that he was (and is) one of few Gallic singers in artistic debt to US and British pop to be beheld with anything approaching awe beyond the republic's frontiers. Several degrees from obvious bandwagon-jumping, Hallyday thrived on a hip sensibility demonstrated by his hiring of fashionable studios in North America, and employment of US session musicians prominent on 1975's *Flagrant Délit* which, like most of his post-*Olympia '67* albums, embraced some Hallyday originals. After teaming up with country-rock *chanteuse* Emmylou Harris for a bi-lingual 'If I Were A Carpenter' in 1985, he would be hammering on foreign doors yet in the mid-1990s with an all-English album and a concert debut at the Royal Albert Hall.

Well before that, Claude François stole a march on Hallyday when 1976's 'Tears On The Telephone' minced into Britain's Top 40. However, it was amassed royalty pay-outs for 'My Way' that had bought him a mansion near Fontainbleau, his final home.

Sacha Distel's best-remembered moment outside France had come with ambulant 'Raindrops Keep Falling On My Head' from 1969's Oscar-winning *Butch Cassidy And The Sundance Kid*. He was not to make much more than the mildest ripples afterwards. Nonetheless, he retained his pulling power in cabaret throughout the globe - unlike Adamo who, though million-selling 'Petit Bonheur' confirmed his status as a national pop attraction, could not duplicate this feat to any large extent in other territories. Jacques Dutronc could no longer take hit records for granted either - so he'd settled down as a 'personality' on French television panel games.

There was a sense of hangover in Gallic pop, what with 'Sugar Baby Love' - shooby-doo-wahs, insane falsetto and spoken bridge passage - *the* hit of 1974, and its perpetrators, The Rubettes, touted in the French press as 'les nouveaux Beatles'. Just as these white-capped Londoners had shut down a translated cover, so Ian Dury vanquished Patrick Duvet and his Sweet Perversions' Frankish version of his 'Sex And Drugs And Rock And Roll' in 1977. Other failed heists of British chartbusters were symptomatic of creative bankruptcy in French and Belgian pop. By the mid-1970s, no less derivative talent surfaced that measured up to Hallyday, Distel or any older contenders who, like the aliens clogging up the charts, were still forever on TV screens, on sell-out barnstormers or blaring from radio and jukebox. For all the 'good' foreheads, chicken necks and belts loosened to the last holes, they still intrigued the young hopeful, envious of their unquiet pasts.

Onto Jacques Brel's frail shoulders thus was pressed the mantle of Howard Hugues of Gallic pop. He might have abandoned the world, but the world hadn't abandoned him - not while factories were in full production, repackaging his albums, and *Jacques Brel Is Alive And Well*

And Living In Paris was keeping his work before the public elsewhere. In 1976, Miche was at large at both the opening night and the revels at Annabel's night club that followed when the authorized Greenwich Village production had come to London's Roundhouse with Mort Shuman[1] understudied by a nervous Kenny Lynch.

Unsolicited covers were still swelling Éditions Pouchenel coffers too. With Carl Wilson on lead vocals, the Beach Boys had taped a hitherto unreleased 'Seasons In The Sun' in 1968. Present at the session[2] was guitarist and arranger Terry Jacks. This former mainstay of Canadian group, The Poppy Family, logged the rendition of the Brel number and disappeared into the Californian night.

Six years later, he eased it from his memory bank; 'lightened up' the last verse; altered the rhythmic accents of the chorus, and sang it himself as the first release by his own Goldfish company. 'It was an inventive treatment,' admitted Rod McKuen (while not granting Jacks a composing credit), 'so I was very glad. He'd taken a song of mine that hadn't been a hit, and made something of it.' Both of them made something of it when currency changed hands for sales of over six million copies. After heading the British chart for a month, Terry followed up with 'If You Go Away': not as gigantic a hit, but enough of one to warrant a second gold disc in March 1977.

Less prominent respects were paid to Jacques by such as Scotland's bombastic Sensational Alex Harvey Band who bedecked 'Next' with both a string quartet and a heavy metal touch-up as the title track of a 1975 album. That David Bowie was still a big Brel admirer too as instanced by his mid-1970s revivals of 'Amsterdam' and, still in his show in 1996, 'My Death'. Furthermore, the hook-line of Bowie's 'Rock 'N' Roll Suicide' quoted 'You're Not Alone (Jef')', and words to 1978's 'Sons Of The Silent Age' were allegedly compiled by the random juxtaposition ('cut-up') of the librettos to 'Old Folks' and 'Sons Of'. Brel had also tinged pieces like 1973's 'Time', a lyrical blending of 'My Death' and Chuck Berry's 'Reelin' And Rockin'', but suffused with Bowie's innate resourcefulness.

As far removed from 'The Legend Of Xanadu' as Bowie now was from Feathers and Anthony Newley, Ken Howard and Alan Blaikley furnished lyrics where needed to *Few And Far Between*, a 'work' by Jean Musy, a bearded Frenchman of similar musical background to François Rauber. Overlooked in 1975, *Few And Far Between* was as mournful as a seagull's cry, particularly after 'Remorse' chased 'Radiance' into 'Child In The Rain' - which I understand to be about a couple whose emotional bonds loosen following the loss of a child whose baleful presence encircles a house in the throes of Yuletide jollifications. It is questionable whether such a *lied* would have been envisaged without Brel's - and Rauber's - pioneering accomplishments.

Consciously or not, Brel also coloured selected items by artists as implausible. The late Harry Nilsson's 'Easy For Me', for example, was an outline of mixed feelings about a dowdy spinster in the same private hell as Scott Walker's 'Rosemary' and its Brel reference points - while, from 1977, Steve Winwood's 'Midland Maniac' featured disconcerting breaks in tempo that echoed the subject's elations and depressions *à la* 'Jef', prior to suicide.

That same year, Brel spilt over into the Blank Generation in which, as punk fanzine *Sniffin' Glue* specified, all you needed were three chords. Brussels threw down a gauntlet with "'Ça Plane Pour Moi', a smash for former department store salesman Roger Jovret who as 'Plastic Bertrand' was added to the meagre list of world-famous Belgians. Within punk's two-minute bursts of aural debris also stood Tom Robinson who was to blast up a rewording of 'Les Bourgeois' - as 'Yuppie Bourgeois Scum' - before seated pupils and their with-it headmaster at Eton public school. From out of the sub-cultural woodwork too had crawled Magazine, whose 'The Light Pours Out Of Me' was penned by Mancunian leader, Howard Devoto, so conscious of its similarity to Brel's 'La Lumière Jaillira' - 'the light gushes out' - that he'd be given to breaking into French whilst performing it.

Significantly, Devoto was to move to Paris - as was Wreckless Eric, a more prominent New Wave songwriter mindful of Brel. The seedy spectaculars of Eric's Len Bright Combo would include 'Julie' - whose sexual athleticism went horribly wrong - 'Someone Must Have Nailed Us Together' - a joyless marriage - and 'Selina Through The Windshield' in which the marketing department of a hair-spray firm affirmed the prod-

uct's lasting hold by crashing a car containing model Selina who was reduced to a bloody pulp but, never mind, her stiffened mane still looked
OK. May I also put forward the raw information, lest we forget, that that
mighty Cerberus the Reading *Evening Post* wrote of my own *What A
Difference A Decade Made* album that 'on occasions, the delivery and
style crossed the influences of Brecht and Brel'?

Inhabiting an artistic area bordered by Brel too were punk founding fathers such as Lou Reed, Iggy Pop, Bryan Ferry - and Ian Dury, described
with vague accuracy in another British daily as 'a sort of dirty old man
of punk' as he spat out in Oi! Oi! Cockney his perspectives on London's
sleazy-flash low-life.

Most new movements that were baring their teeth to the world passed
Jacques Brel by in his Polynesian hideaway. Yet, shortly after he'd jet-
ted back to Hiva-Oa, he felt unexpectedly homesick for Europe. This was
sublimated by the composing of 'Les Remparts de Varsovie' ('The Walls
Of Warsaw') - women as perhaps an expanded metaphor for the imagined or otherwise fiscal difficulties fermenting in the Éditions Pouchenel
offices - and in the buying of land on a hill near the airstrip with a spell-
binding view of nearby Motu Anakee and the splendour of a bay where
dolphins gambolled. By applying for planning permission to build a
house there, Brel burnt his bridges more decisively than the sale of the
Askoy had been a few months earlier.

It would require, nonetheless, an outlay of cash that could, he conjectured, provoke pointed questions when next he communicated with Éditions Pouchenel - whose only consistent money-spinner were his *chansons*, but how much longer would it be before returns on even 'Seasons
In The Sun' diminished? How much longer would anything be? With his
songwriting well not as dry as folk suspected, Jacques sounded out Gerard Jouannest, François Rauber, Charley Morouani and Eddie Barclay
about routing 'some nonsense' for a new album. He concluded each letter by signing himself 'Old Brel'.

NOTES

1. Shuman had found it convenient to take up permanent residency in Paris. Pop obeys no laws of natural selection - which is why, though a debut solo album, La Mort, *had flopped, consequent releases had elevated old Mort to a modicom of renown as a* chansonier *in France. Like Aznavour did before recording in English, he surrendered the fine tuning of his verses to others because, although he spoke French fluently, 'it's very hard to write lyrics in another language. It's full of nuances and I don't feel qualified to write in it.'*

2. In which they also finished 'Cease To Exist' (retitled 'Never Learn Not To Love'), a composition by the homicidal Charles Manson

Chapter Ten
'Le Temps Qui Passe'

Being awash with medications for a debilitating disease that was losing him the race against death was not the firmest foundation for Jacques Brel to resume recording - or was it? As Elvis Presley was about to demonstrate, a pop bereavement could hoick up annual sales from tens of thousands to millions. Before they'd even wiped away the tears, music business supremos would be obligated to meet demand aroused by a life cut short. However much it hurt to do so, they'd have to sanction the rush-release of product while the corpse was still warm - because no matter how poor the entertainer in question's latest disc, it would be bequeathed with a 'beautiful sadness' that would cause even the most peripheral fans to clasp him to their bosoms at least as tightly as they once did. In their heads, he'd be visualized forever in some fixed attitude at the zenith of his powers.

Death would also impede objective criticism. That fate had decreed that the cancer was malignant, and that Brel was to open the door to eternity not long after he sang his last note on tape compounds an involuntarily over-personal consideration of his final *chansons*. Because he found the emotional detachment to tackle those touching hardest on his physical constitution and the phantoms engulfing him is testament to either resignation or relaxed equilibrium, but even if you've only a glimmer of its maker's history, you cannot convince yourself easily that there're only album tracks by a highly-paid pop singer.

For those who collate macabre allusions on record[1], there are many hours of enjoyable time-wasting on Brel's valedictory LP, Chilling lines on 'Orly', for example, may be seen as expressive of the writer's wearied amazement that he was still clinging to life. Morbid lyricism in 'Voir Un Ami Pleurer'[2] and further references to imminent death in other tracks are also obvious to music lovers with better things to do. When studying 'Viellir' with a view to translating it, Mort Shuman understood that 'he (Brel) sensed that he was going and said that he'd like to see a little more of the sky first'.

Without the benefit of hindsight, however, there was every reason for most of his devotees to believe that Brel's 'wilderness years' were behind him, that his health problems were under control, that everything would be OK again, just like it was before he gave up concerts to fritter away his talent and capital on projects that were more intriguing conceptually than in often ill-conceived practice. The uneven quality of his celluloid escapades, his vinyl silence and revelations about his private shortcomings had made the public at large wiser to him, and, to some fans, it was Jacques Brel's misfortune to live on after he'd dumped the bulk of his artistic load.

Yet, nourished by half-truths and media fiction, myth had bestowed a near-superhuman aura on the flesh-and-blood mortal that had generated it - though it was partly the recognition of that very mortality that had enticed him back to the studio. Too much would be expected of Brel, whether the new record was good, bad or, worse, ordinary. A glorious past was a near-impossible yardstick for him to overcome - as impossible as Muhammad Ali regaining his heavyweight title in 1975.

Brel was, however, beyond caring about surpassing any previous standards. The gilding of his legend didn't matter now. The type of well-meaning doctor who sugared bad news, Arthur Gélin had pinned the odds of his patient pulling through at fifty-fifty - a sweet lie that Brel had not swallowed during preliminary work on the album in Hiva-Oa. Armed with just under twenty proposed items - detailed demo tapes, lyrics with no music and nebulous ideas computed in his brain - he and Maddly commenced a reposeful journey to Paris via California and Martinique in August 1977[3].

The flight from Fort de France was the final sanctuary before Jacques would no longer be able to back down, not succumb to not so much a temptation as an impulse to squander some of the precious time he had left - closeted in a subterranean studio, his headphoned ears like braised chops, his vocal cords getting increasingly more tattered, his skull splitting with neuralgia. It was true that, if he lost his nerve, he could always catch the next flight back to the wool-gathering indolence of Hiva-Oa - but, like the Boy who cried Wolf, any further talk of another album would then be shrugged off by the stalwarts to whom he'd communicated not even an approximate date of touch-down at Charles de Gaulle International Airport.

He wanted his return to be so unapproachably low-key as to be almost cloak-and-dagger. After contriving to shuffle out of the glass-domed terminal unnoticed to the taxi rank, Jacques and Maddly - with no prior reservation - put up in a lowly hotel near the Raubers' apartment off the Avenue des Champs-Élysées. Only Dr. Gélin was made aware that they were cocooned there before Brel was ready to face the music. After the best part of a week, the couple checked out. With Jacques' face beaming from the depths of brimmed hat and sunglasses, they showed up at *chez Rauber* where there had always been an open invitation to stay.

François was saddened by Jacques' steadfast refusal to contact or be contacted by any members of his family, going as far as forgoing urgent treatment in keeping Gélin - still in constant touch with Miche - in the dark about his present whereabouts. Fear of his cover being blown broadened to Brel relaying his felicitations rather than speak person-to-person when Clairette Oddera rang the Raubers from Canada.

The secret had to be shared, however, with Gerard Jouannest who, dropping everything, came over to give his opinion on what Jacques had to offer. Nothing of unreserved brilliance leapt out of Rauber's cassette machine however much Gerard willed it. The lyrics were as ageless as ever, but the melodies, he told François and Jacques, were monotonous for the most part, but, outfitted with suitably inventive arrangements of diverting instrumental timbres, they could be made to pass muster.

He would also remark that Jacques' vocal resonance had deepened to bass-baritone. Nevertheless, it regained its higher register as the team muddled through exploratory rehearsals round Gerard's piano at the house in Rue De Verneuil that he shared with a then absent Juliette Greco. Brel's expressed hopes of decamping for a recording complex in Switzerland had to be thwarted, but, no longer the night bird, he got his way over the musicians working conventional Parisian office hours with an 8 a.m. start and an hour off for lunch.

When the day's toil was over, he would repair perhaps to a sumptuous restaurant meal or, defying doctor's orders, hazard getting mellow in clubs that were attractive for their strict membership controls, tariffs too highly priced for Joe and Joan Average, lighting that made all look suntanned and fit, and a firm stipulation that no photographers were to be admitted. From a retinue that frequently included Maddly, her mother and Evelyne, her sister, someone would usually be delegated to keep sober enough to watch over him when his head drooped or his laughter got shrill.

The word got out that he was back, and there wasn't a newspaper editor in France who wouldn't promise a fortune for a Brel exclusive or an up-to-the-minute photo. *Paris-Match* hooked the biggest fish with several shots (including one of Jacques threatening the photographer) spread over two autumn editions.

He was also the most wanted party guest in the city. A forgathering in his honour at Lino Ventura's house brought together representatives from almost every trackway of Jacques' professional life in Paris. The most piquant reunion was with Georges Brassens who recalled once more the bag of nerves that had sung to him in the Bobino changing room. That seemed like a previous existence during a companionable evening that bred more selective reminiscences and coded mirth, and was blighted only when the superstitious host and, to a smaller extent, Maddly became unmistakably upset when Jacques' graveyard humour got the better of him.

Eddie Barclay was not in evidence at many of these celebrations - if that's what they were - and looked in at only one of the sessions that he'd block-booked for eight weeks in a studio in Avenue Hoche, a few streets away from the Raubers. It wasn't all smiles between Jacques and Eddie - who had vetoed the Swiss jaunt as too expensive.

The sessions got underway in a mood of evaporating bad grace from Brel, the Barclay label's biggest asset and biggest liability. Seated in the vocal booth, he made clear his desire for it to be as 'live' as possible - no arguments, no overdubs and on to the next number - rather than let gadgetry and superimposition intrude upon the grit by permitting a too premeditated vocal to float effortlessly over layers of treated sound. In any event, it was not beneficial for him to be kept hanging about during some boring mechanical process at the console. Neither was he to risk raising his pulse count by plunging into the heart of those occasional episodes in which a murmured debate about, say, degree of echo on a keyboard track would scale such a height of vexation and cross-purpose that console assistants would slope off for an embarrassed coffee break until the flare-up subsided to a simmering huff.

A discernable sense of urgency was captured through the necessity of getting Jacques' contribution in the can within three takes before fatigue robbed him of even sufficient concentration to decipher jargon-ridden directives through the talkback. As his singing grew more limp and bedraggled, engineers were sometimes thunderstruck at how much more belligerently alive his first raspy crack at a given *chanson* seemed when the tape was rewound. Down in one was 'Les Marquises', blazing with the acerbity of one with enough desolations to start World War III. Indeed, almost everything he did had all the brisk finesse and some of the mistakes - deliberate or otherwise - that only an old pro giving a virtuoso performance could make, but at least it was an artist doing something he was good at, even if he was too far gone to learn new tricks.

When Barclay came by, he spoke of negotiations for his man to make an album of duets with Barbra Streisand that would surely make Jacques something more in the North American 'quality' pop mainstream. Others present looked away, having ascertained - at least subconsciously - that there might be no more Brel for Eddie to release after - or if he even finished - the work in progress. As he had at Lino's get-together, Jacques attempted to defuse the surreal, uneasy atmosphere by jesting about it - and there were recorded moments of levity such as two comic recitations - 'Histoire Française' and 'Le Docteur' - though these, along with 'Le Detour' (a more recent spoken-word piece) were to be remaindered from the album, along with five songs in varying states of completion that an emphatic Brel ordered not to be released, not even posthumously.

Of its twelve selections, nearly half were in a 'ballad' style levelled unswervingly at both the listener to the bedsit stereo and those addressed in the verses whether 'Messieurs les Flamingants' in 'Les F...', 'Le Bon Dieu' (in the familiar 'tu'), or 'Jojo'. No self-indulgent concealment, the latter *chanson* - with the merest adjustment - could be applicable to any departed confidante with whom 'we speak in silence of old times'. The overbearing shadows of 'L'Âge Idiot', 'Fernand' and 'J'Arrive' - and Aznavour's 'Le Palais De Nos Chimères' of 1970 - impinge upon a chorus that began: 'Six feet below ground, Jojo, you are not dead...'

No-one could deny that Brel had kept his lyrical ship on course as most of the tracks were affiliated to some aspect of previous themes. Death was only one of several reiterated as strongly in 1977 as they had been in 1957 and 1967. It was the way he resystemized the old, old messages that made them brand-new all over again.

'Les F...' fired at the same targets as 'Les Flamandes' and 'La La La'. If in more oblique fashion to 'Amsterdam', 'Les Remparts On Varsovie' dealt with prostitution, while 'Orly', like Ces Gens Là', juxtaposed the plight of the poor with romantic trauma - just as 'Voir Un Ami Pleurer' did distant war, pestilence and subways 'full of the drowned' of less head-on significance than an intimate's distress uncovering the 'Jef'-esque inner child in him.

Brel lived to see record store windows bloom with the album's splendour when he and Maddly stopped off in Paris after a late summer holiday in Sicily. Though the musical outcome was as satisfactory as it could have been, Jacques wasn't enamoured with the gatefold jacket's plain-and-simple artwork: his surname printed over a background of a cloudy-blue sky.

He claimed to detest the publicity campaign too. With nothing to lose, he had been in a position to call the shots to Barclay Records about marketing procedure. It was, he said, to be non-aggressive with no sneak previews or even tip-offs about when and where the LP would be available. If there was the slightest security leak, wild horses wouldn't drag him out to utter one solitary syllable on its behalf.

Given the parochial character of the Gallic music business and associated media, this was a tall order - and one that Brel had probably calculated would be disobeyed somehow or other, thus providing the excuse for him to leave the product to fend for itself. He could then leave what he called the 'great sadness' of Paris in a letter to Marc Bastard, and scuttle back to tranquil Hiva-Oa with Maddly. *En route*, he intended to take in Switzerland (to look up old pals from the flying school), Tunisia, Hong Kong, Thailand and India. Life was too short to mess around plugging records on talk shows or pose for any more soft-focus photographs for Barclay.

As the artist wasn't going to co-operate, the company's press office felt justified in interpreting his commands as the Light Brigade had Lord Raglan's at the Crimea. As a result, the approach was as gimmicky as it could be within Brel's prescribed limits. Each review copy was to be sealed in a metal container with a digital lock, see, to build up the tension like a bomb taking forever to explode in a Hitchcock movie. At precisely 12.51 p.m. on 17 November 1977 - the afternoon before it was to be unleashed on the world - telephonists in every branch of Barclay's would transmit the combination to the listed radio stations, television networks and newspaper offices.

First, there'd be the tactile thrill of handling the cover - and in the inner sleeve picture, Jacques Brel looked of such indeterminate age (thanks in part to dark room jiggery-pokery) that he'd emit much of the lustre of a fresh sensation to those young enough not to have fully grasped who he was. Their parents would will the record to top the charts anyway as a verification of the lost value of someone singing a song as opposed to producing a production.

Finally, an element of morbid inquisitiveness - embellished by erroneous hearsay that royalties were to be donated to cancer research - plus Brel's crafty avoidance of interviews, and the mentions of his own inscrutability in 'Les F...' would all add to a determination to pick the bones of meaning from what France's daily *L'Express* had presupposed to be 'the most mysterious album'.

Before the needles slid into the respective vinyl grooves, there'd long been sufficient advance orders on the first pressing of one million to slam it straight in at Number One in all French and Belgian territories. Over six hundred thousand customers stampeded into the shops on the first day as if the new Brel discs and cassettes were being given away, thereby beating the world record set two years earlier by US sales of Pink Floyd's *Dark Side Of The Moon*

Across the time zones, an observedly disgusted Brel had caught the hyped-up first broadcasts on his wireless in Hiva Oa. He remembered the previous spring when Claude François was never off the airwaves after the domestic accident involving high voltage that had dispatched him on 11 March. Like the central figure in 'Le Tango Funèbre', his life - marred by divorce and maladies such as chronic insomnia - was laid bare during a media field day as 'Clo-Clo' was mourned in microcosm as passionately as Elvis Presley had been.

That was what the future held for Jacques Brel too. Other than that, all he had to look forward to was the past. Correspondence from Atuona was full of both retrospection and apologies either in advance for expiring too early or, like England's Charles II, for being so long a-dying.

In July 1978, he fell so ill that it was necessary to fly him to Tahiti as the *Jojo* had flown the woman in labour from Motu Anakee to Hiva Oa. He quantum-jumped further up the scale of emergency when a cancer specialist, Lucien Israel, tut-tutted the invalid's distrust of antibiotics and anticoagulants, and his repudiation of the recommended twice-yearly check-ups. As there was little that could be done in Tahiti to arrest the spreading growth discovered in the remaining lung, Dr. Israel advised praying for a miracle and a post-haste flight to France.

In Paris, escorts steered Brel quickly to the Hotel George V, but this predictable hiding place was rumbled by predatory reporters, and its switchboard jammed with enquiries. Huddled under the bedcovers, Jacques ordered the posting of security guards and such total denial of his presence that even a call from Chantal in Brussels was not put through to a suite as truly impregnable as Howard Hugues' Las Vegas penthouse. Nevertheless, Chantal - if it was her - span what must have been a very likely tale to elicit the intelligence that her father might buy perhaps another year or two of life if he underwent immediate radio- and chemotherapy available at the Hartmann clinic, an outbuilding of the American infirmary in Neuilly - though this would mean a regular run by ambulance from the Franco-Moslem hospital in the suburban calm of Bobigny where he was admitted under the name of 'Jacques Romain'.

False names, decoy tactics and secret destinations did not fool the press, and curtains at both locations would be drawn each morning to reveal a phallanx of newshounds outside the main entrances, the lobby being too crowded with more of the same. As the old stag weakened, the hounds grew bolder - bolder than they'd been at the Brussels Hilton in 1974. One diligent snapshotter perched up a tree, his long-distance lens surveying perpetually what an educated guess said was Brel's window, while, with notebook at the ready, his more brazen colleague from the same journal skulked throughout the duration in the toilets on the same floor in order to buttonhole seat-bound Brel acolytes that had wriggled through the twittering throngs. Another muckraker almost made it through the wall of bodyguards, costumed as a priest come to administer last rites.

Paris-Match outdid competitors again with three candid shots splashed among four pages of commentary in August, and the following month, a feature of comparable length built round a quote about his worsening condition from a 'spokesperson' and a fuzzy double-page picture of a bandage-draped Brel with a bloated face that looked less lived-in than completely derelict, his claw-like fingers clutching two minders holding him upright as he shambled towards a conveyance for Neuilly. 'The way he was treated was absolutely horrid,' lamented Mort Shuman (whose own cancer was to kill him thirteen years later), 'Even the lowliest of dogs has the right to die with peace and dignity. They had no right to humiliate him in the way they did.' Brel's solicitors and the petitioned Parisian judge were of the same mind, and, though thousands of copies had been distributed to newsagents already, the rest of the magazine's September edition was seized on the grounds of gross invasion of privacy.

Death seemed to be sparing the plaintiff as the swelling in his lung shrank from the size of a melon to that of a clementine. This was sufficient for Brel, now bearded to the cheek bones, to purchase from his plight just under a month's respite. He insisted that he was on the mend when by coincidence Claude Lelouch was conducted to a table adjacent to his in a diner where Jacques was spending an evening before a three-week break in the countryside between Geneva and Marseilles. In parenthesis, the next morning, it was necessary to shake off pursuing press by hiding in a closet in the airport's public conveniences for two hours.

Resigned to staying in Europe *pro tempore* with the reckless expectation that he might survive this latest onslaught of symptoms, he and Maddly hunted rural Provence for a house that was less important than the space between it and the nearest neighbours. However, on one such expedition, Jacques perceived the tell-tale pangs - hacking coughs, panting and hampering weight on his chest - that forewarned of another collapse.

He surfaced from delerium on a stretcher being borne into the Franco-Muslim hospital. On the way to Room 305, he stirred, and his sticky eyelids parted as if slit with a knife. There was a flicker of a smile as his hand tightened in Maddly's. Apparently, this had been so much more acute than any previous attack that blood-clotting was obstructing his one remaining bronchial tube. Maddly's glance was all he needed to comprehend that this time Death would take him without effort.

The flame was low as a reported halting but purposeful 'Je ne vous quitterais pas' emerged from his lips when a nurse removed the oxygen mask to let him drink a requested tumbler of Coca-Cola. At 2.30 am on Monday, 9 October 1978, the only sounds audible were the bleep of the cardiograph and the boots of some half-awake night porter clacking about echoing corridors when Jacques Brel, his eyes dull like vapoured glass, sank into a coma. His feeble breathing slackened, and, while Paris yet slept, the spark went out.

NOTES

1. Death Discs *by A. Clayson (Sanctuary, 1997) is recommended.*
2. *Covered by Juliette Greco who had begged to issue her version before Brel's original.*
3. *The month of Elvis Presley's fatal heart attack*

Epilogue

Brel Epoch

In Holland where she'd spent the weekend, it was dawn when Chantal was shaken from her dreams to take a call from Arthur Gélin. During her stop-starting drive through rush-hour Brussels a few hours later, she was misted by regret at not visiting Papa in his Pacific island shangri-la as she looked at without seeing the chalked headlines on newspaper stands and electronically-transmitted images of him in electrical goods shops as the car radio babbled like an idiot relation. The morning news was how Pierre Brel, spluttering into his shaving mirror, learned of the release of his little brother's soul.

Even today, members of the family can hardly bear to touch upon that creepy day. One or two sick jokes were already circulating among the press corps awaiting them at the hospital's black carnival. After the embalmer's priority attentions, the body had been laid in an open casket amid the white statuettes and candles of the chapel where Miche, the daughters, Maddly, the Raubers and others close to him clustered. At this lying-in-state, France's had been the most quoted remark: 'He's happier where he is now' - and, afterwards, a loitering photographer freeze-framed the embrace of wife and mistress, united in grief.

Flags were already at half-mast, and, into the evening, Gallic wireless stations broadcast the dead man's music continuously in place of listed programmes. As twilight thickened, *France-Soir* - the organ that had once urged him to run back to Brussels where he belonged - had banner-headlined Brel's passing across its front page with the same type it had used to announce the death of Pope John Paul I only a fortnight before. 'Brel will always live,' proclaimed the article, 'He is the least dead among all of us.'

Meanwhile, journalists on the morning tabloids were shoving together adulatory tributes, quite rightly allowing that Brel's was a greater loss to popular culture than that of Clo-Clo, but distorting the old stories even more. Not knowing or caring anywhere as much about him, sister periodicals abroad assumed that their readers didn't either. In Britain for example, there were obituaries in broadsheets like *The Guardian* and *The*

Times, but not a word in the *Daily Express* and most of the other tabloids about his death or the spectacle of his send-off: a cavalcade of police motorcycle outriders as the coffin was transported like crown jewels to Charles de Gaulle airport on 14 October for shipment to the South Pacific.

While Miche returned to everyday activities in Brussels - where she is still based (as are most of her six grandchildren and their mothers) - Maddly would accompany the coffin to Altuona, where she was to remain for a while prior to gravitating back to France to do whatever energy and willingness would do to further the Brel cause. Palpable evidence of her devotion was to include published memoirs and reflections of her life with Brel, and hands-on involvement in *Jacques And Maddly*, a musical drama that centred on the final years in the Marquesas - where his remains had been interred with the simplest of ceremonies in the small necropolis on Hiva Oa, a fastness forever unreachable and outlandish to the commonplace Brussels pen-pusher, supermarket check-out girl or asphalt-layering road-mender. Yet, to one such as this, Jacques Brel would always be eternally Belgian.

The country was to declare 2003 the Year of Jacques Brel, an omnipotence epitomised by an exhibition in Brussels containing such minutiae as a comb with a few of his hairs entangled in it, and a baguette half-eaten by him. Yet, though Belgium thus displayed an official - and, sometimes, severely tested - pride in him, even at the very end of his days, Brel re-opened so deep a wound with 'Les F...' that, just as news of Elvis Presley's death had provoked a malicious cheer in a basement club frequented by London punks, so a person or persons unknown took the trouble to spray 'BREL EST MORT. HURRAH!' along railway cuttings between Brussels and Liège. Conversely, the Metro station behind Vanneste and Brel was renamed after the firm's most famous and notorious employee.

If not now the biggest ape in its particular cardboard jungle, Vanneste and Brel was still prospering - and, with modernized interiors, other of Jacques' old haunts in both Brussels and Paris still bore their original appellations, though the Théâtre Des Trois Baudets had become La Locomotive, a discotheque with occasional 'live' acts. Marking the demise of the music hall too, cabaret clubs like L'Écluse had closed down altogether.

The *chanson*, however, prevails, albeit in more markedly differing regionalized shades. Canada, for instance, leans towards jazz while acts from Britanny and Provence betray roots in traditional folk music, exemplified today by Toulouse's remarkable Les Fabulous Troubadours. Likewise, Belgium still spawns contemporary talent such as Michel Desaubies and Bernard Bruel. Across France too, up-and-coming *chansoniers* like Benjamin Biolay and Christophe Miossec ring changes and sing fine songs, but somehow quite a lot of them look and sound just like Jacques Brel.

One that doesn't is MC Solaar - alias Claude M'Barali, an African immigrant to Paris - who, in the 1990s, wove *chanson* into the *braggagio* of rap (or was it *vice-versa*?), and was described by Juliette Greco - still with her finger on the pulse - as 'a gardener of words'. If appearing as different to a *chansonier* in the grand tradition as the Moon to the Earth, this prime executant of French-language rap represents not only a new direction in his 'sampling' from revered *chanson* sources (notably on the albums *Prose Combat* ('fighting prose') and 1997's *Parardisiaque*), but also a culmination of all that has gone before in his Brel-esque dialectical declamations of swelling anger and alienation; commentaries on social iniquities and hypocrisy; self-denigrating outlines of his amorous adventures; use of acoustic guitar and orchestral strings, and a flair for rapid-fire literariness and wordplay, albeit welded to disco rhythms and perfunctory - or totally absent - melodies.

In Anglo-Saxon areas, however, any debt to Brel by Grandmaster Flash, MC Hammer, LL Cool J and other of MC Solaar's role-models was not acknowledged, and he had even more negligible effect on the one-line lyrics and recurrent synthesizer *arpeggios* that were common ingredients of trance, techno, acid-house, hip-hop, trip-hop, jungle, ragga and further sub-divisions that out-of-touch pop pundits tended to lump together as 'The Modern Dance'. This was partly because 'club culture, which doesn't rely so much on spoken language, has opened a lot of doors.' Thus spake Nicolas Godin of Air, a Versailles duo who thus became UK Top Forty contenders in 1998 with 'Sexy Boy', signalling a French invasion of MTV by such as Daft Punk, Motorbass, Cassius, Kid Loco and Mellow.

In Britain, to all intents and purposes, Brel had been the exclusive property of undergraduates flirting with bohemia before becoming teachers.

Any mainstream interest had declined in ratio to Scott Walker's retreat from pop in the early 1970s. The Terry Jacks windfall apart, Brel's output as a composer was unnoticed by everyman for years until the likes of David Bowie, Ultravox and A Teardrop Explodes confessed the influence of him (and Walker). This precipitated belated and frequently empty revaluation by music press hacks as well as the issue of expedient compilations like 1981's *Scott Walker Sings Jacques Brel.*

Throughout the next fifteen years, there were further posthumous resurgences of Brel's popularity. Some came indirectly through cultural burglars like Malcolm McLaren whose *Paris* album featured *chanteuses* of Françoise Hardy vintage. Furthermore, Brel put the icing on songs like Scritti Politti's 'Lions After Slumber' - which borrowed from 1958's 'Litanie Pour Un Retour' - and less specifically on, say, the doom-laden exorcisms of Joy Division. Most of these products attracted as many people who'd read reviews in *The Guardian* as those who'd scanned the *New Musical Express.*

Brel - or, to be precise, his estate - was to derive more pragmatic benefit when 'Jackie', a spin-off single from Marc Almond's *Jacques* tribute album, peaked at Number Six in the UK - and a 'Seasons In The Sun' by Irish 'boy band' Westlife was to be the final British Number One of the twentieth century. Far less impressive commercially but more intrinsically likeable had been a 1988 Brel EP by Nick 'Momus' Currie. Brel was also very much alive and well in Jarvis Cocker's gauche *après*-punk romanticism which drew much from an adolescence spent in Sheffield, a grimy pivot of industrial enterprise closer in character to Brussels than London.

Much as he might gainsay it, Scott Walker is still under the Brel spell too. He'd sunk his teeth into the regrouped Walker Brothers' *Nite Flights* in 1978 and, six years later, the solo offering *Climate Of Hunter* with the same relish as he had 'Jackie' and 'Next'. One critic depicted the latter album as the fount of 'the most terminal songs ever written' - and you can understand why. Like cattle marked for the abattoir - or the soldiers queueing in 'Au Suivant' - most tracks on *Climate Of Hunter* had numbers rather than names. It was just as well with some of them - especially 'Track Seven'. Otherwise, would you request a disc-jockey to spin something called 'Stump Of A Drowner'? Ten years on, Walker hadn't shaken off Brel, as instanced in the very title of challenging *Tilt*'s opening piece,

'Farmer In The City', referencing perhaps 'L'Homme Dans La Cité', the Brel-Rauper opus from 1958.

Tilt would seem almost catchy in comparison to 2006's *The Drift*, embracing a libretto that resembles the plot of some wild dream that seems perfectly comprehendable until the sleeper wakes - or maybe I haven't read the books or seen the films necessary for comprehension - set to tunes that verge on the atonal, and arrangements that seem at times to dart randomly from section to indissoluble section. Fragments of Schoenberg, Penderecki and composers of that 'difficult' persuasion surface - and, though I detected a shadowy link to 'Jailhouse Rock' in 'Jesse' (an abstraction of an imagined conversation between Elvis Presley and his stillborn twin) only drums and electric guitars put *The Drift* even remotely in the realms of pop, even the most morbidly surreal psychedelia.

On a more accessible plain had stood a 1988 reconstruction of *Jacques Brel Is Alive And Well And Living In Paris* at the Donmar Warehouse in Covent Garden, dignified one night by the presence of the widow in the audience. Retaining *de jure* say-so over Éditions Pouchenel copyrights, Miche had encouraged the production team to commission and work from fresh interpretations, recommending those of a Professor Arnold Johnson of Western Michigan University, whose translations she considered more accurate than those of Shuman and Blau - and McKuen. 'Our American producers approached us first of all,' affirmed co-director Sebastian Graham-Jones, 'with the idea of putting on a London production of *Alive And Well*, but we had no interest in it because it's very American college cabaret and shallow, not a fitting tribute. Then when the Brel estate invited us to start from scratch, we jumped at it. Ours is a much darker show. It has a lot more moods to it.'

Even if Jacques Brel had still been around in 1988, how could we have ever known his true feelings about this update of *Alive And Well*? Do we ever see a man? Do we only see his art? I mean this most sincerely, friends. There's no glimmer of an answer to these questions unless we can investigate the impossible: videos of, for example, the domestic scene *chez* Brel in September 1954 when Catherine Sauvage paid her visit; to be a fly on the wall in the dressing room before the last hurrah in Roubaix, or to sample with our own sensory organs Pierre Brel's realisation that his younger sibling was a national icon.

We can also speculate endlessly about how it might have been. Brel could have been surely another Aznavour, selling out a regular month's residency at the Sands in Las Vegas. In dry-cleaned pullover and made-to-measure slacks, he'd stroll down Memory Lane with an amused medley in French and swing gently through 'Seasons In The Sun' - 'we 'ad joy, we 'ad furn/we 'ad seezuns in zuh surn' - before switching gear with sombre 'If You Go Away'. That his latest album, *Brel Sings McKuen*, is much like the one before is sufficient recommendation for those matronly members of his international fan club to continue following him round the world's citadels of 'quality' entertainment.

Yet for a man typecast by tidy-minded journalists as a 'pop singer', he was in truth an odd fish, this Jacques Brel. After a period of appearing to uphold safer showbusiness values, he chose to walk an increasingly rugged artistic pathway that, if not to *Tilt-The Drift* extremes, finally transcended what is generally recognized as pop. He desired but has never been given an entirely new classification for what he did, having concluded that 'making a *chanson* is neither a major nor minor art. It isn't an art at all. It is a very poor domain because it's limited by a whole series of disciplines. There is nothing more exacting than to put a note of music above a word.'

With this in mind, he could have been a catastrophe. While able to hold a tune and find his way around a guitar, he was no hybrid of Scott Walker and Manitas de Plata. More to the point, his early attempts at songwriting aroused little enthusiasm. In truth, he wasn't that brilliant at anything until almost-but-not-quite too late. Yet, as the world continues to discover, Jacques Brel was a possessor of original, if vulnerable, genius rather than anything as common as mere talent.

Appendix One

Can the Anglo-Saxons sing the Gauls?

In spring 1996, just after I completed the first edition of this tome, I undertook a series of one-nighters in the north-east of England with Denny Laine, once of The Moody Blues and then Wings. He and I were also contracted to make ourselves pleasant at a charity record fayre at the University of Northumbria. My motives for partaking in this jaunt were not entirely selfless as it presented an opportunity to plug my literary and musical catalogue (mostly via regional radio shots), and sell and autograph records and books. Certainly, I was looking forward to the ego-massage of being a 'celebrity' again after hermit-like months of driving myself into a clinical depression over Jacques Brel.

Almost three years later, the fellow reared up again when I contributed two tracks - 'Next' and 'Sons Of' - to *Ne Me Quitte Pas: A Celebration Of Jacques Brel* in which a cast ranging from 1960s pop stars to acclaimed denizens of the 'roots' scene delivered a selection of the Great Man's works. It was to be one of *Folk Roots'* 'Albums of the Year', having already attracted rave notices such as 'hugely entertaining. Jacques would've approved' (*Rock 'N' Reel*); 'everything here is pretty much equal to the doomed romanticism that was Jacques Brel's trademark' (*Record Collector)*, and 'these eighteen performances reel you into a complex emotional landscape of understated dynamics and dark aesthetics' (*Folk On Tap*). Next, a revue featuring key participants and embracing linking narrative as well as music went on the road, filling venues with across-the-board audiences of both Brel devotees and those interested generally in Gallic culture. Without exception, response was enthusiastic everywhere, whether Brighton's Barn Theatre, the Chester Festival of Literature, the Tower Arts Centre in Winchester or Whitby Pavilion.

By 2001, the 'English chanson' community was of sufficient immensity to sustain seven consecutive nights at South London's Bread-and-Roses auditorium, and, the following autumn, the release of *Nine Times Two: Contemporary English Chanson*, an album containing two tracks each by nine of its brand-leaders. More insidiously, venues like Brighton's Café Prague, the Blue Hours at Newbury's Greenham Arts Centre,

Club TGV in North London, the Drill Hall up the West End and Reading's Rising Sun Institute were embracing *chanson*, following the example of Pirate Jenny's, a monthly evening in Stoke Newington's Vortex Jazz Bar. Named after a character in *The Threepenny Opera*, during a ten-year run, Pirate Jenny's worked up a mid-week audience for 'quality acts that people rarely get to perform in such a sympathetic context,' remarked its founder and host, Des de Moor, 'No matter how experienced they are, the really top talents always seem to go that extra mile at Jenny's. It's a bit like a mutual support group for misunderstood *chansoniers* and their fans.

'Pirate Jenny's came about in 1994 as a way of presenting meaningful but accessible songs that didn't quite fit either jazz clubs, acoustic folky places or poetry evenings. I started to run into performers with similar interests who had the same problem. Some of them were also doing small theatres, which seemed too formal - so I decided it would be nice if we all had a place to play. Pirate Jenny's was the only club to have regularly sold out the Vortex on a Monday, traditionally the deadest night of the week - with no funding and no media support other than listings. We've always had a respectable crowd - including regulars who come even if they don't know the acts because they respect my judgement'.

The most pivotal event to nudge English chanson from haphazard cells of activity into cohesion - at least in London and the Home Counties - was the launch at Pirate Jenny's of *Ne Me Quitte Pas: Brel Songs By...*, a feather in the cap of Irregular Records (also responsible for *Nine Times Two*). Among those present in both the audience and on the boards were Dave Berry - who had found himself the sudden Presley of the Flatlands after performing in customary cobra-like fashion at 1965's Knokke Song Festival - 'social surrealist performance poet/musician' Attila the Stockbroker ('a huge fan for twenty years, having been introduced to Brel while perfecting my French - or rather Bruxellois - as a member of a wild Brussels rock group, living in a squat in Schaarbeek'); John Forrester, a hard-hitting lyricist with 'the rare gift of turning bare, raw emotion into commercial music' (*Taplas*), and punk methuselah Charlie Harper of The UK Subs. One of many showstoppers was a 'Les Bonbons' from Robb Johnson, who emerged from the folk circuit as the principal catalyst in the development of the movement, principally by establishing Irregular Records. Moreover, the gifted Johnson's compositions have been covered by such disparate artists as bluesman Mike Cooper and cabaret diva Barb Jungr.

Almost as inevitable as Valentino recording 'Kashmiri Song', was Jungr's reinvention of Edith Piaf's 'No Regrets'. Yet if Barb is English chanson's Piaf, its Roy Orbison is de Moor with his supple baritone and a repertoire exemplified by 'Joey's Dream', building from muttered trepidation to neo-operatic anguish.

Conversely, Neurostar, once house band at Club TGV, traded in a unique brand of synthesizer technology and Eurotrashy charm before mainstay Steve Lake went solo, often sharing bills with the remarkable Mark Astronaut, Welwyn Garden City's representative - and, based where London bleeds into Surrey, Project Adorno, who, in a different manner to MC Solaar, superimpose rap - or, as they call it, 'electronic beat poetry' - onto the increasingly more complex grid of English chanson.

What, therefore, is the common denominator? By its most basic definition, 'chanson' means 'song'. This means that the contents of, say, The Pussycat Dolls' *Doll Domination* are like those of *Nine Times Two* just as Mrs. Mills and Theolonius Monk are both pianists. The difference, according to Robb Johnson's haiku-like sleeve notes, is that *Nine Times Two* is 'grown-up songs for grown-up people'.

'English chanson is concerned with a knowledge and understanding of mainland Europe songwriting culture,' opines Attila the Stockbroker, 'and its application in an English context. In this country, few have been prepared to step outside the traditional "folk" or "rock" genres and use what can best be described as the "European cabaret" style - because we have no tradition of this.'

'For me, the parents of English chansons are music hall and the simple popular song of the post-war period,' reflects Barb Jungr, 'which sort of comes into its own in the 1960s and beyond. Think "Pictures Of Lily" by Pete Townshend.'

'There's also the German satirical cabaret tradition,' adds Des de Moor, 'and the Brecht repertoire, and lesser known genres like the *kleinkunst* and cabaret of the Low Countries. All this makes English chanson seem like a slavish imitation of European models, but it's more about a particular attitude to songwriting and a particular kind of mood or feeling - which is to be brave, intelligent, challenging, emotionally sophisticated. Don't be afraid of being poetic and expressive, exploring language and form and of tackling a wide range of big subjects, but keep your work direct and accessible with a dose of wit: the polar opposite of the typically puerile, banal, repetitive and derivative modern chart hit written by committee - except for the accessible bit.'

'There's something in the way sub-text is used,' agrees Barb Jungr, 'the greater emotion, the reaching within for something. There is a musical simplicity that is not naive or dull, but that allows the word, the emotion to lead.'

Project Adorno dispense with melody altogether. Other acts beneath the canopy of English chanson defy succinct description. 'We're a category-obsessed country when it comes to the arts,' concludes Des de Moor, 'and *chanson* falls between too many stools. It's too sophisticated and intelligent for pop, too contemporary and emotional for folk and roots, too simple and accessible to count as art or classical music, too urban-sounding and not exotic enough to be world music, too vocal and text-based and not improvised enough to be jazz. You're also struggling against the British penchant for philistinism and a reluctance to confront emotions except archly and at a distance. Quite a few of us have had to endure critics airing their embarrassment at emotional honesty in public - and as for daring to set poetry to pop music, it's about as suspicious as a red-blooded young lad wanting to prance about in tights at ballet school.'

Information about Ne Me Quitte Pas: Brel Songs By... *and* Nine Times Two: Contemporary English Chanson *and the stage presentation of the former is available via www.alanclayson.com*

Appendix Two

Chronology

*In a man's life, there are two important dates: his birth and his death.
Everything in between doesn't matter much'* - Jacques Brel

1883
Birth of Romain Brel (father) in Zandevoorde, Belgium

1896
Birth of Elisabeth 'Lisette' Lambertine (mother) in Brussels, Belgium

1921
Birth of Georges Brassens
Amand Vanneste founds cardboard carton merchandising company
3 Dec. Marriage of Romain and Elisabeth in Brussels

1922
13 Aug. Birth of Pierre and Nelly Brel (brother and sister) in the
Belgian Congo
Sept. Death of Pierre and Nelly in the Belgian Congo

1923
19 Oct. Birth of Pierre Brel II (brother) in Brussels

1924
Birth of Georges 'Jojo' Pasquier
Birth of Charles Aznavour (Shahnour Verenagh Aznavourian)

1926
30 Dec. Birth of Thérèse 'Miche' Michielsen in Brussels

1929
8 April Birth of Jacques Romain Georges Brel at approximately 3 am in
138, Avenue du Diamant, Brussels
Birth of Jean Corti

1931
Romain Brel becomes co-director of Vanneste and Brel

1933
Birth of François Rauber
Birth of Gerard Jouannest
Birth of Rod McKuen

1934
Sept. Jacques is enrolled at École Saint-Viateur

1936
Birth of Mort Shuman

1940
April Germany invades Belgium

1941
Sept. Jacques commences studies at L'Institut Saint-Louis

1944
Birth of Scott Walker (Noel Scott Engel)
Birth of Maddly Bamy
Sept. Belgium liberated by the Allies

1947
May Publication of the first edition of *Le Grand Feu*, a magazine that contains contributions by Brel
Aug. Jacques starts work at Vanneste and Brel
Dec. Jacques joins La Franche Cordée

1948
1 June Jacques begins military service

1949
1 June Jacques completes military service
Jacques elected president of La Franche Cordée

1950

1 June Marriage of Jacques and Miche in Maison Communale, Brussels

1951

6 Dec. Birth of Chantal (daughter) in Brussels

1952

Jacques adopts the stage alias 'Berol' to sing on *La Vitrine Aux Chansons* radio programme

1953

March Release of first record, 'La Foire'/'Il Y A'
May Jacques performs at Knokke-le-Zoute song festival
1 June Jacques resigns from Vanneste and Brel
20 June Philips recording test in Paris, France
Meeting with Georges Brassens
12 July Birth of France (daughter) in Brussels
Sept. Parisian stage debut at Théâtre Des Trois Baudets, 90, Boulevard de Clichy

1954

July Jacques' debut at the Olympia, 26, Boulevarde Des Capines
First night of month-long tour of France with Catherine Sauvage, Phillipe Clay and Dario Moreno

1955

Release of debut album
May Jacques begins national tour with Suzanne 'Zizou' Gabriello
Oct. Tour of Algeria with Dario Moreno, Sydney Bechet and the Milsons (with Jojo Pasquier)
Nov. Jacques appears at the De La Mer in Amsterdam
Dec. Jojo Pasquier becomes Jacques' general factotum

1956

March 'Quand On N'A Que L'Amour' reaches Number 3 in the national chart

23 July Fourth tour of France with Pierre-Jean Vaillard, Nicole Louvier, Guy Beart and Les Trois Minestrels.
Jacques stars in film short, *La Grande Père De Monsieur Clement*

1957
Release of *American Debut* album by CBS

1958
19 August Birth of Isabelle (daughter)
Charley Marouani becomes Brel's manager

1959
20 Nov. Jacques co-headlines at the Olympia

1962
March Jacques signs to Barclay Records
Oct. Foundation of Éditions Pouchenel

1963
Feb. US stage debut at New York's Carnegie Hall
3 April Jacques presents an edition of *Rendez-Vous De La Musique Europe* radio programme
Jacques narrates a performance of Prokofiev's orchestral fairy tale, *Peter And The Wolf*

1964
January Death of Romain Brel
March Death of Elisabeth Brel
Release in Britain and USA of *Music For The Millions (À L'Olympia)* album

1965
May Performance of *Les Trois Histoires De Jean De Bruges* symphonic poem at the Parisian Conservatory of Music
Oct. Tour of USSR
Dec. One of Jacques' two sell-out concerts at Carnegie Hall is attended by Mort Shuman

1966

June Jacques' first long-haul piloting of an aircraft
Oct. Final concert at the Olympia
Nov. Jacques performs for the first and only time in Britain at London's Royal Albert Hall

1967

16 May Final concert appearance
Jacques stars in first major movie, *Les Risques Du Métier*
Dec. 'Jackie' by Scott Walker reaches No. 22 in UK Top 30

1968

Commencement of three-year run of *Jacques Brel Is Alive And Well And Living In Paris* musical at the Circle In The Square, Greenwich Village, New York
12 Nov. *L'Homme De La Mancha* musical opens at the Théâtre de la Monnaie, Brussels

1969

June *L'Homme De La Mancha* closes at the Théâtre des Champs-Elysées, Paris

1970

27 Jan. Cancellation of *Le Voyage Dans La Lune* musical two days before premiere at the Théâtre de la Monnaie
March Jacques becomes a fully-qualified aeroplane pilot

1971

Film directorial debut with *Franz*
Nov. Maddly Bamy becomes Jacques' constant companion

1973

May *Far West* represents Belgium at Cannes film festival

1974

April 'Seasons In The Sun' by Terry Jacks tops UK chart for four weeks

1 July Jacques gains yachtsman's certificate
24 July Jacques begins proposed circumnavigation of the globe in
L'Askoy II
27 Aug. Death of Jojo Pasquier
Nov. Jacques undergoes major surgery to relieve diagnosed cancer

1975
Nov. *L'Askoy II* docks in Hiva-Oa in the Marquesas.

1976
Jacques rents house in Atuona, Hiva-Oa
Jacques Brel Is Alive And Well And Living In Paris opens at London's
Roundhouse

1977
18 Nov. Release of *Brel*, the last album

1978
9 Oct. Death of Jacques Brel in Paris

Appendix Three

Compositions

Issues of discs by Jacques Brel outside France, Belgium and their dominions were irregular until a posthumous schedule of CD repackagings
and DVDs (notably, 2006's three-disc *Comme Quand On Était Beau* by
Universal) was implemented in Britain, North America and other English-speaking territories. These have included interviews, in-concert performances, film clips - and hitherto unheard items, most controversial-
ly, the 1977 tracks that Brel had deemed too below standard for release.
Commercial pragmatism outweighed his wishes, and these appeared on
2003's *Brel Infinitely* album. Other compositions were performed by Brel
long before he gained his first recording contract. More useful than a dis-
cography, therefore, is the following list of *chansons*, grouped under the
years in which they were first published.

1953
Il Y A/La Foire/La Haine/Grand Jacques (C'Est Trop Façile)/Le Diable
(Ça Va)[1]/Il Nous Faut Regarder/C'Est Comme Ca/Il Peut Pleuvoir/Le Fou
Du Roi/Sur La Place

1955
Il Pleut/La Bastille

1956
S'Il Te Fois/Qu'Avons-Nous Fait Bonnes Gens/Pardons/Les Pieds Dans
Le Ruisseau/Quand On N'A Que L'Amour/Heureux/Les Blés/Ce Qu'Il
Vous Faut

1957
Prière Paienne/L'Air De La Bêtise/Saint Pierre/J'En Appelle/La Bourée
Du Celibataire/Demain L'On Se Marie

1958
Au Printemps/Je Ne Sais Pas/Dors Ma Mie/Dites Si C'Était Vrai/Le
Colonel/L'Homme Dans La Cité/La Lumière Jaillira/Voici/Litanies Pour
Un Retour/L'Aventure/Dis-Moi Tambour

1959
Seul/La Dame Patronesse/La Valse De Mille Temps/Ne Me Quitte Pas/
Isabelle/La Tendresse/Les Flamandes/Voir

1960
La Mort/La Colombe

1961
Je T'Aime/L'Ivrogne/Marieke²/Le Moribund/Le Prochain Amour/Vivre
Debout/Les Prenoms De Paris²/Clara/Les Singes/

1962
On N'Oublie Rien/Les Biches/Madeleine/Les Paumes Du Petit
Matin²/Zangra/La Statue/Les Bourgeois²/Le Plat Pays²/Une Île/
Bruxelles/Le Caporal Casse-Pompom/Rosa²/Les Filles Et Les Chiens/
La Parlote/Les Bigotes

1963
La Toison D'Or/Chanson Sans Paroles/La Fanette/Les Fenêtres/Les
Vieux/Les Toros/J'Aimais/Quand Maman Reviendra

1964
Je Prendrai/Amsterdam/Les Timides/Le Dernier Repas/Les Jardis Du
Casino/Pourquoi Faut-Il Que Les Hommes S'Ennuient (from the film
Un Roi Sans Divertissement)/Titine/Jef/Les Bergers/Le Tango Funèbre/
Mathilde/Les Amants De Coeur/Les Bonbons/Au Suivant

1965
Je M'En Remets A Toi/Il Neige Sur Liège/Ces Gens-Là/La Chanson De
Jacky/Fernand/L'Àge Idiot/Grand-Mère/Les Despèreres/Un Enfant/La
Baleine³/La Sirène³/L'Ouragan³

1967
À Jeun/Fils De/La Chanson Des Vieux Amants/La La La/Les Coeurs
Tendres (from the film *Un Idiot À Paris*)/Le Cheval/Le Gaz/Les Bon-
bons '67/Mon Enfance/Mon Père Disait

1968

Comment Tuer L'Amant De Sa Femme/J'Arrive/Je Suis Un Soir D'Été/
La Bière/L'Éclusier/L'Ostendaise/Regarde Bien Petit/Vesoul/L'Homme
De La Mancha[4]/Un Animal[4]/Dulcinea[4]/Vraiment Je Ne Pense Qu'A
Lui[4]/Je L'Aime[4]/Pourquoi Fait-Il Toutes Ces Choses[4]/Sans Amour[4]/
Le Barbier[4]/Le Casque D'Or De Mambrino[4]/Chacun Sa Dulcinea[4]/La
Quête[4]/Gloria[4]/Aldonza[4]/
Le Chevalier Aux Miroirs[4]/La Mort *[not the 1960* chanson *of the same
title]*/Chanson De Sancho[4]

1969[5]

Allons Il Faut Partir/Chanson D'Adelaide/Chanson De Christophe/La
Leçon De Geographie/Recitatif Lunaire/Chanson De Victorine Differ-
ents Lunaries Choeurs/Chanson De Victorine/Chanson De Cowboy/
Chanson De Cowboy II/Chanson De Christophe Pops Cowboy/Finale

1970[6]

Buvons Un Coup/Mourir Pour Mourir/Les Porteurs De Rapières

1972

La Chanson De Van Horst (from the film *Le Bar De La Fourche*)/

1973

L'Enfance (from the film *Far West*)

1977

Jaures/La Ville S'Endormait/Viellir/Le Bon Dieu/Les F.../Orly/Les
Remparts De Varsovie/Voir Un Ami Pleurer/Knokke-Le-Zoute/Jojo/Le
Lion/Les Marquesas

The pieces below were written between 1948 and 1953

Ballade/Le Troubadour/Bruxelles *[not the 1962* chanson*of the same ti-
tle]*/De Deux Vielles Notes/Belle Jeanette/Les Paves/L'Orage/Les
Deux Fauteuils/Ne Pensez Pas/Les Gens/Departs/Je Suis L'Ombre Des

Chansons/À Deux/L'Ange Dechu/Les Enfants Du Roi/L'Accordéon De La Vie/Si Tu Revenais.

These Brel chansons were first released by the artists in brackets

Vielle (Juliette Greco)/Je Suis Bien (Juliette Greco)/Les Crocodiles (Sacha Distel)/He! M'Man (Mirielle Mathieu).
'Ode A La Nuit' and 'La Chanson De Zorino' were sung by Lucie Dolene in the 1969 Hergé cartoon film *Le Temple Du Soleil*.
A tape of Brel singing Rod McKuen's 'The Lovers' in 1964 is thought to have been destroyed by fire in 1967. Lyrics in French by Brel were rendered as 'To You' on a *McKuen* album in 1972.
'Les Moutons' and 'Le Pendu' were commissioned for, respectively, a French election campaign in February 1967, and a television spectacular in the Netherlands.
Tracks written and recorded by Brel but not selected for his final album included 'Mai '40', 'Avec Elegance', 'Sans Exigences', 'L'Amour Est Mort', 'La Cathédrale', 'Le Docteur', 'Histoire Française' and 'Le Detour'.
'Un Avion' and nine further items were penned with Maddly Bamy.
'Place De La Contrescarpe' - a song about the main square in Paris's Latin Quarter - on the 1965 TV show, *Chansons Pour Un Ami* - and 'Le Petit Chemin, a Jean Sablon favourite, broadcast on *Le Château De Chansons* in 1969, are among extant non-originals performed by Brel.

NOTES

1. On some vinyl pressings and later formats, this title was rendered as 'Ça Va (Le Diable)'.
2. Also recorded in Dutch; 'Les Paumes De Petit Matin' being retitled 'De Nuttelozen Van De Nacht', 'Le Plat Pays' as 'Mijn Vlakke Land', and 'Les Bourgeois' as 'De Burgerij'. There exists too Dutch versions of 'Les Signes' (as 'De Apen') and 'On N'Oublie Rien' (as 'Men Vergeet Niets').
3. From the symphonic poem Les Trois Histoires De Jean De Bruges, *narrated by Brel and sung by Christophe Benoit.*
4. From the musical L'Homme De La Mancha.
5. All 1969 compositions are from the musical La Voyage De La Lune.
6. All 1970 compositions are from the film Mon Oncle Benjamin

Fondation Internationale Jacques Brel

France Brel is executive supervisor of the Foundation Internationale Jacques Brel, a concern that houses a museum, library and archive collection, and dispenses an array of quality merchandise associated with Jacques Brel. This includes posters, badges, lithographs, interview cassettes (such as *Brel Parle 1971*), books, CDs, videos (notably *Les Adieux De Jacques Brel À L'Olympia*), DVDs (notably, the *Brel: Comme Quand On Était Beau* box-set) and *Jef*, a quarterly magazine. The foundation also awards scholarships, supports charities and promotes Brel recitals by such as Michel Desaubies, Bernard Bruel and Jacques Grillot as well as dramas based on Brel texts like 1996's *Le Vent Du Nord*.

For further information, contact:

Fondation Internationale Jacques Brel, 11, Place de la Vielle Halle aux Bles, 1000 Brussels, Belgium.
Telephone: +32 (0) 2511 1020Fax: +32 (0) 2511 1021
web-site: www.jacquesbrel.be

Appendix Five

Selective Bibliography

Such is the volume of literary spin-offs (nearly all in French) both before and after his death that someone ought to write a book about books about Jacques Brel. Therefore, rather than attempt a long - and probably incomplete - list of dry titles, it makes more sense to comment briefly on four recommended items that are still in print and comparatively easy for readers in English-speaking countries to obtain.

Clouzet J. and Vassal J. *Jacques Brel* (Seghers, Paris, 1964)
There is much food for thought in the opening essay which leads into an in-depth interview with the subject; a small but intriguing plate section, and librettos referred to in the text.

Todd O. *Jacques Brel: Un Vie* (Robert Laffont, Paris, 1984)
Though accepted by Fondation Internationale Jacques Brel as a standard work, this is rather heavy going at times, and has a tendency to flit back and forth chronologically. Nevertheless, its appendices contain a list of the tomes that stood on Brel's bookshelves in Atuona; the original titles of his early *chansons*, and further detailed information that a certain type of enthusiast would not find too insignificant to be without value.

Bamy M. *Tu Leur Diras* (Gresivaudan, Paris, 1981)
Maddly's compassionate 'insider' effort is drawn from Brel's unfinished memoirs, his attempts at writing about his experiences on his death bed, what she could recall of his verbal reminiscences, and her own first-hand knowledge.

L'Oeuvre Intégrale De Jacques Brel (Robert Laffont, 1982)
An essential compilation that embraces every extant lyric that Brel committed to paper.

The Brel music portfolio that can be bought most readily in non-French-speaking territories is that containing some of Mort Shuman and Eric Blau's translations for *Jacques Brel Is Alive And Well And Living* In Paris (Chappell/Intersong, 1968).

Appendix Six
Film Appearances

1956
La Grande Père De Monsieur Clement
1967
Les Risques Du Métier
1968
La Bande À Bonnet
1969
Mon Oncle Benjamin
1970
Mont-Dragon
1971
Les Assassins De L'Ordre
1971
Franz (available on video)
1972
L'Aventure C'Est L'Aventure
1972
La Bar De La Fourche
1973
Le Far West
1973
L'Emmerdeur
1976
Jacques Brel Is Alive And Well And Living In Paris

About The Author

Born in Dover, England in 1951, Alan Clayson lives near Henley-on-Thames with his wife Inese. They have two sons, Jack and Harry.

A portrayal of Alan Clayson by the *Western Morning News* as the 'A.J.P. Taylor of the pop world' is supported by *Q*'s 'his knowledge of the period is unparalleled and he's always unerringly accurate.' He has penned many books on music - including the best-sellers *Backbeat*, subject of a major film, *The Yardbirds* and *The Beatles Box* - and has written for journals as diverse as *The Guardian, Record Collector, Ink, Mojo, Mediaeval World, Folk Roots, Guitar, Rhythm, Hello!, Drummer, The Times, The Independent, Ugly Things* and, as a 'teenager, the notorious *Schoolkids Oz*. He has also been engaged to perform and lecture on both sides of the Atlantic - as well as broadcast on national TV and radio.

From 1975 to 1985, he led the legendary Clayson and the Argonauts - who reformed in 2005, ostensibly to launch *Sunset On A Legend*, a long-awaited double-CD retrospective - and was thrust to 'a premier position on rock's Lunatic Fringe' (*Melody Maker*). A DVD, *Aetheria: Alan Clayson And The Argonauts In Concert*, was issued in 2009.

As shown by the existence of a US fan club - dating from an 1992 *soirée* in Chicago - Alan Clayson's following grows still as well as demand for his talents as a record producer, and the number of versions of his compositions by such diverse acts as Dave Berry (in whose backing group, he played keyboards in the mid-1980s), New Age outfit, Stairway - and Joy Tobing, winner of the Indonesian version of *Pop Idol*. He has worked too with The Portsmouth Sinfonia, Wreckless Eric - producer of the latest Clayson album, *A Windmill Too Far* - Twinkle, The Yardbirds, The Pretty Things, The Astronauts, Mungo Jerry and the late Screaming Lord Sutch among many others. While his stage act defies succinct description, he has been labelled a 'chansonnier' in recent years, partly because of his contributions to the 1998 CD collection, *Ne Me Quitte Pas: Brel Songs By...* and as a mainstay of the associated theatre presentation. Performances and record releases since may stand collectively as Alan Clayson's artistic apotheosis were it not for a promise of surprises yet to come.

Further information is obtainable from *alanclayson.com*

Other books by Alan Clayson

Call Up The Groups: The Golden Age Of British Beat, 1962-67
(Blandford, 1985)
Back In The High Life: A Biography Of Steve Winwood
(Sidgwick And Jackson, 1988)
Only The Lonely: The Life And Artistic Legacy Of Roy Orbison
(Sidgwick And Jackson, 1989)
The Quiet One: A Life Of George Harrison (Sidgwick And Jackson,
1990
Ringo Starr: Straight Man Or Joker? (Sanctuary, 1991)
Death Discs: An Account Of Fatality In The Popular Song
(Sanctuary, 1992)
Backbeat: Stuart Sutcliffe: The Lost Beatle (With Pauline Sutcliffe)
(Pan Macmillan, 1994)
Aspects Of Elvis (Ed. With Spencer Leigh)
(Sidgwick And Jackson, 1994)
Beat Merchants (Blandford, 1995)
Jacques Brel (Castle Communications, 1996)
Hamburg: The Cradle Of British Rock (Sanctuary, 1997)
Serge Gainsbourg: View From The Exterior (Sanctuary, 1998)
The Troggs File: The Official Story Of Rock's Wild Things
(With Jacqueline Ryan) (Helter Skelter, 2000)
Edgard Varese (Sanctuary, 2002)
The Yardbirds (Backbeat, 2002)
John Lennon (Sanctuary, 2003)
The Walrus Was Ringo: 101 Beatles Myths Debunked
(With Spencer Leigh) (Chrome Dreams, 2003)
Paul McCartney (Sanctuary, 2003)
Brian Jones (Sanctuary, 2003)
Charlie Watts (Sanctuary, 2004)
Woman: The Incredible Life Of Yoko Ono
(With Barb Jungr And Robb Johnson) (Chrome Dreams, 2004)
Keith Richards (Sanctuary, 2004)

Mick Jagger (Sanctuary, 2005)
Keith Moon: Instant Party (Chrome Dreams, 2005)
Led Zeppelin: The Origin Of The Species
(Chrome Dreams, 2006)
The Rolling Stones Album File (Cassell, 2006)
The Rolling Stones: The Origin Of The Species
(Chrome Dreams, 2007)
Beggars Banquet (Flame Tree, 2008)

Index

A

B